# Totalitarian Money?

Kevin Dowd's *Totalitarian Money?* provides a comprehensive critique of proposals to establish CBDCs (Central Bank Digital Currencies) around the world. He argues that they are economically inefficient, as they provide no benefits that cannot be obtained by other means. He explains why CBDCs are dangerous to financial stability and personal freedom as they enable digital currency to be weaponised against people to comply with the political or social agendas of those in control. Dowd reveals that, despite being promoted by central banks as the next 'big thing', public demand for CBDCs is negligible and they have been rejected by the public wherever they have been introduced. Evaluating the track record of countries that have introduced CBDCs, Dowd explores their drawbacks and explains why the private sector is better equipped to provide a retail digital currency to the general public.

Kevin Dowd is professor of finance and economics at Durham University Business School. He is a prominent critic of central banking whose previous books include *Competition and Finance* (1998), *Alchemists of Loss* (with Martin Hutchinson, 2010) and *The Experience of Free Banking* (second edition, 2023).

# Totalitarian Money?

## *The Case against Central Bank Digital Currencies*

KEVIN DOWD
*University of Durham*

CAMBRIDGE
UNIVERSITY PRESS

Shaftesbury Road, Cambridge CB2 8EA, United Kingdom

One Liberty Plaza, 20th Floor, New York, NY 10006, USA

477 Williamstown Road, Port Melbourne, VIC 3207, Australia

314–321, 3rd Floor, Plot 3, Splendor Forum, Jasola District Centre, New Delhi – 110025, India

Cambridge University Press is part of Cambridge University Press & Assessment, a department of the University of Cambridge.

We share the University's mission to contribute to society through the pursuit of education, learning and research at the highest international levels of excellence.

www.cambridge.org
Information on this title: www.cambridge.org/9781009758444

DOI: 10.1017/9781009758482



First published 2026

*A catalogue record for this publication is available from the British Library*

*Library of Congress Cataloging-in-Publication Data*
NAMES: Dowd, Kevin author
TITLE: Totalitarian money? : the case against central bank digital currencies / Kevin Dowd, University of Durham.
DESCRIPTION: Cambridge, United Kingdom ; New York, NY : Cambridge University Press, 2026. | Includes bibliographical references and index.
IDENTIFIERS: LCCN 2026002425 (print) | LCCN 2026002426 (ebook) | ISBN 9781009758444 hardback | ISBN 9781009758468 paperback | ISBN 9781009758482 ebook
SUBJECTS: LCSH: Central bank digital currencies
CLASSIFICATION: LCC HG1710.26 .D69 2026 (print) | LCC HG1710.26 (ebook) | DDC 332.4/048–dc23/eng/20260410
LC record available at https://lccn.loc.gov/2026002425
LC ebook record available at https://lccn.loc.gov/2026002426

ISBN 978-1-009-75844-4 Hardback
ISBN 978-1-009-75846-8 Paperback

And he causeth all, both small and great, rich and poor, free and bond, to receive a mark in their right hand, or in their foreheads:

And that no man might buy or sell, save he that had the mark, or the name of the beast, or the number of his name.

Book of Revelation 13:16–17, King James Version

# Contents

# Figures and Tables

FIGURES



TABLES

# Acknowledgements

I would like to express my thanks to all who offered me comments on the manuscript: Jim Allan, Nick Anthony, David Blake, Geoff Blanning, Romke Bontekoe, Jim Bovard, Roger J. Brown, Dean Buckner, Dave Campbell, Dave Cronin, Jim Dorn, Safiah Dowd, Anthony J. Evans, James Forder, Charles Goodhart, Steve Hanke, Vernon Hill, Martin Hutchinson, Doug Jackson, Lars Jonung, Gordon Kerr, Mahjabeen Khaliq, Duncan Kitchin, J. P. Koning, David Llewellyn, Bob Lyddon, David McGrogan, Norbert Michel, Allistair Milne, Anneliese Osterspey, Thorsten Polleit, Jim Rapp, John Skar, Ewen Stewart, Stan Szynkaruk, Jeff Tucker, Fran Villa, Kevin Villani, Keith White-Hunt and Basil Zafiriou.

I also thank Robert Dreesen, Sable Gravesandy, Julene Knox and Claire Sissen of Cambridge University Press, and especially Raadhiyah Anees, for their advice and assistance getting it through to publication.

# Preface

This book explains why CBDCs – Central Bank Digital Currencies – are a truly terrible idea. A central bank has no legitimate reason for providing a retail digital currency to the general public: the central bank should let the private sector do that and stick to its knitting, as the private sector is much better at retail-facing activities. Digital currencies issued by central banks make no economic sense and pose major dangers to individual rights and civil liberties.

My primary focus in this book is to establish that CBDCs provide absolutely no tangible benefits: everything that a CBDC could achieve, could be better achieved using alternatives. But it is important to recognise that CBDCs are also dangerous, not least because they enable digital currency to be weaponised against people and used to control them. CBDCs are nothing less than a route to a tyranny. Tolkien put his finger on this issue in *The Lord of the Rings* when he wrote: 'One ring to rule them all. One ring to find them. One ring to bring them all and in the darkness bind them.'

The good news, however, is that the public instinctively realise that CBDCs have nothing useful to offer them and have rejected them everywhere they have been introduced. Yet the central bank elite and the array of established interests promoting them – the Atlantic Council, the Bank for International Settlements, the International Monetary Fund, the World Bank, the World Economic Forum and numerous central banks and governments across the world – have bought into the CBDC hype in the deluded fantasy that CBDCs can somehow be made to work as if by a sufficiently determined exercise of their 'will'. But they overlook the point that no amount of 'will' can substitute for a public acceptance that does not exist. It is already clear that the great CBDC policy experiment is turning out to be an almighty flop and their foolishness in promoting a dead horse will become all too apparent in time.

# 1

# The Case against Central Bank Digital Currencies

## 1.1 INTRODUCTION

For preliminary purposes, we can define a Central Bank Digital Currency (CBDC) as a digital currency issued by a central bank to retail customers.

When digital technology was in its infancy nearly fifty years ago, there was a sense that future developments in IT would pose a major threat to financial privacy and ultimately to civil liberties. This threat gave rise to a pro-privacy 'cypherpunk' movement whose efforts led to major improvements in cryptography and ultimately made it possible to build new private digital currencies – Bitcoin and the many 'altcoins' that followed – based on the principles of secure cryptography.

Over the past decade, however, the pendulum has swung back towards centralisation and control and given rise to CBDCs. These have proven to be popular among central banks and ruling elites all over the world; CBDCs would allow these groups to benefit from immense increases in their power to control 'their' populations, to the point where central banks could potentially monitor and control their every transaction. To quote Agustín Carstens, the General Manager of the Bank for International Settlements in a 2020 speech: 'The key difference with the CBDC is the central bank will have *absolute control* on the rules and regulations that will determine the use of that expression of central bank liability, and also we will have the technology to enforce that [absolute control]' (Carstens, 2020). This power could be used to strengthen and reinforce the elites' power, promote their own political agendas and silence dissidents. Such concentration of power is inconsistent with the core principles of a free society and, as such, is wrong on principle.

Interest in CBDCs among central bankers has grown rapidly over recent years: the overwhelming majority of central banks have active CBDC development projects and a few have implemented CBDCs already.

However, CBDCs are not so popular among the general population. In the United States, a May 2023 poll by the Cato Institute (Ekins and Gygi, 2023) reported that only 16 per cent of the American public would support the Federal Reserve (the Fed) issuing a CBDC, while 34 per cent were opposed. Twenty-two per cent said they were likely to use a CBDC while 78 per cent said they were unlikely to use one. Results also revealed that a CBDC was about as popular among the population as the government installing surveillance cameras inside their own homes. In the United Kingdom, a 2023 joint initiative by the Bank of England and the UK Treasury was met by a huge public backlash as over 51,000 people expressed their concerns about the initiative during a public consultation. And in countries where CBDCs have already been implemented, the results have been distinctly unimpressive. Everywhere they have been tried, CBDC take-up has been almost homeopathically low despite gimmicky inducements and noisy public campaigns to promote their adoption. Should other countries also adopt them, as seems likely, we might reasonably expect similar results. The CBDC bandwagon is on course to become an enormous flop. Then in late 2024, Colombia, Canada and Australia all paused their CBDC programmes and, on 23 January 2025, US President Donald Trump signed an Executive Order effectively banning CBDCs in the United States.

Thus, the battlelines are drawn for a momentous struggle that will play out over the next few years: we have the elites who support CBDCs, because CBDCs give them more power, and we have the hoi polloi, who oppose CBDCs on the grounds that our self-appointed elites have more than enough power and privilege already.

## 1.2 SUMMARY OF MAIN ARGUMENT

The first point to appreciate about a CBDC is that it is quite unnecessary. Assume, as seems reasonable, that the private sector has at least the same technological capabilities as the public sector. If there is a market niche for a CBDC-type financial instrument, then the private sector could fill that niche at least as well as the public sector could fill it. Given that serious reservations have been expressed about the public sector issuing a CBDC (of which more below), then the wisest course of action would be for the public sector to allow the private sector to fulfil that niche by issuing a derivative known as a *dollar stablecoin* (or pound stablecoin, or whatever) or a *synthetic CBDC*.[1] And since the private sector is issuing stablecoins successfully already, then we know that the demand for an instrument to fill that niche exists. But there is no need for a *Central Bank* Digital Currency as such; that niche is already filled with a financial product that is, as we shall see later, also superior to an actual CBDC. Hence, a CBDC is not only unnecessary, but cannot match what the private sector already successfully delivers.

The main argument in this book is a simple one: that CBDCs offer no benefits to the public that cannot be better achieved using existing tools; at the same time, CBDCs entail substantial disadvantages and risks. These include the risks that CBDCs pose to the stability of the banking system, their inefficiency compared to private alternatives and especially the risks to civil liberties that come from giving the central bank an immensely powerful instrument of surveillance and control. We would be wise to reject them.

As the Canadian monetary blogger J. P. Koning wrote in 2021: 'I've listened to all the arguments made for issuing a CBDC in Canada or the US. It seems to me that everything that a CBDC is supposed to fix can already be achieved by another existing process or institution—and these alternatives are typically cheaper and less risky'(Koning, 2021). At the same time, adopting a CBDC would give policymakers major headaches and expose them to considerable new risks. To quote an American Bankers Association statement to Congress, 'The proposed benefits of CBDCs to international competitiveness and financial inclusion are theoretical, difficult to measure, and may be elusive, while the negative consequences for monetary policy, financial stability, financial intermediation, the payments system, and the customers and communities that banks serve could be severe' (American Bankers Association, 2021, p. 2).

Consider the main proposed benefits of a CBDC. Advocates say that a CBDC would provide consumers with *safe electronic money*. However, money holders are already entitled to safe bank accounts that benefit from government deposit insurance. It is not clear what benefit a new 100 per cent safe money would offer them.

[1] More on stablecoins below.

There is the argument that a CBDC *counterbalances monopolistic or oligopolistic tendencies* in the banking system. But the counterargument is that there are more natural ways to make the banking system more competitive than introducing a new state monopoly. For example, authorities could reduce existing regulatory barriers to entry and they could make it easier for new firms (including foreign firms, fintechs and private firms that issue private digital currency backed by riskless central bank currency aka the synthetics and stablecoins mentioned earlier) to enter the market.

One often hears claims that CBDCs would make the *payments system more efficient* but these claims unravel on close examination. In the US, the key barrier to clearing efficiency is not the lack of a CBDC, but the bankers' opening hours that the Fed still maintains. Move to 24/7 service and payments efficiency would considerably improve. Regulators in countries with better-functioning financial systems typically found no payments efficiency role for a CBDC and the biggest barrier to cross-border payments efficiency is not the absence of a CBDC but the existence of Anti-Money Laundering/Know Your Customer (AML/KYC) regulation that needlessly increases banks' regulatory compliance costs but is almost completely ineffective in achieving its main objective, which is to control criminal money transfers and the businesses underlying them.

Relatedly, it is sometimes said that CBDCs would make for more *efficient relief and stimulus measures*. However, relief payments are not slow because of the payment mechanism, but are slow because of information problems. As Koning (2021) observes, 'If those problems are solved, payments can be quickly sent electronically via regular bank accounts' but if 'those problems are not solved, a CBDC would do little to improve matters'. For governments to provide more rapid relief in future, they need to assemble information on how recipients wish to be paid. 'This is a simple fix' that 'doesn't require building an entirely new payments system' (Koning, 2021).

The most common argument for CBDCs is that they would *improve financial inclusion* – that is, they would help more people to become banked. However, a CBDC does *nothing* to address the reasons why people might not have a bank account and is likely to give them additional reasons to avoid banks. Many such people distrust banks, value their own financial privacy or cannot afford a bank account, despite a range of cheap accounts being offered to them. Also, to the extent that inclusion is an issue, the private sector is better equipped to deal with retail issues than the central bank and is well on the road to resolving it already. If central banks really wish to promote inclusion, they could do so in other ways, such as by reducing regulatory compliance costs to make bank accounts cheaper to hold.

It is sometimes suggested that CBDCs would *improve financial privacy* and provide more privacy than the private sector could. Such claims have it the wrong way round, however. The fact is that the private sector can deliver whatever levels of financial privacy customers might demand, but are restricted from doing so by state regulation, especially AML/KYC regulation. No central bank proposes CBDCs that deliver more privacy than that permitted under those regulations. Indeed, far from enabling greater privacy, CBDCs are a major and obvious threat to it.

Then consider that CBDCs are *dominated* by (that is, are never preferable to) synthetic CBDCs. Synthetic CBDCs are superior in every way – they avoid conflicts of interest and monopoly, promote financial stability, better mitigate cyber-vulnerabilities and so forth, while CBDCs perform worse across all points of comparison. There is *never* any rational reason to prefer a monopolistic CBDC to competitive synthetics.

For all these reasons a CBDC is merely a solution in search of a problem. To quote Facebook co-founder Chris Hughes:

> Well, I came to this excited about the idea of a central bank digital currency. I saw all the positives and everything that felt like it was worth exploration. And then, after spending a year talking to lots of experts researching it, reading everything I could get my hands on, thinking about the political dynamics of all of it, I had a day when I was whiteboarding it out and I just took a step back and said, 'This is really a solution in search of a problem.' We can solve all of these very real problems with other public policy interventions, and creating a CBDC is mostly just hype. (quoted in Brancaccio et al., 2022)

CBDCs are dominated by synthetics and do not offer any benefits that alternatives cannot deliver. There is also no problem to which a CBDC is the natural solution.

The CBDC project itself reflects confused thinking by its proponents. In problem solving, one should start with the problem to be solved, then find a solution that works. However, CBDC advocates start with a proposed solution, but then struggle to backfill it to find a problem it solves. To quote Dr Doug Jackson, the founder of e-gold:

> CBDCs are a terrible idea and central bank interest in the topic has the earmarks of a fad. Every proposed benefit of CBDCs could be provided at lower cost and risk by an alternative approach that would not require the operational participation of any government central bank.

> Moreover, strategic emphasis on CBDCs . . . fails to address multiple chronic – in some cases centuries enduring – problems with legacy monetary, payments and financial systems. . . . A clean sheet of paper approach to identifying these problems and their origins, undertaken at an appropriate level of abstraction and informed by historical data, would enable a systematic analysis revealing core principles and design requirements for possible remedies.
>
> [But this] was not the process that led to discussions of and pilot projects involving CBDCs. All such activities started with advocacy by certain constituencies for blockchain or DLT [distributed ledger technology] schemes and then backfilled to find a rationale for why/how these protocols might be needed or useful. (Jackson, 2019, p. 1)

CBDCs also entail substantial downsides: First, there is the risk that a CBDC would disintermediate the banking system by encouraging bank depositors to convert their deposits into CBDCs. Such an effect would draw deposits out of the banking system and make the banking system both less stable and less efficient. Financial stability problems can also arise out of the contradiction between the need to maintain an elastic CBDC supply, on the one hand, and proposals to reduce CBDC-induced financial disintermediation by issuing CBDCs in restricted quantities, on the other. This contradiction could potentially lead to a situation in which a surge in the speculative demand for CBDC could overwhelm supply constraints and see CBDC prices exceed their 'parity' prices, and thereby further aggravate financial instability.

Second, CBDCs are inefficient for a number of separate reasons: (i) Central banks are not good at retail-facing activities and will never be able to compete against private payments providers who are specialists in such activities. (ii) A central bank that offers payments services and regulates the financial system is conflicted, and it is unreasonable to expect that a conflicted regulator could ever deliver an efficient outcome: the central bank would always be inclined to promote its own payments systems against others'. (iii) CBDCs are more exposed to financial instability than are private sector firms because of single point of failure issues. (iv) Monopolistically issued CBDCs are subject to the usual efficiency drawbacks of monopolies that we see in other areas of the economy – they provide less choice, they charge higher costs, they are slower to innovate and so on. As former Bank of England governor Lord King observed, it would be somewhat odd to try to increase competition by creating a state monopoly. (v) CBDCs are subject to a negative seigniorage problem. The public would be reluctant to pay for them when they could choose to hold deposits that yield them a positive return instead. The banks would be reluctant to pay for them because CBDCs yield them no return and cost them the returns they could have achieved on bank deposits. So the only way to pay the costs of hosting CBDC wallets would be for the central banks to subsidise them. Thus, in adopting CBDCs, the central bank would be shifting from a system that previously worked well to one that can only be sustained by an ongoing public subsidy. The need for this subsidy implicitly acknowledges the inefficiency of the CBDC system and also violates the principle that the central bank should be neutral between different payments approaches.[2]

Third, CBDCs entail serious financial privacy concerns including the possibility of being weaponised against their users. CBDCs can be used to target anyone whose views are deemed to be unacceptable to those in authority, and those targeted could be subject to penalties that could be as severe as being digitally ostracised from the monetary economy. Such weaponisability is fundamentally at odds with the core principles of a free society.

Fourth, for CBDCs to work as intended, it is essential that the public trust central banks to manage the new powers that CBDCs would give them without abusing that trust, but there is no good reason for the public to give them that trust, and evidence, such as the UK public's backlash against the Britcoin proposal, indicates that the UK public do not trust them. The same would appear to be the case elsewhere. Yet central banks remain tone deaf to public concerns on this issue.

Fifth, going further, CBDCs are opposed by both the general public and the banks, and central banks have no practical chance of achieving widespread adoption against strong public opposition. The fact that so many central banks are determined to do their utmost to promote them, merely shows how out of touch they are with the public mood.[3]

Sixth, we should consider CBDCs' track record. Advocates of CBDCs cannot point to a single case where a CBDC has made a country better off. They have been tried and abandoned in Finland and Ecuador. Ongoing CBDC experiments in the Bahamas, China, Jamaica, the countries of the

[2] If the CBDC bears an interest rate, there is the problem that a CBDC would introduce a second interest rate that is risk-free. Even small movements in the spread between the original risk-free rate and the CBDC rate could then trigger large flows of funds seeking to exploit arbitrage opportunities between them. This problem is a major threat to financial stability and has the potential to make monetary policy much more difficult to implement than it already is.

[3] One should also consider the impact of the collateral damage that has been or could be created by efforts to introduce a CBDC. The most obvious example to date is the highly destructive assault on cash undertaken by the Nigerian central bank in furtherance of its policy to promote a CBDC.

East Caribbean Currency Union and Nigeria have extremely low take-up. Evidence from these experiments indicates that when people have alternatives to CBDCs they much prefer those and the average per capita holdings of CBDCs is negligible. Above all, these experiences indicate that the overwhelming majority of people in these countries do not want a CBDC.

Enthusiasts for CBDCs are presumably aware that the public do not want them, but simply cannot bring themselves to respect their wishes. To quote Dr David McGrogan from Northumbria Law School:

> It is, though, a sign of the times that what ordinary people want, or don't want, is not generally considered to be a relevant factor in decisions about policy. What the technocrat wants *is good* by definition, because it is the product of his expertise; the only relevant question to ask is how implementation should take place. Since implementation of a CBDC is thought to need widespread adoption, then people will be made to adopt it. Hence, we see an awful lot of emphasis in the CBDC literature on the question of how it is that people will be cajoled, nudged, persuaded, hoodwinked, or coerced into adoption – given that it must, self-evidently, ultimately be in their best interests [whether they recognise that or not]. (McGrogan, 2024c)

Yet the fact remains that retail CBDCs would provide no tangible benefits and entail serious problems that could be avoided by not introducing a CBDC in the first place. It is as simple as that.

The case for CBDCs should be dismissed.

## 1.3 LAWRENCE H. WHITE ON CBDCS

In a recent presentation (White, 2024) Lawrence H. White offers a succinct analysis of the basic economics of CBDCs. He destroys the case for CBDCs in half a page:

- First, that money balances are a private good because they are rival in consumption and excludable in supply, so the market does not fail to provide money efficiently. It follows that CBDCs would not provide greater consumer welfare than private alternatives.
- Second, CBDCs would be inefficient at retail payments because central banks have no experience at retail and are not set up to perform retail functions.
- Third, CBDCs would reduce the efficiency of credit allocation, because credit allocation would become politicised due to imposition of government mandates.

- Fourth, CBDCs would become a financial panopticon – the central bank would be able to see (and control) all financial transactions. Thus, a CBDC would threaten financial privacy.
- Fifth and finally, a CBDC would stifle dynamic innovation.

## 1.4 BEWARE THOSE WHO ARE PROMOTING CBDCS

It is also worth keeping in mind that a whole raft of major international organisations are pushing hard for CBDCs. These include the vast majority of central banks, many governments, the Atlantic Council, the Bank for International Settlements, the European Union, the International Monetary Fund, the World Bank, the United Nations and, of most concern of all, the World Economic Forum (WEF), which meets regularly at Davos in Switzerland.

The WEF has its own agenda, the ghastly Great Reset, based on the idea that the Covid-19 pandemic gives them the opportunity to 'reset' the world as they would have it. In the words of J. B. Shurk:

> The mission objective of the World Economic Forum (WEF) is remarkably simple: the smartest, best people in the world should rule everyone else. In WEF parlance, their schemes of total supervision and behavioral modification will create a 'sustainable' future for humanity. Humans become nothing more than 'things' to be counted, shuffled, categorized, tagged, monitored, manipulated, and controlled. They become nothing more than cogs in the WEF's great trans-humanist, technocratic machine.

Shurk continues:

> Separated from all its pretensions about 'saving the world' from unchecked population growth and climate apocalypse, the WEF is nothing new. Its foundations have been around at least since the time of Plato, when two and a half millennia ago the Greek philosopher proposed that the ideal city-state would be ruled by 'philosopher kings'. Just as Plato surveyed the world and predictably concluded that people from his own vocation should logically govern everyone else, the World Economic Forum's global 'elites' have come to a strikingly similar determination. ... For a half-century, the WEF's members have been on a quest to devise the perfect global government without any say from Western nations' voting populations, and to no-one's surprise, those same 'philosopher kings' have nominated themselves to do the ruling. How convenient. (Shurk, 2023)

They propose a future in which the rest of us are merely 'useless eaters', superfluous humans who will 'own nothing and be happy' and whose sole purpose is to be reduced to eternal serfdom to serve their WEF masters and live at their pleasure. Digital vaccine passports will provide universal tracking of every person's movements but also ensure stick-and-carrot compliance with mandatory orders during periodic declared 'health emergencies'. Personal carbon footprints will measure each individual's 'culpability' for climate change and record everything a person eats and everywhere a person goes, all the time 'nudging' citizens with digital rewards or penalties to modify behaviour towards the government's preferred standards. People will be pushed into 'Fifteen Minute Cities' in which tens of millions can be crammed into small apartment complexes, and move through a maze of entrances and exits accessed solely through digital ID verification and approval. Everyone will get a Guaranteed Annual Income 'enough to keep them sated with avocado toast and vanilla lattes while they watch cat videos at the local Starbucks', as Doug Casey (2022) puts it. Government 'narratives' will dominate dissenting opinion via government-allied platforms that ridicule and censor the thoughts and words of dissident opinions, free speech will be labelled as dangerous 'misinformation' and much of it will be criminalised.

Of course, the WEF also promotes CBDCs that would allow governments not only to track every citizen's income and purchase history in real time but also to limit and control what a person may spend depending upon government-determined social credit scores that are based on how far they conform to government-imposed standards.

The whole WEF programme was condemned in no uncertain terms by Archbishop Carlo Maria Viganò:

> For months now, despite the deafening silence from the media, millions of citizens from every nation cried their 'NO!' No to the pandemic folly, No to the lockdowns, to the curfews, to the imposition of vaccines, to the health passports, to the blackmails of the totalitarian power enslaved to the elite. It is a power that reveals itself as intrinsically evil, animated by an infernal ideology and driven by criminal purposes. A power that now declares that it has broken the social contract and considers us not as citizens but as slaves to a dictatorship ... (Viganò, 2021)

> My appeal for an Anti-Globalist Alliance – which I renew today – aims precisely to constitute a movement of moral and spiritual rebirth which will inspire ... those who do not want to be enslaved as slaves to the New World Order. A movement that at the national and local level will be able to find a way to oppose the *Great Reset* and that coordinates the denunciation of the coup that is currently in progress. (quoted in Ellwood, 2021)

Amen to that.

To quote my friend the *Bear's Lair* journalist Martin Hutchinson:

> productivity growth, which has already been declining worldwide since the imposition of major environmental controls in the 1970s, will fall to a negative level . . . and will remain there indefinitely. Humanity's life experience, which has been improving beyond all imagination in the two and a half centuries since the Industrial Revolution, will begin to decline, and will continue doing so as long as Great Reset policies are in effect. The Anti-Industrial Revolution will thereby, slowly but inexorably, destroy our civilization. (Hutchinson, 2022, pp. 295, 310)

But wake up! This is just a bad dream from the same part of the world that bought us the Third Reich 80 years ago, the Frankenstein fantasy in the 1820s and Rousseau in the 1750s. We don't have to accept such fates!

Those of us who reject this naked power grab could make a good start by rejecting CBDCs as one of its core pillars.

## 1.5 ORGANISATION OF THIS BOOK

This book is organised as follows.

Chapter 2 discusses the background and history of CBDCs.

Chapter 3 provides an overview of the economic issues involved with CBDCs.

Chapter 4 introduces the concept of *synthetic CBDCs* or *dollar stablecoins*, privately issued digital currencies backed by riskless central bank money, and the related concept of *narrow bank*s, banks that hold all their reserves in deposits at the central bank. It suggests that these have a number of significant attractions over actual CBDCs and that one would never rationally prefer a CBDC to them.

Chapter 5 outlines the more interesting controversies surrounding CBDCs, focussing in particular on those controversies in the UK, the US and Sweden, and gives a brief overview of the current state of play of CBDC projects around the world.

Chapter 6 examines CBDC experiences to date. These experiences suggest that the public willingness to adopt CBDCs is negligible: there is no significant public demand for CBDCs in any country that has implemented them.

Chapter 7 discuss purported macroeconomic uses of CBDCs but suggests that these are questionable.

Chapter 8 discusses the ways in which CBDCs could undermine the banking system by disintermediating it.

Chapter 9 addresses the argument that CBDCs would increase financial inclusion by encouraging more people to get a bank account. However, we suggest that a CBDC would do nothing to improve financial inclusion and would actually give the financially excluded even less reason to open a bank account than they already have.

Chapter 10 examines the importance of the right to financial privacy and discusses how CBDCs would threaten to end any financial privacy that still exists.

Chapter 11 discusses how CBDCs could be used to weaponise currency to punish or incapacitate dissidents or anyone else the ruling regime took a dislike to.

Chapter 12 proposes an alternative agenda to the current one preferred by many central banks, which is to establish CBDCs and abolish cash. This alternative agenda would involve a restoration of a gold standard in financial privacy and propose a legislative framework to guide how payments media should be regulated in a market economy. This framework would prohibit central banks from engaging in any CBDC activity, establish rules to permit different types of private payments media to compete against each other on a level playing field and have the central bank remove itself from the provision of *any* payments media. The reforms needed are extremely elegant and very simple.

# 2

# Background and History of Central Bank Digital Currencies

Main Points

Central Bank Digital Currencies (CBDCs) arose as a reaction by central banks to the threats posed to their currencies by cryptocurrencies, and, in particular, to the threat posed by Facebook's proposed Libra cryptocurrency.

Over the past decade, central banks have been caught up in an ill-conceived 'CBDC mania', attempting to design CBDCs without thinking the fundamental issues through.

This mania will prove to be embarrassing when its underlying folly becomes obvious for all to see.

## 2.1 DIGITAL CURRENCY

*Currency* is medium of exchange used to facilitate trade in everyday life. Traditional currency, aka cash, took the form of a physical coin or banknote with a specified face value at which it normally traded. A *digital currency*, however, is currency that exists only in digital or electronic form as an entry on a digital ledger. The notion of digital money in general terms, for example as in 'the money in your digital bank account', goes back many decades, but we are specifically interested here in the digital equivalent of a banknote with its attendant attributes of being generally acceptable, homogeneous, portable, divisible, liquid, etc., and which can be used to make anonymous transactions. However, whereas physical currency can be costly to store and is difficult to spend at long distances, digital currency is neither.

In 1992, three Bay Area computer scientists launched a new mailing list, the members of which they called cypherpunks.[1] They shared the conviction that the newly emerging internet would soon become an important battleground in the struggle for human freedom: once governments understood the significance of the internet, they would soon want to control and censor it. They also understood that there was one key tool to protect the internet's security, cryptography, the mathematics of codes and coding. Their first task was to break the US government's hold on strong encryption, which it regarded as a munition, and this objective was soon achieved, helped by the growing recognition that e-commerce itself needed encryption also.

However, the cypherpunks also realised that a truly free digital commons also needed its own native form of money, a money that the government could not control. But designing such a monetary system posed problems that were difficult to solve. A number of such systems were proposed – David Chaum's 'DigiCash' in 1990, Adam Back's 'HashCash' in 1997, Wei Dai's 'b-money' in 1998 and Nick Szabo's 'BitGold' in 2005. However, all these systems were subject to one flaw or the other, and none of them took off.

## 2.2 BITCOIN

The breakthrough then came with the launch of Bitcoin. On 31 October 2008, a writer calling himself Satoshi Nakamoto distributed a paper, 'Bitcoin: A Peer-to-Peer Electronic Cash System', to a cryptography mailing list. This article set out the principles underlying his proposed new digital currency, Bitcoin. Nakamoto starts with the problem of how to dispense with the need for a trusted intermediary to block attempts to double-spend an electronic currency instrument. What was needed, he said, was an electronic payment system based on cryptographic proof instead of trust, which would allow any willing parties to transact directly with each other without the need for a trusted third party. Transactions that are computationally impractical to reverse would protect sellers from fraud and generate computational proof of the chronological order of transactions and escrow mechanisms could be implemented to protect buyers.

[1] This discussion draws on Qureshi (2019).

On 11 February 2009, Nakamoto further explained the thinking behind Bitcoin in an email announcing its launch:

> The root problem with conventional currency is all the trust that is required to make it work. The central bank must be trusted not to debase the currency, but the history of fiat currencies is full of breaches of that trust. . . . With e-currency based on cryptographic proof, without the need to trust a third-party middleman, money can be secure and transactions complete.[2]

The system works as follows. A trade is made and put out with others made around the same time in a block for confirmation by the network; the putative trade is posted on a digital ledger known as the blockchain. A block is to be confirmed about every ten minutes. Users known as 'miners' race to approve a block which they do by solving a difficult-to-solve mathematical problem ('proof of work') on their computers whose solution is easily verified; the first confirmed to have solved the problem is rewarded with a gift of newly created bitcoin; from the miners' perspective, it is as if they are mining for bitcoins, but from the perspective of the Bitcoin system, their function is to confirm transfers. The level of difficulty of the mathematical problem is adjusted continuously to ensure that a constant flow of bitcoin is produced over any short period, but the flow of newly produced bitcoin decreases periodically over time so that the total supply of bitcoin will approach an upper limit of 21 million. Miners also receive competitively determined transaction fees. The Bitcoin system works automatically except for occasional tweaks by its steering committee. There is also no single point of failure so there is no easy way to control it or shut it down.

The first block of bitcoin was mined on 3 January 2009. Transaction levels were very low at first and the price barely moved – in a famous early transaction, Laszlo Hanyecz paid 10,000 bitcoins for two pizza deliveries – but trading volume increased and its price eventually took off.[3]

Figure 2.1 shows bitcoin prices over the period 2010–2025. At the start of the plot, the bitcoin price was $0.07 on 19 July 2010; by 5 May 2025 the price was $ 95,729.05. At the same date, its current market capitalisation was £1.87 trillion.[4]

Bitcoin was the first in a new class of currencies known as cryptocurrencies. From 2011 onwards, thousands of further cryptocurrencies,

[2] Quoted from https://satoshi.nakamotoinstitute.org/posts/p2pfoundation/1/. Accessed 28 December 2025.

[3] For more on the early history of Bitcoin, see, e.g., Marr (2017) or Prasad (2021b).

[4] See https://coinmarketcap.com/currencies/bitcoin/. Accessed 17 January 2026.

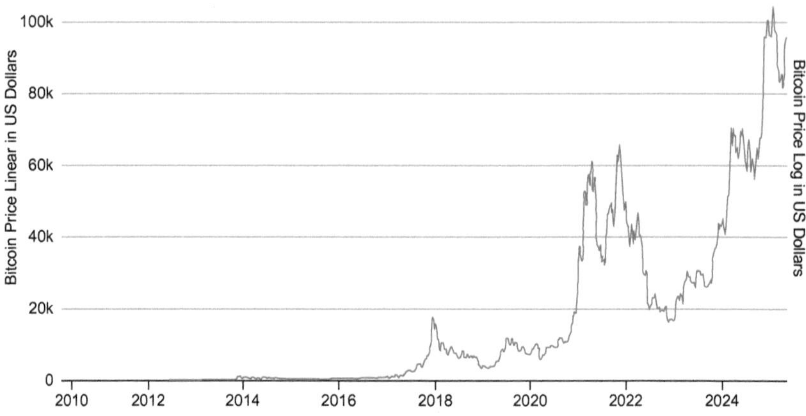


FIGURE 2.1 Bitcoin price chart, 2010–2025
Notes: Figure plots Bitcoin average weekly dollar price on y-axis from 19 July 2010 to 5 May 2025. Source: https://buybitcoinworldwide.com/price/ posted by Highcharts.com. Accessed 6 May 2025.

known as altcoins, began to be developed based on variations of Bitcoin's open source code. The varieties of altcoin include straightforward bitcoin lookalikes, meme coins, such as Dogecoin based on a Japanese dog, which started as a joke, and utility and governance tokens.[5] Bitcoin's share of the cryptocurrency market was 64.1 per cent as of 6 May 2025.[6] The prices of these cryptocurrencies are extremely volatile by conventional standards.

Since it was launched, much has been made of Bitcoin's potential to compete against and even possibly replace pre-existing currencies and payments systems. However, such speculations do not sit well against Bitcoin's inability to operate at any serious scale: to illustrate, Bitcoin can process perhaps 7 transactions per second, whereas Visa can process about 24,000 transactions per second (see Killian, 2020). As a medium of payment, Bitcoin thus falls a long way behind the transaction capabilities of the big traditional payments methods.

## 2.3 STABLECOINS

A second and more recently developed form of cryptocurrency is a stablecoin, a cryptocurrency issued on a blockchain whose value is

[5] For more on these, see https://101blockchains.com/governance-token-vs-utility-token/. Accessed 4 February 2026.

[6] See https://coinmarketcap.com/charts/. Accessed 6 May 2025.

pegged to that of another currency, commodity or financial instrument, or to some basket of the above. Stablecoins may be pegged to a currency like the US dollar or to the price of a commodity such as gold. Stablecoin issuers maintain their price peg by standing ready to buy/sell stablecoins for US dollars at a 1:1 exchange rate, or by following algorithmic formulas to maintain the peg. Thus, a stablecoin that is pegged to the US dollar should have a value of $1. Stablecoins aim to provide an alternative to the high price volatility of conventional cryptocurrencies, which makes them far less suited than stablecoins for carrying out common transactions.

The largest, Tether, has a market cap of $149.44 billion.[7] Figure 2.2 shows the prices of Tether over the period 2015–2025. The price typically fluctuates very close or equal to $1, its target price. However, there are occasionally larger fluctuations.[8] The prices of other stablecoins show similar patterns.

Stablecoins operate like digital banknotes but without the physical hassle of moving them around; they cut down on the fees, transaction times and potential infringements to privacy entailed by other ways of making peer-to-peer payments. As Lawrence H. White points out

> Stablecoins are most useful for cryptocurrency traders and exchanges. A trader can sell Bitcoin for USDT [or Tether] on one exchange, and buy another coin with the USDT [or Tether] on another exchange, without the hassle and delay of

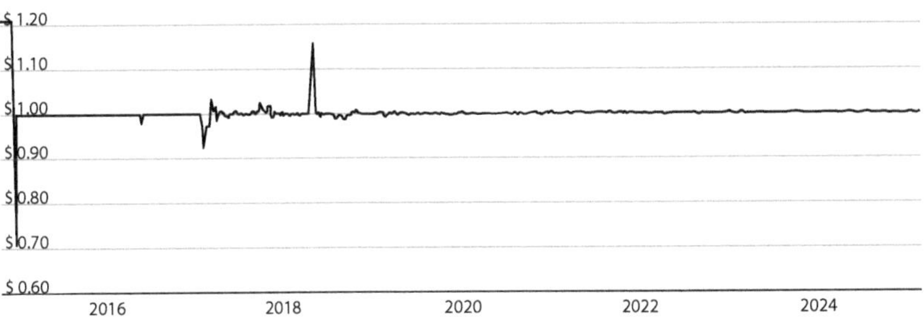


FIGURE 2.2 Tether price chart, 2015–2025
Notes: Figure plots weekly average Tether price (on y-axis) from 7 January 2015 to 5 May 2025. Source: https://coincodex.com/crypto/tether/?period=ALL. Accessed 6 May 2025.

[7] See https://coinmarketcap.com/currencies/tether/. Accessed 4 February 2026.

[8] These larger fluctuations occur at least in part because Tether's terms and conditions allow it to withhold payments under certain conditions. There is more on this issue in White (2021b). Concerns have also been expressed that departures from parity might also reflect doubts about Tether's financial soundness.

> moving funds into a bank account and back out. The usefulness of stablecoins for traders is evident in the way stablecoins have displaced Bitcoin from the role of commonly accepted medium of exchange in crypto markets. Their volume in circulation has grown to more than $100 billion in just a few years. (White, 2021b)

Stablecoins also provide liquidity for traders in (other) cryptocurrency markets and play a role today not just as 'crypto reserves' but also as a source of liquidity across decentralised finance (DeFi) exchanges. They provide a medium for the instantaneous movement of value between exchanges and digital wallets to settle bilateral over-the-counter (OTC) trades or execute cross-border payments (de Bode et al., 2021).

Then there is the question of how regulators should best handle stablecoins. On this issue, I quote United States Federal Reserve Vice Chair for Supervision, Randal Quarles, in 2021:

> In my judgment, we do not need to fear stablecoins. The Federal Reserve has traditionally supported responsible private-sector innovation. Consistent with this tradition, I believe that we must take strong account of the potential benefits of stablecoins, including the possibility that a U.S. dollar stablecoin might *support* the role of the dollar in the global economy. For example, a global U.S. dollar stablecoin network could encourage use of the dollar by making cross-border payments faster and cheaper, and it potentially could be deployed much faster and with fewer downsides than a [Central Bank Digital Currency, of which more presently]. And the concern that stablecoins represent the unprecedented creation of private money and thus challenge our monetary sovereignty is puzzling, given that our existing system involves – indeed depends on – private firms creating money every day. (Quarles, 2021)

In short, stablecoins are a useful and safe addition to the digital ecosystem – and, as we shall soon see, some[9] are a natural alternative to a CBDC.

## 2.4 ORIGINS OF CBDCS

In 2013, J. P. Koning proposed that the Fed take Fedwire, the Fed's real-time gross settlement system, and put it on a distributed blockchain to enhance its resilience. This was the first time that it had been suggested that a central bank might find a use for a blockchain. In October 2014, Koning proposed a scheme that was much more like a stablecoin. The Fed would create a new blockchain or Ripple-style ledger called Fedcoin. It would use its powers of money creation and destruction to ensure that

[9] To be more precise, I am referring here to those stablecoins known as *synthetic CBDCs*, which are discussed further in Chapter 4.

Fedcoin maintained a 1:1 exchange rate against existing Fed money. Deviations in that exchange rate would trigger arbitrage trades to restore parity. The supply of Fedcoin would be left to vary endogenously and unwanted Fedcoins would reflux to the Fed for conventional Fed currency. Fedcoin transactions would be verified by nodes on the distributed ledger. Fedcoin would provide an innovative and cheaper payments instrument than, say, cash. Fedcoin would have no impact on monetary policy except for the possibility of being used with negative rates to implement negative interest rate policies (NIRP). Koning notes the potential destructive effects of Fedcoin for private bank deposits, but suggests letting the commercial banks issue their own versions of Fedcoin – WellsFargCoin and so forth. He then ended with a prescient observation:

> Bitcoin true believers may not like this post, but perhaps they can take something constructive from it. Fedcoin is one of the potential competitors in the distant horizon. Now is the time for the rebels to figure out how to create a stable-price version of bitcoin, before Darth Vader does it himself. Otherwise they may someday find themselves closing down their bitcoin startups in order to write code for the Empire. (Koning, 2014)

Shortly afterwards, David Andolfatto of the St Louis Fed gave a talk about Koning's Fedcoin at the 2015 International Workshop on P2P Financial Systems (29 January 2015) and posted a blog about it on 3 February 2015 entitled 'Fedcoin: On the Desirability of a Government Cryptocurrency'.

> I view Bitcoin as a potentially promising payment system, saddled with a less-than-ideal money and monetary policy. . . .
>
> What is the main problem with bitcoin as a monetary instrument in an economy like the U.S.? It is [that . . .] the exchange rate is volatile and unpredictable. . . .
>
> And so, here is where the idea of Fedcoin comes in. Imagine that the Fed, as the core developer, makes available an open-source Bitcoin-like protocol (suitably modified) called *Fedcoin*. The key point is this: the Fed is in the *unique* position to *credibly* fix the exchange rate between Fedcoin and the USD (the exchange rate could be anything, but let's assume *par*). . . .
>
> Fedcoin is essentially just like digital cash. . . .
>
> The purpose of Fedcoin is to *compete* with other cryptocurrencies – to provide a property that no other cryptocurrency can offer (guaranteed exchange rate stability with the USD). (Andolfatto, 2015)

Andolfatto's post received considerable attention, and interest in CBDCs increased sharply afterwards.

Later that same month, the Bank of England published its 2015 'One Bank' research agenda. This document included a section on digital currencies which raised some of the questions that were to figure largely in the soon to rapidly unfold discussion on CBDCs. These included, for example, the costs and benefits of making central bank digital money accessible to a wider range of holders; should it be remunerated and, if so, how?; how would it affect the monetary policy transmission mechanism?; how would it impact the banks and the availability of credit?; what type of distributed ledger technology (DLT) would be most appropriate?; and how should it be regulated?

The climax of this activity was a keynote address given by Chain CEO Adam Ludwin to a big Fed-IMF-World Bank conference of central bankers and financial regulators in Washington, D.C., on 1 June 2016. His talk was on how blockchain enables a 'new medium of money' that can enable next-generational financial networks to operate on blockchain architectures and also allows a central bank to issue a CBDC. Ultimately, he argued, blockchain networks will lead to a safer and better payments system and CBDC will be its foundation.

However, a much underappreciated point is that it did not make any sense for a *central bank* to adopt a bitcoin or Ripple-style distributed ledger, as was now commonly presumed. The purpose of the distributed ledger was to allow a decentralised system to operate that could run itself and did not depend on any one entity to manage it. A Bitcoin-style distributed ledger is much slower and does not easily scale, and being able to scale is hugely important in the digital payments business. Moreover, blockchains such as the Bitcoin one are expensive to operate because they consume a lot of computer and electrical power to solve the mathematical problems on whose solution the system's performance depends.

An alternative to a distributed ledger is an old-fashioned hub-and-spokes system with the payments manager, in this case the central bank, as the hub. Roubini (2018) was correct when he wrote that 'No central banker in his or her right mind would ever swap out that sound system for one based on blockchain.' Before Bitcoin even came along, the experience of Doug Jackson's e-gold system had already shown that a digital payments system could operate at scale and at negligible cost. So, taking into account developments in systems architecture that have taken place since e-gold was shut down in 2005, a natural choice for a central bank was to work with an updated e-gold-type payments system using more flexible scalable architectures that have been developed since then.[10] Put differently, you might adopt a blockchain if you *did not* trust the central bank to manage the

[10] For more on these issues see Jackson (2018, 2020). Mojaloop (see https://mojaloop.io/how-it-works/) is a good example of such a system.

system, but if you *did* trust the central bank to operate the system and especially if you *were* the central bank itself, then you should adopt one of these more recently developed payments architectures instead.[11]

Confusion over this point persists in CBDC circles even now. For example, according to the Atlantic Council CBDC Tracker, among the five currently operational CBDCs (those in the Bahamas, China, the East Caribbean Currency Union, Jamaica and Nigeria), three (those in the Bahamas, the East Caribbean Currency Union and Nigeria) are built on a blockchain-type ledger. This point alone suggests that 3 out of the 5 contemporary CBDCs are built on a major misconception of a basic design principle and so have no realistic chance of ever achieving scale.

## 2.5 THE LIBRA THREAT

On 18 June 2019, Facebook published the white paper for its long-awaited cryptocurrency, the 'Libra'. Facebook's white paper was the most hotly anticipated ever, the more so because of the secrecy surrounding the project. 'The Libra Association's mission is to enable a simple global payment system and financial infrastructure that empowers billions of people', it announced.[12]

David Gerard, the author of *Revenge of the 50 Foot Blockchain*, was not too convinced:

> Libra promises a fabulously efficient financial future – 'paying bills with the push of a button, buying a cup of coffee with the scan of a code or riding your local public transit without needing to carry cash or a metro pass.' Imagine if you could do all of that!
>
> If you're in Europe or Asia rather than the United States, you've had all of that for the past decade or so with the card or phone that's already in your pocket . . .
>
> A lot of the problems that Facebook claims Libra solves are really just US retail banking being a few decades behind the rest of the world—sending money between banks can take days, everything has fees, so many things need a phone

[11] In his Fedcoin posting, Andolfatto says 'I have some serious reservations about the efficiency of proof-of-work mechanisms' so he clearly gets the problem. In a slightly later postscript, he also outlines a centralised version of Fedcoin – which he calls 'Fedwire for all' – as an alternative to the distributed ledger version that featured in the original posting. 'People are asking questions, like why would we want to use an inefficient system like Bitcoin, which consumes vast quantities of electricity, when a centralized system is more efficient', he said (quoted in Todd, 2015). Similarly, in their article introducing a proposed new digital coin called RSCoin, Danezis and Meiklejohn (2016) 'demonstrate, both theoretically and experimentally, the benefits of a *modest* degree of centralization, such as the elimination of wasteful hashing and a scalable system for avoiding double-spending attacks' (my italics).

[12] See https://tinyurl.com/ymymky4d. Accessed 3 February 2026.

call, paper checks are still a thing, and so on. But it's standard in Silicon Valley to propose an all-encompassing international system, and base it entirely on looking out your window in Palo Alto. (Gerard, 2020c)

The white paper revealed that the Libra would operate on its own blockchain and would be backed by a basket of low-volatility assets including bank deposits in various currencies and US Treasuries, which technically makes it a stablecoin, not too unlike Tether USD, but with its price pegged to a basket of five currencies rather than to the dollar alone.[13] The coin would be governed by a non-profit consortium, the 'Libra Association', which would oversee development of the Libra ecosystem from Geneva.

Some twenty-eight partners, including Visa, Mastercard, PayPal and others, had pledged to help build out the ecosystem and would contribute $10 million each to kick start the new Libra Association that would govern the coin and its reserve assets.

The coin was also intended to facilitate payments across Facebook's various smart contract platforms (including WhatsApp and Instagram), as well as a new Libra payments app. The coin's software would be open source and allow developers to build out an ecosystem around it. It could operate like PayPal and would enable, for example, remittances and other payments to be made to people anywhere in the world with virtually no commission. Facebook hoped its app and its mobile first strategy would help plug the 'payments gap' created by 1.7 billion adults across the world being without bank accounts.

Facebook would also spin off a unit called Calibra, which would be separate from Facebook and not share user information with it, to manage the Libra digital wallet, which would be integrated into Facebook's family of apps. It was also hoped that Facebook's new cryptocurrency platform would provide it with a new revenue stream of historic proportions as well as attract even more users to its vast social network.

However, the project evoked a hostile reception because Facebook had a bad reputation for stealing personal data and for other scandals, which regulatory authorities were already investigating, and because Mark Zuckerberg had made a plenty of enemies. 'From the people who ripped your data off, they can now get into your wallet', one observer quipped.[14]

The Congressional hearings in mid July were openly hostile. Senator Sherrod Brown (D-OH) set the tone: '[Facebook] is like a toddler who has

[13] More details of Libra's monetary technicalities can be found in White (2019b).

[14] This quote and the otherwise unattributed quotes that follow are all from Murphy and Stacey (2022).

gotten his hands on a book of matches', he said. 'Facebook has burned down the house over and over and called every arson a learning experience.' On the Republican side: 'I don't trust you guys', said Senator Martha McSally (R-AZ).

The adverse legislative response continued to cause a stir among policymakers after that. In October, Senator Brown warned, 'Facebook is too big and too powerful, and it is unconscionable for financial companies to aid it in monopolizing our economic infrastructure' (Brown, 2019). In November, Representative Jesus Garcia (D-IL) introduced the Keep Big Tech Out of Finance Act, a bill intended to prohibit large technology companies from offering financial services and especially cryptocurrencies (Garcia, 2019).

Facebook executives were taken aback by the Congressional reaction and Libra partners soon started to quit. Senators threatened them with increased scrutiny – 'It's as close to a Sopranos threat as you'll ever read', said an insider[15] – and executives realised they needed to make concessions if they were to win them over. So the project shrunk from one based on a basket of currencies to one based solely on the US dollar, it was rebranded – Libra became 'Diem' and Calibra became 'Novi' – and the headquarters were to be moved to the US to reassure regulators. However, these efforts at reassurance were rebuffed when the Fed finally said no on 29 June 2021, the day before the official launch.[16] Diem's leadership then spent the next six months in a last-ditch drive to rescue the project but to no avail. In January 2022, they announced that the scheme was to be abandoned. Not a single regulator anywhere had given it permission to operate legally.

Murphy and Stacey (2022) offered an interesting epitaph:

> What [Diem executives] failed to realise was that the very fact Facebook had conceived the idea, doomed it. As one government official involved in the process puts it: 'Diem spent years trying to reverse engineer their project to fix all of its faults. But they could never fix being linked to Facebook. It was their original sin.'

[15] The letter of 8 October 2019 from senators Brian Schatz (D-Hawai'i) and Jerrod Brown advised them of a 'proliferation of online child sexual abuse, due to a large part to tech platforms like Facebook. ... If you take this [Libra] on, you can expect a high level of scrutiny from regulators, *not just* on Libra-related payments activities, but *on all* payments activities' (my italics).

[16] The decision had been made on 24 June 2021, when Fed chair Jerome Powell had his weekly breakfast with Treasury Secretary Janet Yellen. Powell told Yellen that he was willing to give the go-ahead for Facebook and its partners to trial Diem. Yellen told him that it was 'political suicide': 'it was his decision to make, but that she would not protect him from the political fallout if he did so', says one person briefed on the conversation. 'And that was the end of Facebook's digital currency' (quoted in Durden, 2024, and Murphy and Stacey, 2022).

## 2.6 THE RISE OF CBDCS

Diem's most notable legacy, however, would appear be that it concentrated the minds of policymakers and regulators on the perceived threat that such a scheme posed to financial stability[17] and on the 'need' for central banks to create competitors to pre-empt future versions of Diem. As Zachary Warmbrodt reported in October 2019, 'Lawmakers and Federal Reserve officials are so concerned about Facebook's plans to launch a new digital currency that they're contemplating a novel response – having the central bank create a competitor', that is, a CBDC (Warmbrodt, 2019).

The reaction in Europe was similar. In September 2019, the European Central Bank's Benoît Cœuré warned in a speech about the 'formidable challenges' posed by Libra and similar private initiatives. It was a 'wake-up call' for central bankers who needed to work on technologies to make payments 'faster and cheaper', he said (Sandbu, 2019). Similarly, in a meeting of EU finance ministers that same month, Bruno Le Maire, the French finance minister, said that 'under current circumstances, we should refuse the development of Libra in the EU' because it risked undermining the 'monetary sovereignty' of governments (quoted in Sandbu, 2019). Then Christine Lagarde, the ECB president, said in an unguarded moment in 2023 that

> The reason I'm personally convinced that we have to move ahead [with a CBDC] is a situation like the one we are in now. . . . I don't want Europe to be dependent on an unfriendly country's currency . . . or dependent on a friendly currency [that] is activated by a private corporate entity like, you know, Facebook or Google. . . . I don't want Meta, Google, or Amazon to suddenly come up with a currency that will take over the sovereignty of Europe.[18]

[17] 'Nothing amplified [financial stability] concerns more than Facebook's announcement of the Libra project last year', said Senator Mike Crapo (R- ID) on 30 June 2020; see www.banking.senate.gov/newsroom/majority/crapo-statement-at-digital-currency-hearing (accessed 3 February 2026). Similarly, de los Rios and Zhu (2020, p. 4) write 'Wide adoption of a digital currency denominated in a different unit of account, such as Libra, presents a significant threat to monetary sovereignty and financial stability.' Without going into details, I think such concerns are overrated – the financial stability 'risk' of private currency supplanting government currency is not much different in principle to the old 'risk' of bank deposits supplanting banknotes and that was never much of a problem in the first place. I would also suggest that concerns about monetary sovereignty are anachronistic and should have no place in a free-market economy.

[18] Lagarde's comments were made when she thought she was speaking in confidence to Ukrainian President Volodymyr Zelenskyy but was actually speaking to pranksters (*Forkcast.news*, 2023).

The word 'sovereignty' is key here. Libra had frightened central banks to their core. Libra was not just a stablecoin like the others, but a global one that had the capacity – so they feared – to scale to a level that posed a major threat to their own powers and interests, including their right to govern, namely, to exercise their 'sovereignty'. Down the road, it even posed a threat to their continued existence.

Add to this threat central banks' fear of the spectre of large tech firms entering financial markets and it soon became clear that they would seek to ban stablecoins or at least regulate them into some corner of the financial system where the dangers they posed could be neutralised.

Thus, Libra unwittingly helped to catapult the CBDC agenda into centre space.

By this point, CBDC mania among central bankers had already taken off. As of 12 January 2026, five CBDC schemes are currently in operation in China, Nigeria, the Bahamas, Jamaica and the eight island countries which are members of the East Caribbean Currency Union. At that same date, the Atlantic Council CBDC tracker reports forty-nine schemes in the pilot or pre-launch stage, twenty in the earlier development stage, thirty-six in the research stage, twenty-one inactive schemes, two schemes have been launched and since abandoned, and six schemes classified as 'other'.[19] All G20 countries were investigating CBDCs, and nineteen of them were at an advanced stage (Bhandhakavi, 2024).

CBDCs were also being pushed strongly by the World Economic Forum, the Bank for International Settlements (BIS), the International Monetary Fund and the World Bank, all of whom exuded a breathless confidence in CBDCs' glittering future. To give just one example, the outgoing governor of the Reserve Bank of India, Shaktikanta Das, said in his farewell speech on 19 December 2024, 'As I see it, CBDC has a huge potential in the coming years, in the future. In fact, it is the future of currency' (quoted in Sarkar, 2024).

However, by 2024, there were also clear signs of pushback. In July, the Banco de la República of Colombia published a report that said, 'there are not sufficient reasons for the issuance of [a CBDC] (retail or wholesale) in Colombia' (Banco de la República Colombia, 2024). In September, both the Bank of Canada and the Reserve Bank of Australia made similar announcements: the former said in a very low key announcement that it

[19] Note that the Atlantic Council CBDC tracker considers the CBDC schemes in China and in the countries of the ECCU as in the pilot stage. See www.atlanticcouncil.org/cbdctracker/. Accessed 3 February 2026.

is 'scaling down its work on a retail central bank digital currency and shifting its focus to broader payments system research and policy development' (Reserve Bank of Australia and Government of Australia, 2024). and the latter said 'There is no clear public interest case to issue retail CBDC in Australia yet' (Bank of Canada, 2024). Then, in January 2025, came President Trump's Executive Order banning CBDCs in the United States.

There are also concerns about why central banks are so keen to promote CBDCs. When one examines the reasons central banks give for pursuing CBDCs, one finds that one reason was because other central banks were also pursuing them: central banks had a fear of missing out. Creating a CBDC because Facebook (almost) created Libra or because China adopted a CBDC is not a good basis for policy, however. A darker reason sometimes suggested is that central banks were keen to expand their power and a CBDC would potentially expand it greatly.

A more sensible approach would have been to consider the problems that needed to be addressed or were worth addressing, and to consider the wider range of reliable technologies available in the payments area that could achieve those ends.

Part of this problem relates to the all-important question of the demand, or not, for CBDCs. As a case in point, consider the following from the speech given by then BIS official Benoît Cœuré in Ljubljana on 10 September 2021: 'We have to ask ourselves why consumers would want a CBDC and what would they want it to do?' (Cœuré, 2021).

The issue, however, is not to ask why consumers *would* want this CBDC that advocates want them to adopt, but first to ask if they *actually* want a CBDC in the first place? There is no evidence to suggest that they do. There is also no point building the product without first establishing that people would buy it, otherwise they will end up building a CBDC equivalent of the Ford Edsel that no one wants. It is a fundamental principle of marketing that a product should solve a problem that the customer has. So what exactly *is* this problem? Answers on a postcard please to Agustín C., c/o BIS, Geneva, Switzerland.

If the private sector introduced an unwanted digital currency, then the budget constraint would eventually kick in and the project would be shut down. However, the CBDC project has no comparable constraint and carries on because the public sector continues to throw good (public) money after bad at it.

That, in a nutshell, is why the Great CBDC Project is failing and why it will turn out down the road to be a major embarrassment to those who promoted it.

I leave the last word to the American banking entrepreneur Vernon Hill: ‘You can’t name me one retailer in this country that has pushed people where they don’t want to go and succeeded.’

# 3

# CBDC Fundamentals

**Main Points**

**CBDCs can be retail or wholesale, but it is the retail CBDCs that are most important.**
**Retail CBDCs are inefficient and could only be accepted by the public if the central bank subsidises them. Thus, they would earn negative seigniorage.**
**Retail CBDC systems are prone to potentially serious instability.**
**Second-generation CBDC systems that offer interest payments pose additional major problems for the central bank.**

This chapter sets out the fundamentals of CBDCs, first we address the taxonomy and then the main economic issues involved with CBDCs.

## 3.1 DEFINITION OF A CBDC

A *Central Bank Digital Currency* (CBDC) is a digital currency which is issued by (and hence is a liability of) the central bank or monetary authority and is denominated in the local government currency unit (e.g., the dollar or pound). The term 'digital' means that it exists as an item on a digital ledger and not as a physical instrument.[1]

[1] Kiff et al. provide an alternative but similar definition: a CBDC is 'a digital representation of a sovereign currency issued by and as a liability of a jurisdiction's central bank or other monetary authority' (Kiff et al., 2020, p. 9).

**Box 3.1 CBDCs vs Cryptocurrencies**

Central Bank Digital Currencies (CBDCs) and cryptocurrencies differ fundamentally in their nature and governance. CBDCs are digital currencies directly tied to a country's official currency. They are issued by and regulated by a central bank. They offer government control and are subject to compliance with existing government regulations.

In contrast, cryptocurrencies like Bitcoin operate on a decentralised blockchain, independent of any central authority. They prioritise decentralisation, autonomy and a certain degree of anonymity but their prices are typically subject to considerable volatility as demand rises or falls.

The distinction between CBDCs and cryptocurrencies is also linked to that between permissioned and permissionless systems. Permissioned systems require user authorisation from the system management to access and participate in the network, and give management control over the network. Permissionless systems promote decentralisation and openness, and allow anyone to join and interact without needing approval.

## 3.2 CBDCS COMPARED TO NEAR SUBSTITUTES

We can compare CBDCs to the following near substitutes:

*Banknotes*: In the US, dollar bills (sometimes also known as *paper currency* or *cash*) are issued by and hence are liabilities of the Federal Reserve, but exist as anonymous[2] physical bearer instruments.[3] CBDCs also differ from conventional non-interest-bearing banknotes in that CBDCs are programmable currency and can in principle bear positive or negative interest.

A programmable currency is a digital or cryptocurrency that allows for the execution of automated, self-executing smart contracts or predefined instructions. These contracts enable transactions and financial operations to occur automatically when specific conditions are met, making the

[2] We say that paper currency transactions are 'anonymous', i.e., are not traceable to the transacting individuals, but we ignore the point that these transactions can be traced if one is able to count and follow the serial numbers.

[3] We gloss over *physical coins*, which play no role in our discussions here.

currency itself capable of carrying out complex, predefined functions without the need for intermediaries.

To quote Cecchetti and Schoenholtz:

> [Paper currency] is supplied elastically to allow the conversion of certain bank liabilities at par into the medium of exchange without limit in as many circumstances as possible. Anyone can hold paper currency. And, it bears zero interest.
>
> The likely characteristics of CBDC are equally clear. To avoid facilitating criminal activity, CBDC *cannot* be anonymous.[4] To truly substitute for paper currency, it will have to be supplied elastically.[5] Individuals will be allowed to hold unlimited quantities; otherwise, there would be circumstances when bank liabilities will not be convertible into CBDC at par. (Cecchetti and Schoenholtz, 2021)

*Deposits at financial institutions and other private means of payment*: These are issued by commercial banks and other private payment firms. These are liabilities of the issuing firm – the firm owes a customer an amount of money equivalent to the money deposited in the customer's account and is responsible for transferring it at their request – and (barring a bailout) are not liabilities of the central bank.

*Reserves with the central bank*: These are the amounts held by financial institutions on deposit with the central bank and are liabilities of the central bank. CBDCs would also be liabilities of the central bank, but come in two broad forms: (a) *wholesale CBDCs*, which are much the same in principle as traditional bank reserves with the central bank; and (b) *retail CBDCs*, which are CBDCs issued to retail users, namely, to firms and individuals across the economy.

The basic taxonomy of CBDCs is illustrated in the Figure 3.1.[6] Along the top row, we have wholesale CBDCs that are issued only to those financial institutions with accounts at the central bank. Along the bottom row, we have retail CBDCs issued to potentially everyone. These in turn can be divided into: (a) account-based retail CBDCs whose users are typically identifiable to the central bank, who would access with account information and have wallets that allow user and transaction authentication and a digital interface;[7] and (b) token-based retail CBDCs whose

[4] See, however, the comments on anonymity a little further below.

[5] Although its developers sometimes envisaged that CBDCs might only be issued in limited quantities. More on this issue later.

[6] One could provide a more elaborate taxonomy (e.g., as in Lloyd, 2023, pp. 34–37, who also includes hybrid systems) but the taxonomy provided in the text suffices for our purpose.

[7] However, it has been suggested that, e.g., the Bank of England might allow payment interface providers (PIPs), intermediaries that would provide account-based CBDCs to

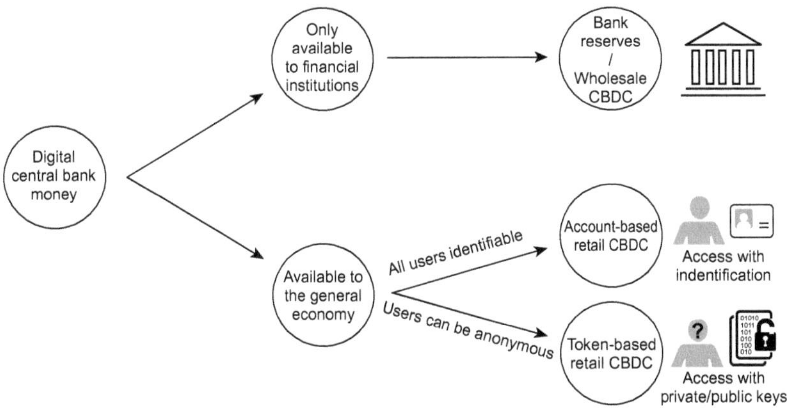


In today's financial system, digital fiat money is available only to regulated financial institutions, in the form of reserves accounts held by commercial banks at the central bank. Wholesale CBDCs would similarly be restricted to financial institutions. Retail CBDCs in contrast are available to the general economy. Account-based retail CBDCs would be tied to an identification scheme and all users would need to identify themselves. Token-based retail CBDCs would be accessed via password-like digital signatures and could be accessed anonymously.
© Bank of International Settlements

FIGURE 3.1 Different forms of CBDC

users are (or could in principle be) unidentifiable to the central bank, and who could access and trade anonymously with public/private keys.

## 3.3 CBDCS COULD BE ANONYMOUS BUT WILL NOT BE

CBDCs could be designed to be anonymous, as shown with token-based retail CBDCs in Figure 3.1. However, in practice governments will not allow them to be anonymous, while occasionally insisting, contrary to the evidence, that governments can provide greater privacy than the private sector can.[8] To quote Lawrence H. White:

> It is of course laughable that a government would itself provide greater privacy in payments than it allows private institutions to provide. . . . The private sector can in fact provide as much financial privacy as customers desire, as numbered Swiss bank accounts once did, and as 'privacycoin' crypto projects today remind us.

the public, with tiered wallets that could allow less stringent identity requirements (and hence more anonymity) for low-value digital pound holdings and transactions.

[8] To give an example, former IMF head Christine Lagarde proposed in a speech in 2018 that a CBDC could 'provide what the private sector cannot . . . privacy in payments' (Lagarde, 2018). However, Lagarde's claim that the private sector cannot protect privacy is just plain wrong: Austrian, British and Swiss banks successfully provided it for many decades until governments pressured them to stop.

> Lack of privacy stems from government [legal] restrictions [against financial privacy], not from private-sector inability [to provide financial privacy]. (White, 2018b)

A token-based CBDC would be most equivalent to 'digital cash' because, like a banknote, it would be a bearer instrument that could be transferred with anonymity. However, a token CBDC would be incompatible with existing AML regimes and could only be issued, if at all, in small amounts. AML rules depend on physical cash being bulky and difficult to move and store securely; people then need to convert it into commercial bank money to spend it; and banks assume the duty of monitoring or blocking its movement. Anonymous digital cash would present no such obstacle.

Thus, in practice, we can rule out anonymous token-based CBDCs as being politically unacceptable to financial regulators unless issued in small amounts.

## 3.4 WHOLESALE CBDCS

A wholesale CBDC (W-CBDC) system is one in which the central bank would hold all CBDC accounts for participating financial institutions and provide all their CBDC payments services, such as cross-border exchange services.[9] Participating institutions would include the big banks, other big financial firms and foreign central banks, and one might imagine that the Fed's wholesale CBDC group would grow over time. However, as Norbert Michel points out:

> With a wholesale CBDC, banks can electronically transact with each other using a liability of the central bank. Because that is essentially what banks do now, transact and settle (electronically) using reserve accounts held at the Fed, there aren't very many new and interesting wholesale CBDC policy issues [because in effect] *the Fed has had a wholesale CBDC for decades*. (Michel, 2022b, my italics)

Others might disagree with his claim that wholesale CBDCs do not give rise to new or interesting policy issues, but one cannot deny that the Fed has had a wholesale CBDC for decades, albeit without calling it that.

[9] Leading examples of wholesale CBDCs are Fnality and RTGS Global, which can potentially offer a range of wholesale market services, especially repo and cross-border exchange, that are currently impractical, costly or infeasible because of limitations on wholesale RTGS access and operating hours. For a more detailed treatment of W-CBDCs, see Lloyd (2023, pp. 135–141).

One such issue is a major rift in the W-CBDC world between those who support the BIS's Project Agorá and those who support the most established cross-border CBDC, Project mBridge, spearheaded by the People's Bank of China (PBOC). The proposed solution is to create multi-currency CBDC exchanges, but as Bryce Elder (2024) points out, 'it's already gone VHS vs Betamax', that is, two competing incompatible standards, and in October 2024, the BIS formally pulled out of mBridge. The result is that even central bankers are, at the time of writing, losing confidence in W-CBDCs being the most promising fix for cross-border payments (see Elder, 2024).

There is also some confusion on central banks' part about the underlying technology. In an email to me of 22 January 2022, Doug Jackson explained this confusion as follows:

> To me the so-called W-CBDC ('wholesale') conceit is the epitome of stupid. Most advanced economies have used ... current account balances at the central bank, which can be held/used only by domestically chartered depository institutions – as the medium of final settlement for intermediated payments for decades. Recasting [these] as CBDCs betrays the 'Cool Kids' New Clothes' memes that have infected central banks, causing them to imagine, counterfactually, that [distributed ledger technology] is somehow superior to more-efficient and straightforward protocols/technologies.

These points are well-taken, but we will have little further to say of wholesale CBDCs and will focus henceforth on retail CBDCs instead.

## 3.5 RETAIL CBDCS

A retail CBDC is one in which the CBDC is attached to ordinary people and firms and potentially tracked as it passes from one owner to the next. We have already explained that retail CBDCs can be either token or account based, but they might also come in one of two further forms – a *direct* CBDC system, in which the central bank would manage all CBDC accounts, and an *indirect* CBDC system, in which the central bank would issue all CBDCs, but leave their management to a bank or other intermediary (e.g., a non-bank fintech firm).

### 3.5.1 Direct Retail CBDCs

The direct model is attractive for its simplicity, because it does not involve any other institutions. However, the direct retail model is quite impractical because central banks have neither the expertise, manpower nor the desire to take on the technical issues related to AML/KYC rules:

A direct model would require the central bank to take on responsibility for account administration – for example, account services (including providing ongoing balances), AML/KYC monitoring, transaction verification, dispute resolution and provision of any mobile banking applications. For some perspective on the workforce required, the 17 largest [US] banks employ over 14,000 people in AML/KYC compliance alone; the industry total is likely closer to 20,000. If nationalized, this workforce would constitute a government agency roughly the size of the Department of Energy or the Environmental Protection Agency. And that is only AML/KYC.

Lastly, the financial sector also would lose access to data that comes with processing transactions; the effect on FinTech firms that count on monetizing that data would be particularly significant. The government would hold that data. Thus, consumers and businesses would gain privacy vis-à-vis the private sector and lose it vis-à-vis the government.

Thus, there is a strong consensus among central banks and other analysts that a direct model is unworkable … (Baer, 2021, pp. 4–5)

Those, such as Bordo and Levin (2019)[10] or Roubini (2019),[11] who argue that the central bank can provide such services for free through a direct system are simply mistaken. Indeed, central banks do not even have a comparative advantage in retail payment services, that is, they cannot provide transferable deposit accounts to individuals and businesses at lower cost than commercial banks do, much less that they can provide such services at zero cost. Zero-cost service is a fantasy.

White writes:

[Even managing] retail accounts in a way that satisfies users, as we see in a competitive environment where providers have every incentive to be cost-efficient, is far from zero-cost. Commercial banks invest capital in branch offices and ATMs. They employ tellers, customer service representatives, and 'phone bankers' for such tasks as processing account applications (including identity verification), dealing with cash and foreign exchange, answering customer questions, and resolving disputes. Central banks have little experience at providing such consumer services. According to the Bureau of Labor Statistics, depository institutions in 2016 employed 444,000 tellers and 120,700 customer service

[10] Michael Bordo and Andrew Levin have asserted, incorrectly, that a direct CBDC would be 'a practically costless medium of exchange' (2019, p. 392).

[11] Roubini: 'It would be a completely efficient system. It would be almost virtually costless. It would be safe. … It would reduce a lot the transaction costs. … [Y]ou can do it for free with the central bank. And of course it will dominate the deposits that individuals have in their private commercial banks' (quotes from YouTube video cited in White, 2019a).

> representatives. Meanwhile the BLS estimates that the Federal Reserve in 2016 employed about 100 tellers and 300 customer service representatives. . . .
>
> Implication: if the Federal Reserve were to take over the provision of retail demand deposits, it would have to hire more than 400,000 employees[12] away from commercial banks to give the same level of consumer service as the banks currently do. Note that the profit motive, together with the weeding-out of loss-making firms, impels commercial banks not to add employees inefficiently, beyond the point where the additional services they provide are as valuable to consumers as they are costly to the bank. The Federal Reserve faces no such motive or discipline. Presently the Federal Reserve System has around 20,000 employees. If my estimate is in the ballpark, taking over retail payments would be more than a twenty-fold expansion of its workforce. (White, 2019a)

Moreover, it would be quite unreasonable to expect a command-and-control government agency with no retail experience to provide better retail service as a state monopoly than the private sector firms that currently make their living providing such services under competitive conditions. The likely outcome would be a system that falls short on customer service or loses money at taxpayers' expense, or both. This is the outcome we have seen at public monopolies like state-owned liquor stores and the US Postal Service, and at state-owned retail enterprises such as Petro-Canada. Retail payment services do not become more efficient by moving them into a bureaucratic public sector agency.

Underlying these issues is that proposals for CBDCs rely implicitly on what Deirdre McCloskey and Alberto Mingardi (2020) call 'the myth of the entrepreneurial state', the idea that innovation is top-down and state-led. However, economic history shows that successful innovation tends to be bottom-up and profit-driven, and state-led enterprises often do more harm than good because they do not need to make profits to continue in business and can distort markets indefinitely while supported by taxpayer subsidies. At the most basic level, proposals for CBDCs fail to address the most elementary questions, in particular, why would we expect someone with no skin in the game to do better than those who do have skin in the game, and why would we expect good retail service from people with no experience at providing it, and who have little to gain by doing a doing a good job at it, or to lose by doing a bad job?

[12] White also provides a breakdown of his numbers, which I do not repeat here.

**Box 3.2 The Balance Sheet Impact of a Switch from Cash or Deposits to CBDC**

*Switching from cash to CBDC*: Banknotes and CBDC are just two different types of central bank liability, so a switch from banknotes to CBDC affects the composition – but not the size – of household and central bank balance sheets. The household swaps one asset (cash) for another asset (CBDC) and the central bank swaps one liability (cash) for another liability (CBDC). Although banks may facilitate this conversion from cash to CBDC, the process has no impact on the size of the banking sector's balance sheet.

*Switching from deposits to CBDC*: A shift from deposits into CBDC has the same impact on bank balance sheets as a withdrawal of banknotes from an ATM or bank branch, reducing both the assets and liabilities of the bank and shrinking the bank's balance sheet. This means that net shifts from deposits to CBDC (partially) disintermediate the banking sector. For example, if a household wants to convert £10 of deposits to CBDC:

- The household tells its bank to make a £10 payment from its deposit account to its CBDC account (in effect, 'withdrawing' CBDC just like with cash).
- The bank debits (i.e. reduces the value of) the household's account by £10.
- The bank tells the central bank to transfer £10 from its reserves account to the household's CBDC account.
- The central bank debits (reduces the value of) the bank's reserves account, and credits (increases the value of) the household's CBDC account, by £10.
- The composition of the household's assets changes, because it now holds £10 less in deposits and £10 more in CBDC. But there is no change in the overall size of the household's balance sheet.
- The composition of the central bank's liabilities changes: it now has £10 less in reserve liabilities and £10 more in CBDC liabilities. But there is no immediate change in the size of the central bank's balance sheet.
- However, the commercial bank has lost both £10 of reserves (an asset) and £10 of deposits (a liability). Its balance sheet has contracted by £10.[13]

[13] This text is reproduced with permission from Bank of England (2020, Box 4, p. 36).

### 3.5.2 Indirect Retail CBDCs

The alternative is an indirect retail CBDC system in which private institutions would provide the front-end services, as they do today for conventional operations. In this latter system, consumers would hold their CBDC account at a bank or other firm – say PayPal or Amazon – in a digital wallet. The obligation to provide CBDC on demand would fall to the intermediary rather than the central bank. However, instead of these intermediaries booking transactions on their own balance sheets as is the case today, they would simply update the record of who owns which CBDC balance. The central bank then avoids the operational tasks of opening accounts and administering payments, as private intermediaries would continue to perform retail payment services. In effect, the intermediaries would become an agent of the central bank.

However, it is important to understand that a customer holding CBDCs is much like a customer holding cash in so far as neither provides funding to banks. Baer and Nelson explain:

> we have spoken with many smart people – policymakers, bankers, journalists – who believe that in fact a CBDC would continue to provide funding to banks and thereby support their lending. …
>
> That is wrong – really wrong.
>
> The defining characteristic of a CBDC is that it is a direct obligation of a central bank. In the United States, a CBDC would be an obligation of the Federal Reserve in the same way as a $20 Federal Reserve note. …
>
> Thus, if a CBDC is to remain a CBDC to the business or consumer that owns it, it could not be 'deposited' in a bank, because then it would become a liability of the bank. It could be transferred into a customer's digital CBDC wallet managed by the bank and held in custody – like an equity security or money placed in a safety deposit box – but for it to remain a CBDC, the liability for repayment must continue to rest solely and completely with the central bank. And that means it cannot at the same time also be a liability of [a] bank, used to fund loans and other bank assets. It cannot fund both Fed assets and bank assets. (Baer and Nelson, 2021, p. 1)

However, left unexplained 'is why or how a bank would continue to perform those extraordinarily expensive and burdensome agency functions when it no longer received the low-cost funding benefit that comes with carrying a deposit' (Baer, 2021, p. 5, my italics). Thus, a system of indirect retail CBDCs would be *more expensive* to operate than a payments system based on conventional bank deposits. To quote Sam Callahan:

> Retail CBDC accounts would require compliance with AML/KYC rules and would significantly increase the burden and costs for the compliance and

cybersecurity departments of these private financial institutions. There are also the operational costs of building and maintaining all of the technology to be interoperable with the CBDC payment infrastructure. There is the cost of creating wallets, maintaining the systems, and guaranteeing access to these new CBDC accounts. More importantly, there is no clear revenue stream to compensate the private sector for providing these new services. (2023, p. 9)

One must also bear in mind that neither commercial banks nor their customers would have any reason to bear these additional costs of their own free will. To quote a letter from the Independent Community Bankers of America:

Compliance functions are not costless – far from it – and therefore creating the technical and compliance infrastructure for CBDC wallets will require a compensation model that could include charging fees to users. The fees banks will be required to charge in order for CBDC wallets to be a viable business will significantly offset any potential benefit to financial inclusion presented by a CBDC. Currently, the price of deposit accounts to customers is subsidized both by a bank's ability to lend against deposits and to collect interchange fees on transactions. Neither of these business models will be available with a CBDC, so customers may likely be required to pay for access to wallets with an account maintenance fee to offset bank investments to provide and maintain these services. (quoted in Callahan, 2023, p. 10)

## 3.6 INEFFICIENCIES IN CBDC PAYMENTS SYSTEMS

If retail CBDCs are more expensive to operate than a traditional payments system, then retail CBDCs must be inefficient and those involved would not rationally wish to use them.

CBDCs are also inefficient in so far as the attention and energy put into the promotion of CBDCs distracts central banks from considering more promising agendas that get crowded out in the process. Such alternative agendas include promoting other ways to improve payments systems efficiency, promoting synthetic CBDCs or promoting a more level playing field between different payments system providers. Resources are then wasted on promoting CBDCs which could have been more productively employed elsewhere. These 'opportunity cost' problems are a big deal, because once any particular agenda is adopted, the alternative agendas foregone in the process are soon forgotten.

There are also cross-border payments efficiency issues. To quote just one claim on this subject: 'CBDCs would enable more efficient remittances from one country to another. This would significantly reduce the costs of sending and receiving currency, as well as increasing competition in the financial sector' (quoted from Hustle Escape, no date). However, the simplest way to improve cross-border payments efficiency is not to create a wholesale CBDC, but to reduce the burdens created by grossly excessive AML regulation. As Baer (2021, p. 3) observed, 'The solution to revitalizing correspondent networks and speeding cross-border transactions has always been obvious: establishing objective, pre-defined criteria for [AML regulations] and sanctions compliance and granting banks a safe harbor from enforcement if they meet them.' Moreover, this point is true regardless of whether the payment is in commercial bank money or in a CBDC.

## 3.7 INEFFICIENCIES IN US PAYMENTS SYSTEM DUE TO SLOW SETTLEMENTS, NOT THE ABSENCE OF A CBDC

If one looks at the current US payments system, the main problem with it is not that it lacks a CBDC, but that payments settlement is way too slow. 'America's payment system seems more like it belongs to a developing nation than to one of the wealthiest countries on the planet', wrote Aaron Klein and George Selgin in 2020. US banks can easily take a few days to grant customers access to their own deposits. The consequences for poorer Americans can be dire, as they are forced to turn to payday lenders or pay high bank overdraft fees. As Klein and Selgin continue:

> Yet the Fed itself deserves much of the blame for the slow pace of clearing U.S. payments. While other nations were modernizing their payment systems, the U.S. fell further and further behind. . . .
>
> [The problem is that] . . . the Fed hasn't announced making significant steps that could speed many payments up a lot sooner.
>
> Those steps include improvements to the Fedwire and the National Settlement Service [NSS], two 'wholesale' payment services the Fed uses to move funds between different banks. . . . Fedwire and the NSS keep limited weekday hours, and don't open on weekends and holidays. . . .
>
> Though it could make a huge difference, keeping Fedwire and NSS open longer is relatively easy. It's also one of the few payment-system reforms that nearly all payments-industry stakeholders support. (Klein and Selgin, 2020)

This issue of extending opening hours has been going on for nearly a decade and was one of the main recommendations of the 332-member Faster Payments Task Force the Fed established in 2015! Yet in deciding to launch FedNow [which came online in 2023] – a far more ambitious and controversial project – Fed officials set aside the simpler reform, bizarrely saying they needed more time to 'explore' it. Then, when asked about it before Congress in March 2023, the Fed chair simply said, 'I'm not sure why we are not 24x7' already (Anthony, 2023b). The issue has gone on for so long that the Fed has forgotten about it!

So how can one argue that a retail CBDC is necessary to improve payments efficiency when all the Fed needs to do to improve payments efficiency is to *remember* to have its own NSS and Fedwire systems increase their own opening hours instead?

This problem is also a peculiarly American one as other developed countries with better-functioning financial systems see no payments efficiency case for a CBDC. For example, Philip Lowe, the governor of the Reserve Bank of Australia, recently observed, 'To date, though, we have not seen a strong public policy case to move [towards a CBDC], especially given Australia's efficient, fast, and convenient electronic payments system' (Lowe, 2021). Similarly in other countries we already see public and private sectors moving to provide cheaper, faster, more reliable and more accessible retail payments systems that operate both within and across borders. For their part, the euro area has the TIPS system, with a processing time of 10 seconds at a cost of €0.002 per transaction, the UK has Faster Payments, Canada is testing Real-Time Rail (RTR), and so forth, and none of these payment systems requires a CBDC (Cecchetti and Schoenholtz, 2021).

## 3.8 CBDCS COULD DESTABILISE THE FINANCIAL SYSTEM

Perhaps the first point to note here, emphasised by Milne (2024), is that there is a contradiction between the central bank promoting a CBDC, on the one hand, and greater adoption of the CBDC increasing the threat to financial stability, on the other hand. In this case, two key objectives of the central bank (i.e., promoting the CBDC and maintaining financial stability) are in direct contradiction with each other: promoting the one undermines the other. This contradiction is intractable if the central bank issues a CBDC, but does not arise if it does not.

Absent a crisis of confidence, the most likely causes of a payments system disruption are getting hacked, the whole grid going down or a widespread electrical system failure.

The absolute worst-case scenario would be a high-altitude electromagnetic pulse attack or a recurrence of the 1859 Carrington geomagnetic event, the most intense geomagnetic storm in recorded history (see, e.g., Oliver and Svalgaard, 2005). Such a scenario could easily knock out all digital networks including all digital currency systems, not to mention the electrical grid that powers them. It could then take months to get the grid working again. In such circumstances paper currency might be the only safety net to prevent societal collapse. Such events could happen at any time. Less severe coronal events are fairly commonplace. One such event knocked out Quebec's power grid for 9 hours in 1989 and another caused air traffic chaos in Sweden for some hours in 2015 (Pandey, 2024).

Moreover, public sector payments systems – including those operated by central banks – are especially vulnerable to IT problems and on a potentially greatly amplified scale that poses genuinely systemic risks. If implemented with inadequate security protocols, a CBDC could substantially amplify the scope and scale of many of the security and privacy threats that already exist in the financial system.

Hacking is a particular concern. Throughout the period between 2011 and 2015, and doubtless ever since, the Fed has been under constant assault by hackers, was said to be 'compromised frequently' and experienced more than fifty breaches, and this figure does not count any attacks directed at regional Federal Reserve banks (*Reuters*, 2016).

To give a spectacular example, the Federal Reserve Bank of New York fell victim to a successful hack known as the 'Lazarus heist' by a group of North Korean hackers in February 2016. They stole $101 million from it in a cyber-attack carried out via the Bank of Bangladesh. But for extreme good luck, the amount stolen could easily have been almost a billion dollars. It was a 'total fluke' that the name 'Jupiter' was part of the address of a Philippines bank to which the hackers sought to move their money. However, quite by chance, 'Jupiter' also referred to the name of an oil tanker and shipping company under US sanctions against Iran. The cyber-attack triggered concerns about the latter 'Jupiter' and spurred the New York Fed to examine the fake payment orders in more detail, and only then was the hack brought to light (see Das and Spicer, 2016). This case highlights the Fed's vulnerabilities like nothing else ever could, by Jove!

Another example of the dangers posed by computer problems was the CrowdStrike outage that occurred on 19 July 2024, which led to a failure in about 8.5 million Microsoft Windows computers and caused huge disruption to many diverse industries, governments, emergency services and websites. Though it only lasted a day, overall costs of the outage were estimated to be at least $10 billion (see Lian, 2024).

Leaving aside garden-variety central bank operating failures, which are all too common, there are also two potential events we would absolutely wish to avoid. One is a situation where a hacker cracks the computer code that generates the CBDC in such a way that it can mount double-spend attacks against the system and allow it to create and spend the same units of e-currency over and over again. Any such breakthrough could destroy the integrity of the CBDC system. Another is an attack on a 'single point of failure', the failure of which could crash the whole system. A CBDC always has at least one single point of failure, that is, the CBDC programming itself. Such a failure has already happened – the East Caribbean Central Bank's DCash CBDC crashed in early 2023 shortly after it became operational, and it took seven weeks to get it back online.[14] We can never be sure that some other CBDC would not also crash in the future. Were that to happen, the results could be disastrous, especially if the CBDC had become widely accepted and large numbers of people had become dependent on it.

We shall have more to say on CBDCs and financial stability in Chapter 8, where we shall consider how CBDCs could disintermediate the banking system.

## 3.9 INTEREST ON CBDCS

The current first generation of CBDCs bear no interest, positive or negative. In this respect, current CBDCs are like cash that bears a zero return. However, we could envisage CBDCs bearing non-zero interest rates, and these could be positive or negative.

In general terms, we could presume that if CBDC interest rates were in some sense 'too high', then demand for them might become high and excessive, and CBDCs might pull too many funds away from other investments and destabilise the financial system in the process.

We could also speculate that CBDC interest rates should in some sense be 'compatible' – for want of a better term – with returns on other assets, but there are no obvious rules to guide the CBDC interest rate setter. Keynesian economists might welcome this room for additional monetary policy 'discretion' – a new policy instrument is always handy from their perspective – but I worry about the room such an instrument gives policymakers to do a lot of damage by blundering around.

In the current monetary system, there is only one risk-free rate of interest, the interest rate on short-term Treasury bills. By 'risk-free', we mean that the instrument involved, a Treasury bill, is conventionally

[14] We shall say more on this episode in Chapter 6.

deemed to be free of the risk of government default.[15] Other interest rates include premia to compensate the holder for the various market, credit and even operational risks that the holder takes on, and the relationships between different interest rates are well understood.

However, once an interest-bearing CBDC is introduced, then we have a second interest rate that could also be regarded as free of default risk. There then arises the tricky question of how to set it relative to the traditional central bank interest rate and making a mistake could have serious consequences and lead to possible monetary pandemonium. Even small movements in the spread between the two 'risk-free' rates could then trigger large flows of funds seeking to exploit the arbitrage opportunities it might create. These flows into and out of CBDCs could cause considerable financial instability and thereby put pressure on the CBDC interest rate setter to get the CBDC interest rate 'right' without much guidance on how to do so. They would also need to prevent the CBDC interest rate from becoming an administered interest rate that could easily fall out of line with market interest rates. We have here a recipe for truly major instability which is purely down to the setting of the CBDC interest rate, a problem that does not even exist if there are no CBDCs.

At the same time, we also need to remember that a CBDC is unlikely to gain much traction with commercial banks or the public unless it provides them with incentives to manage or hold CBDC wallets. This consideration would suggest that central banks would need to offer banks payments to manage their CBDC accounts and offer holders positive interest rates on their CBDC holdings. The costs of the payments involved imply that CBDCs would earn their issuers a negative seigniorage. This negative seigniorage reflects the inefficiency of CBDCs as payments media.

My advice is not to bother. There is no point introducing a complicated CBDC system that is costly, difficult and risky to manage, to replace an original system that worked better precisely because it had no CBDC.

## 3.10 MAIN ARGUMENT SUMMARISED

We started by defining a CBDC and comparing it to various existing near substitutes, and explained the difference between token and account CBDCs.

[15] I gloss over the fact that each of the three big rating agencies – Fitch, Moody's and S&P – gives US debt a rating that is slightly below default risk-free. For present purposes, we can regard the rate on US debt as being 'very close to default risk-free'.

We explained that a CBDC could be, but will not be, anonymous, for essentially political reasons.

We then explained the difference between wholesale and retail CBDCs, observing that wholesale CBDCs raise no new policy issues that are of any particular interest to us.

Focussing then on retail CBDCs, we set out the difference between direct retail CBDCs and indirect retail CBDCs and explained that the central bank does not have the capability to manage direct CBDCs itself. Thus, the only practical way to deliver CBDCs is indirectly, through other financial institutions.

However, indirect retail CBDCs would pose the problem of who would pay for the costs of those institutions maintaining CBDC accounts for their customers: neither the customers nor the financial institutions have any incentive to bear those costs themselves. Such considerations suggest that *retail CBDCs would be opposed by both the public and the banks* and that CBDCs would need to be subsidised by the central bank if retail customers are to be induced to hold them. They also suggest that CBDCs are a more expensive payment system to one based on traditional deposits, which, in turn, tells us that *CBDCs are an inefficient payment system.*

We discussed the fraught, even intractable, questions relating to the payment of interest rates on CBDCs.

Finally, we discussed the various instabilities to which CBDC systems are prone.

We have here multiple compelling reasons for CBDCs to be dismissed.

# 4

# Private Digital Currencies

## Main Points

This chapter deals with private sector digital currencies,[1] focussing especially on synthetic CBDCs, private digital currencies that are fully backed by riskless central bank currency.

Market evidence indicates that the public are very enthusiastic about synthetics and even more so about private digital currencies in general, especially in Asia, Africa and Latin America.

## 4.1 SYNTHETIC CBDCS

A *synthetic*[2]*CBDC* is a form of digital money that is issued by private firms rather than a central bank but is fully backed by riskless central bank money. A synthetic CBDC is similar to a stablecoin that is backed by central bank currency as opposed to a stablecoin that is backed by other assets.[3]

[1] In truth, the language of 'private digital currencies' is a little outdated, and 'private digital payments systems' seems more up to date. However, I prefer to stick with 'private currencies' for consistency across the book. If they wish, readers may interpret the terms 'private currencies' and 'private digital payments systems' as equivalent here.

[2] On the meaning of the term 'synthetic', see Adrian and Mancini-Griffoli: 'The term "synthetic" [implies] ... that CBDCs as a form of money can be recreated using different building blocks' than those in actual CBDCs (Adrian and Mancini-Griffoli, 2019, p. 14).

[3] The difference is that a stablecoin as defined earlier, in Chapter 2, is issued on a blockchain, whereas a synthetic per se is not.

In a 2019 International Monetary Fund report,[4] Tobias Adrian and Tommaso Mancini-Griffoli discuss how a synthetic CBDC could be created. J. P. Koning explains:

> it is possible to synthesize a version of CBDC by allowing fintech companies and other e-money providers to keep accounts at the central bank. Customers would in turn hold accounts at these fintechs. As long as fintechs always back each customer dollar (or yen or pound) with a dollar at the central bank, then it is as if customers are holding dollars at the central bank. Voila, we have effectively synthesized CBDC.
>
> The main difference between CBDC and synthetic CBDC is who is maintaining the end relationship with the customer, the central bank or the fintech. As Adrian and Mancini-Griffoli point out (and I agree), it makes a lot of sense to prefer the synthetic CBDC. To begin with, a central bank may have better things to do than manage customer relations. (Koning, 2019b)

Here is how Adrian explains his system, which he calls eMoney:

> eMoney is a means of payment and a store of value fully backed by fiat currency. It is the digital equivalent of a pre-paid card. eMoney, in my definition, can be issued as tokens or accounts, settled in a centralized or decentralized fashion. eMoney thus also includes a version of 'stablecoins' that is fully backed or collateralized by fiat currency …
>
> … if eMoney providers can keep client funds as central bank reserves, and if these are protected from other creditors, then, by proxy, eMoney users can hold, and transact in, a central bank liability. Isn't that the very definition of CBDC?
>
> Synthetic CBDC has notable advantages relative to … full-fledged [CBDCs] … Synthetic CBDC outsources several steps to the private sector: technology choices, customer management, customer screening and monitoring including for [AML etc.] purposes, regulatory compliance, and data management – all sources of substantial costs and risks. The central bank merely remains responsible for settlement between trust accounts, and for regulation and close supervision. (Adrian, 2019)

Similar proposals have been couched in terms of *narrow banking*. The business model of a narrow bank is simple and transparent, because such a bank holds 100 per cent of its deposits as reserves at the Fed. Consequently, such deposits can accrue interest at essentially the same rate as IOR (Interest on Reserves) less a small margin to cover the bank's operating costs, rather than the lower return on overnight repos. Such a bank would have 'no need for FDIC [Federal Deposit Insurance Corporation] insurance or access to the Fed's discount window, because its deposits would be inherently safe and

[4] See Adrian (2019) for the original speech setting out the idea and Adrian and Mancini-Griffoli (2019) for a more detailed analysis.

liquid. The only step that hinges on Fed approval is the creation of a master account at a Federal Reserve bank in which the narrow bank can hold its funds and accrue IOR' (Bordo and Levin, 2019, p. 399).

Appropriately designed, narrow banks are also immune from the dangers of runs or failures.

## 4.2 ADVANTAGES OF SYNTHETIC CBDCS

Synthetic CBDCs have a number of major advantages over CBDCs issued by the central bank:

### 4.2.1 Synthetics Allow the Private Sector and the Central Bank to Play to Their Strengths

For central banks, a synthetic CBDC is far cheaper to operate and less risky than an actual CBDC. The central bank merely sets the rules of engagement and the private sector takes the commercial risks involved. A synthetic also preserves the comparative advantage of the private sector to innovate and interact with customers with the central bank's core mission in setting and enforcing a rulebook of bank behaviour.

### 4.2.2 Synthetics Avoid Central Bank Conflicts of Interest That Arise When the Central Bank Regulates Firms That It Also Competes Against

Synthetics avoid the conflicts of interest that would otherwise arise if the central bank both competes against commercial banks or private payments providers and also regulates and supervises those firms. Any regulatory system that allows such conflicts of interest is indefensible on principle, because the central bank must be presumed to be partial towards its own payments media and to be hostile towards those issued by other parties. A retail CBDC system can therefore be dismissed on this ground alone, precisely because it competes against private payments systems that the central bank also regulates. By contrast, a synthetic CBDC entails no such conflict of interest, because it is issued by private sector firms that have no regulatory authority.

### 4.2.3 Synthetics Avoid Drawbacks of Monopoly Provision

The central bank issuing CBDCs would imply a monopoly based on the central bank's own preferred design. This puts pressure on the central bank to get that design 'right' on day one. However, any such model would almost certainly be flawed, possibly in major ways, and weaknesses in the initial design would likely become ossified and difficult to change.

By contrast, the synthetic CBDC proposal allows open competition between a variety of digital currency models and avoids the restrictiveness of a homogeneous 'one size fits all' approach. Competitive forces would weed out the weaker models, leading to synthetic CBDCs that improve dynamically over time as issuers learn from their mistakes and correct them. Instead of the central bank having to design the 'right' CBDC model on launch day, we allow market forces to discover a variety of different and evolving digital currency models instead, and to tell us which work best. In the issue of currency as in so many other areas, a dynamic competitive process that corrects itself is much to be preferred to a monopoly process whose flaws are more difficult to identify and to correct, and whose rigidity would stifle future innovation. Indeed, there seem to be no circumstances at all in which CBDCs would be rationally preferred to synthetic CBDCs.

George Selgin puts it this way:

> I think that the Fed is very poorly equipped to offer directly retail digital payment services. ... The Fed is one firm. ... I can't imagine it providing different kinds of specialized digital payment services. There's going to be one business model that it's implementing, whether it deals with banks or not. I don't think we need that. I think we need new a plurality of digital payment service suppliers. I think if we had that, there'd be little, very little if anything, that the Fed's own product would be capable of adding to the mix. (Selgin, 2021c)

One can make a similar point from first principles. It is usually accepted that monopoly provision of a good or service is inefficient: a monopoly reduces competition, increases costs and stifles innovation, all of which are classic inefficiencies. It must then be presumed that these same considerations apply to monopoly in payment systems too, that is, CBDCs are *inherently inefficient because CBDCs are central bank monopolies.*

### 4.2.4 Synthetics Avoid Negative Seigniorage

Synthetics would also avoid the negative seigniorage that CBDCs would likely return if they are to gain acceptance. If a synthetic were to earn a negative profit, the issuer would soon abandon it. Thus, market forces would eliminate unprofitable synthetics and, in the long run, the only synthetics to survive would be profitable ones.

### 4.2.5 Synthetics Tend to Stabilise the Financial System

Synthetics would enable those who invest in them, such as large corporations, to earn IOR instead of the traditionally lower returns they could earn from overnight repos. So if a crisis were to occur, investors in more risky assets could switch to synthetics and earn IOR rather than the return on repos. In this sense, synthetics help to promote financial stability relative to a situation where synthetics did not exist.

Synthetics also avoid the single point of failure problems that arise with a CBDC. Should the issuer of a synthetic CBDC fail, holders would be compensated from the central bank money that functions as their reserves, and the gap in the market that would occur from the failure would soon be filled by competing CBDCs.

## 4.3 THE FED OPPOSES NARROW BANKING

Given the many advantages of synthetics, it might then come as a surprise to learn that the Fed is opposed to them (or, to be precise, to narrow banks, but synthetic CBDCs and narrow banks are equivalent). As Koning observes:

> The Fed has refused to provide TNB [The Narrow Bank] with a master account. TNB has responded by suing the Fed for failure to connect it to the payments system.
>
> Something is obviously troubling Fed officials. This March [2019], the Fed issued an advance notice to the public concerning a potential change to its rules. Regular banks would continue to earn the full interest rate from the Fed, says the notice, but any bank that keeps a 'very large proportion' of its assets in the form of balances at the Fed would earn a lower reward.
>
> In other words, the Fed is floating the idea of destroying the narrow-bank business model before it can ever be tested in the market. After all, if narrow banks like TNB can only get a significantly inferior rate from the Fed, they won't be able to provide their depositors with deposit rates that are competitive with traditional banks. (Koning, 2019a)

In response to these comments, John Cochrane observes:

> JP [Koning] thinks narrow banks, if allowed, will remain limited, offering an alternative to overnight repo to large corporations. That's already a big advance in financial stability. I have greater hopes. Central banks cannot operate retail digital currencies. Who do you call when you forgot your password? But narrow banks are the ideal institutions to provide the retail-facing end of digital currencies. The sooner the better. (Cochrane, 2019)

Instead of trying to destroy this business model, the Fed should be promoting it. Let private providers compete in providing a central bank-sanctioned version of synthetic CBDC to the masses. If synthetic CBDC does not succeed, there would be no damage to the central bank's reputation. If synthetic CBDC did succeed, the central bank need not worry about its attention being diverted by the day-to-day concerns of dealing with a retail clientele. Instead, the Fed potentially puts itself in the untenable position of promoting the inferior product while simultaneously trying to destroy the superior one!

Now consider the following thought experiment. Image two individuals, Bill and Ben. Bill prefers synthetics and Ben prefers CBDCs. They can, however, agree to allow synthetics as a thought experiment. If the demand for them takes off, then Ben has to make the case that the synthetics should be replaced with an actual CBDC, namely, that the competition between synthetics should be replaced with a central bank monopoly CBDC. Thus, the issue becomes *whether one should prefer competition or monopoly* in the market for these products. On the other hand, if the market rejects synthetic CBDCs, then we can infer that there would be no demand for CBDCs either, because CBDCs are inferior to synthetics; if the market rejects the superior product, we can reasonably infer that it will reject the inferior one also.

I would suggest that this thought experiment gives us a helpful way to think about CBDCs and the conclusions from it suggest that permitting synthetics could bring great benefits at best and do no harm at worst. On the other hand, if one believes that CBDCs are best, then one has to make a convincing argument for the benefits of monopoly provision over competition, a task that no self-respecting economist would ever wish to take on.

## 4.4 MARKET SUCCESS OF STABLECOINS

We also have to consider that stablecoins have been highly successful in practice. Stablecoin market cap grew from under $1 million at the start of 2016 to $2332 billion[5] by April 2025 and most of these stablecoins are dollar ones. By comparison, the amount of CBDCs issued worldwide so far amounts to a little over $3 billion, about 1.4 per cent of the amount of stablecoins in existence.

Consider then their potential for the Asia Pacific region, where nearly half of the 1.8 billion online population regularly uses an e-wallet and

[5] See https://coinmarketcap.com/view/stablecoin/. Accessed 6 May 2025.

e-wallet penetration by the unbanked population was predicted to reach 58 per cent by 2025 (Chan, 2023). Mr Chan goes on to write

> Stablecoins and the blockchains on which they travel offer unparalleled utility as a new, unified infrastructure for payments, commerce and capital markets built directly into the internet. Together, they lay the foundation for a new 'internet of money' that enables financial value to move anywhere, at any time, almost instantly, at less cost, in a permissionless way so that everyone with an internet connection can access it.
>
> This infrastructure enables financial value to travel just like email, text, video and other types of internet data – easily, efficiently and at close to zero cost. … Stablecoins can facilitate near-instant, near-free payments in-country, within regions and across the world. In 2022, stablecoins settled about $7 trillion compared to $14 trillion at Visa and Mastercard. (Chan, 2023)

One can imagine that stablecoins have a number of important uses. These include:

*Cross-border payments*: Commercial trade in Asia was estimated in 2022 to be nearly 65 per cent of the region's $35 trillion GDP (Chan, 2023). Stablecoins can offer major efficiencies for businesses that need to send funds across borders, whether to suppliers or employees.

*Trade finance*: For trade to take place, many of the region's small to medium enterprises must secure trade financing such as letters of credit, trade loans, guarantees and insurance. The Asian Development Bank estimates that the trade finance gap in Asia is about $510 billion. Stablecoins can help plug this gap by offering easier access to dollars over the internet.

*Remittances*: Traditional cross-border payments are riddled with inefficiencies including high costs, slow processing times and layers of intermediaries that are no longer necessary, with significant additional friction for recipients who lack bank access. According to the World Bank, the global average cost for sending remittances stood at 6.35 per cent in early 2024, and in some cases as high as 20 per cent (Advani, 2024). By enabling direct transactions between the sender and receiver, stablecoins reduce the number of intermediaries, deliver faster and more cost-effective payments and bring particular benefits to the unbanked.

Some regulators within the region are also responding positively to stablecoins, especially in Singapore, Hong Kong and Japan. Recent reforms in all three of these countries are broadly sympathetic to stablecoins, establishing frameworks that allow stablecoins to be issued provided that they are backed at least 100 per cent by investments in liquid low-risk assets and subject to regular independent audits, and do not apply to stablecoins based on an algorithmic link to the underlying currency.

One might reasonably speculate that regulatory tolerance for stablecoins worldwide is likely to increase in the future and that the demand for stablecoins in the marketplace will continue to rise.

## 4.5 STUNNING MARKET SUCCESS OF PRIVATE DIGITAL CURRENCIES

Yet the success of stablecoins, impressive as it is, pales in comparison to the success of private sector digital currencies more generally.

### 4.5.1 Chinese Private Digital Currency

By a big margin, the most successful money in the world is Chinese private digital currency. China's private mobile payments industry began in 2004 with the launch of the Alipay wallet app, Alipay being a payments provider that is owned by Ant Financial, which is part of the Alibaba Group. Its user base had grown to about 1.3 billion by 2023. A second private payment provider is WeChat Pay, a payments provider that is part of the WeChat family owned and operated by Tencent. It was founded in 2011 and had 900 million users by 2023. Together, these two firms leapfrogged hundreds of millions of people from cash and straight into mobile payments and together now have well over 90 per cent of the Chinese online mobile payments industry.

As Global Coin Research (2018) observes 'Alipay and Wechat pay did not have actual assets backing its payment system for over 10 years. Yes, you read that right. OVER 10 YEARS. To be specific, it was more like 14 years.' In fact, only in January 2017 did the PBOC first impose a reserve requirement, mandating that third-party payment companies keep 20 per cent of their customer deposits at commercial banks in single custodial accounts that bear no interest. This requirement was strengthened to 50 per cent in April 2018 and rose further to 100 per cent in January 2019.

By this point, Alipay and WeChat Pay had all the features of synthetic CBDCs and all the features of stablecoins except that they were issued by firms without using a blockchain. Which raises an interesting question for the PBOC: How does it justify prohibiting stablecoins when China's big digital payments operators are so similar to them?

### 4.5.2 The Growth of Private Digital Currencies in Africa and Asia

Turning to the broader picture, 'mobile phones and the Internet have enabled the growth of mobile money accounts in regions with limited banking infrastructure', writes Edouard Matthieu (2024). 'These accounts provide simple financial services like deposits, transfers, and payments to hundreds of millions of people.' However, as Figure 4.1 shows, the number of active mobile money accounts globally has grown from 13 million in 2010 to more than 640 million in 2023, a growth of 4,923 per cent.

In the early 2010s, the adoption of mobile banking was almost exclusive to Sub-Saharan Africa, but the more recent years have seen growth primarily in South East Asia. By 2023, the number of mobile money accounts had risen to 334 million in Sub-Saharan Africa, 125 million in South Asia and 131 million in East Asia and the Pacific.

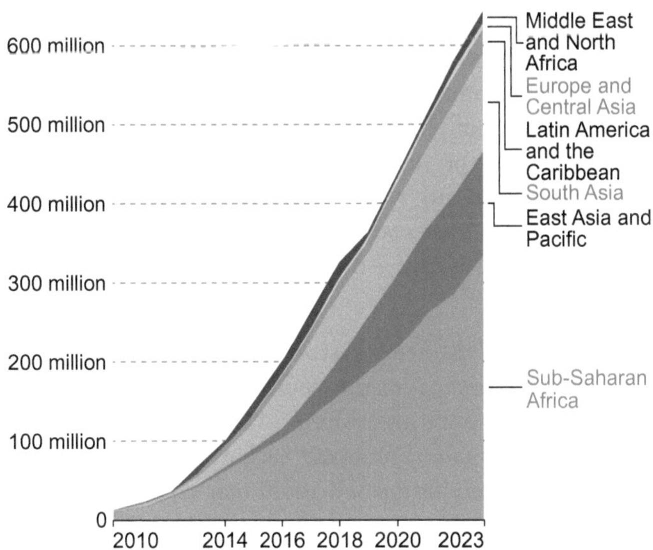


FIGURE 4.1 The growth of mobile money accounts, 2010–2023
Source: GSM Association; Matthieu (2024).

This growth is driven by an increase in the number of mobile phones and by the spread of and ongoing improvements in QR payment technology that enables digital payments to be made. According to a recent study by Juniper,[6] the volume of QR code payments in South East Asia is expected to skyrocket by 590 per cent by 2028, reaching 90 billion transactions, up from 13 billion in 2023. The significant increase in the region and other developing markets is due in considerable part to the 'financial inclusivity' by which QR payments allow unbanked users to transact digitally.

The experience of private sector digital payments providers demonstrates without doubt that such payments systems have been remarkably successful and across the world. By comparison, as we shall see further in Chapter 6, the experience of CBDCs is quite the opposite: CBDCs do not hold a candle to private digital currencies.

## 4.6 CAPITAL ADEQUACY AND LIQUIDITY REGULATION FOR PRIVATE DIGITAL CURRENCIES

Finally, it is reasonable to ask whether unregulated private currency systems might pose financial instability problems. The answer is that such problems might arise if nothing is done to address that possibility, but the solution is simple: firms could be required to maintain minimum capital and liquidity standards.

Consider how these might apply to private payments providers which issue synthetic CBDCs or stablecoins. In theory, one might argue that these firms do not need any regulation because they already have their payments backed by at least 100 per cent central bank money. However, in practice – and for prudence – one might add a regulatory framework that ensures:

- periodic audits of the firm's reserves;
- that the peg between payments media and reserves is based on actual reserves, and not some algorithm;
- that the firm maintains minimum 'cash in till'-type liquidity ratios;
- that the firm maintains a small additional capital requirement; and such like.

The primary concern should be to ensure that private currencies are safe enough to maintain public trust in their continued convertibility into

[6] See https://tinyurl.com/4a66fb3f. Accessed 4 February 2026.

central bank currency and thereby maintain continued trust in currency throughout the financial system, whether that currency be private or public.

Payments firms that offer private digital currencies that are not synthetics or stablecoins could have their capital adequacy regulated in much the same way that big payments firms such as Visa or Mastercard are regulated today.[7]

Finally, one should point out that potential instability problems do not need to be addressed by state-sponsored capital adequacy regulation as such. They could also be addressed by private 'banking clubs' of the sort discussed by, for example, Goodhart (1988), Gorton and Mullineaux (1987) or Dowd and Hutchinson (2010), whereby bankers took action themselves to maintain equivalent standards to those that modern central bankers might take. These banking clubs both invented and enforced 'regulatory' standards, and banks voluntarily chose to join such clubs and submit to these standards because membership of the club sent a signal of respectability to the public and bankers always want respectability. Examples of such clubs are to be found in the pre-Fed United States or nineteenth century Britain, and these systems of private banking regulation were at least as effective as modern central banking regulation has been.

## 4.7 CONCLUSIONS

Synthetics and stablecoins have many advantages over CBDCs and we can safely say that there are no circumstances in which one would rationally prefer a CBDC to either. We can also frame the issue in simple monopoly vs competition terms, which gives us further reason to prefer the synthetics or stablecoins to a CBDC. The rapid growth of synthetics and stablecoins since 2016 indicates that there is a large potential demand for them among the public. However, there are also more general private digital currencies and the demand for the latter across much of the world is positively leaping ahead.

The key issue for the central bank is whether it should be just a rule setter or a rule setter who also builds products. Dante Disparte got it right in 2022 when he wrote that a CBDC could 'end up becoming the equivalent of the FAA [Federal Aviation Authority] flying planes and building jet engines as opposed to designing competitive rules-based safe conduct in

[7] For an example of such an approach, see Financial Conduct Authority (2024).

the skies' (quoted in Sutton, 2022). The purpose of the central bank should not be to design, produce and then fly the actual planes, but it should be to design and enforce the safety rulebook that private producers would use when they make the planes. Those 'planes' might be synthetic CBDCs, stablecoins or other forms of private digital payment systems, and market forces alone should determine how well any digital payment systems might fly – or not.

In other words, the central bank should set the rulebook by which synthetics and other forms of private digital payment system are allowed to operate, but it should not actually produce a CBDC itself. The central bank and private producers should each play to their time-honoured roles, one to hold the ring, and the other to compete in it.

## APPENDIX: TRUST ISSUES BETWEEN STATE AND PRIVATE CURRENCIES

The Merriam-Webster's dictionary defines 'trust' as 'assured reliance on the character, ability, strength, or truth of someone or something'.

Central bankers' overriding concern is to 'try to ensure that ... the essential societal public trust provided by central banks is maintained' (Lloyd, 2023, p. 21) and I agree. This statement presumes, however, that central bank currency is 'trusted' by the general public. Such an assumption is usually a reasonable one so let's accept it for the moment. We might also say that the public trust the central bank enough to use the currency it issues. As an aside, I would, however, point out that this latter claim does not imply that the public trust the central bank enough, say, to accept the Bank of England's views on CBDCs, but that is a separate issue.

In correspondence, Mr Lloyd elaborates on his thinking. 'The trust of the public is paramount', he writes and I agree. The issue then arises of the mechanisms that would promote trust and he raises the subject of blockchains and DLT as means to do that. He then writes:

> Private money channels tend to use blockchains, where the trust is embedded within the blockchain. Bitcoin is a good example of *internalised* trust within the partner network. This is fine until there is interaction with the real outside world. Moreover, Bitcoin does not provide full clearance and final settlement, a requirement for the creation of *universal* trust. It is for this reason, whether within national jurisdictions (where cash usage will eventually disappear) or between jurisdictions, that final settlement via CBDCs is required. Such a system does not preclude private money channels, including stablecoins and tokenised

commercial bank deposits to be used as liabilities, but enables final settlement of these liabilities via **central banks' digital currencies**. In global cross-border terms this can be achieved ... via a unified ledger. ... the principal reason for central banks pursuing CBDCs, using DLT, is to ensure universal trust in fiat currencies and overall financial stability.[8]

This is a clever argument, but I would respond by saying, first, that blockchain/DLT is a secondary issue, and second, that the emboldened term 'central banks' digital currencies' is best understood as old-fashioned 'central bank reserves held at the commercial banks'. We could call these a CBDC if we wish, but if we do so, we should call them a W-CBDC and be careful to make clear that they are not a retail CBDC. I would then paraphrase his argument as saying that if cash disappears, then there is more (indeed, total) reliance on central bank reserves held at the commercial bank as the ultimate settlement medium that ensures universal trust in fiat currencies and underpins financial stability.

However, we cannot always assume that a central bank currency is always trusted by the general public. To give a counter-example, Ecuador has a history of repeated defaults and these defaults were a major reason why its central bank abandoned its CBDC in 2018 (and we shall discuss this subject further in Chapter 6). Put simply, the Ecuadorian population trusted private institutions and the dollar more than they trusted the central bank, and the Ecuadorian CBDC failed as a result.

[8] Private email correspondence between Michael Lloyd and Kevin Dowd, 2024. Italics are his emphasis, but the bold emphasis is mine.

# 5

# CBDC Controversies in Different Countries

Main Points

This chapter looks at the CBDC controversies in the UK, the US and Sweden.

In the UK there was a high-level discussion centred around an important House of Lords Report into the Bank of England's CBDC proposals. There was also a large and highly critical public response to a joint Bank of England-HM Treasury 'consultation' on the subject. A memorable phrase from these discussions was that a CBDC was a solution in search of a problem.

In the US the Fed's CBDC proposals ran into a whirlwind of opposition and sparked various anti-CBDC bills in Congress. A number of senior Fed officials played an active role in public discussion of CBDCs, and almost all of them were critical. CBDCs were eventually prohibited by President Trump when he re-entered office in January 2025.

Swedish discussions of CBDCs are interesting because of the way they highlight the connection between CBDCs and the prospect of a cashless economy. The Swedish case is also interesting because a report by Anna Kinberg-Batra in 2023 offered a blueprint for how cash payments could be protected as digital payments become ever more popular.

The chapter also offers a brief global overview of CBDC initiatives – these are widespread but there are currently only five at the implementation level.

In this chapter we discuss the more interesting controversies surrounding CBDCs in different countries, focussing particularly on those controversies in the UK, the US and Sweden, and give a brief overview of the current state of play of CBDC projects around the world.

## 5.1 THE CBDC CONTROVERSY IN THE UNITED KINGDOM

We start with the United Kingdom.

In 2015 the Bank of England published its big picture 'OneBank' research agenda, a key feature of which was the issue of digital currencies. Initially, the Bank of England focussed on how it could use DLT to design a CBDC. The Bank was not quite right about the distributed ledger, however. It failed to appreciate why the Bank of England of all people would want a distributed ledger that does not require a trusted third-party or guardian of the payments system when the very existence of the Bank of England was predicated on the presumption, especially by the Bank of England, that that trusted guardian *was* the Bank of England itself. A Bitcoin-style distributed ledger is a highly inefficient technology that cannot operate at the scale needed for a national payments system.

In 2016, two University College London cryptocurrency researchers, George Danezis and Sarah Meiklejohn, who were working with the Bank under its 'OneBank' agenda, published an article, 'Centrally Banked Cryptocurrencies', which set out a framework for a central bank cryptocurrency, which they called RSCoin.

The new innovation with RSCoin is that whereas Bitcoin's ledger is maintained by users all over the world, the RSCoin ledger would be maintained at the central bank. RSCoin would be a closed, 'permissioned' blockchain offering the advantages of digital currencies – fast and cheap transactions permanently recorded in a shared distributed ledger – but instead of anonymous miners, only the central bank and vetted financial operators would be allowed to validate RSCoin transactions. Whereas Bitcoin has a lack of scalability that arises due to its reliance on broadcast and its need to expend significant computational energy in proofs of work, RSCoin's more centralised ledger avoids the wasteful hashing required in proof of work systems and potentially allows RSCoin to achieve the scalability required for a national digital payments system.

The central bank would maintain the power to control the supply of RSCoin, to ensure that its monetary policy decisions applied to the crypto-currency as well as to conventional national currency.

### 5.1.1 'Britcoin'

In March 2020, the Bank of England published a discussion paper (Bank of England, 2020) about a possible UK CBDC. In response, in April 2021, the then-UK Chancellor of the Exchequer, Rishi Sunak, announced that he was setting up a joint UK Treasury-Bank of England Taskforce to co-ordinate exploratory work on the subject. Soon after, Sunak tweeted the single word 'Britcoin' (Jones and Milliken, 2021).

In May 2021, Bank of England Deputy Governor Sir Jon Cunliffe said that it is 'probable' that the United Kingdom will launch a CBDC, but that no decision had yet been made on when to introduce it (I. Lee, 2021). With this statement, experienced Bank observers could sense that Cunliffe had tipped the Bank's hand – the decision *had* been made, but the Bank was going through the motions of a public 'conversation' on the subject due to the public's extreme sensitivity to it.

David McGrogan observes:

> This is what British political commentators like to call 'pitch-rolling'. Public bodies, forgetting that the electorate lives and breathes, think that there exist in society people who are actually fooled by phrases like 'no firm decision has been taken', and that talking in this way will soften people up for an eventual announcement. Those of us who live in the real world, meanwhile, know perfectly well what is really going on: the digital pound will soon be upon us, whichever party happens to be in government at the time, because those in charge clearly like the idea. So best get used to it. . . .
>
> The digital pound, and the way it is being set up, offers no clear advantage to the 'user', but, again, that isn't the point. The advantages are obvious to those doing the governing, and that is ultimately what motivates the entire project . . .
>
> To this mindset, there is absolutely nothing wrong with the notion that it should actually effectively own people's money and allow them to 'use' it on sufferance . . . the direction of travel is obvious. (McGrogan, 2024a)

In June 2021, the Bank released a discussion paper, 'New Forms of Digital Money', setting out its thoughts on a CBDC and posing some questions on which it invited public feedback.

### 5.1.2 House of Lords Report

The Bank's proposals received a stinging response from the UK House of Lords in its Report, *Central Bank Digital Currencies: A Solution in Search of a Problem?* published on 13 January 2022. Its chairman, Lord Forsyth, said on its release:

> The introduction of a UK central bank digital currency (CBDC) would have far-reaching consequences for households, businesses, and the monetary system. We found the potential benefits of a digital pound, as set out by the Bank of England, to be overstated or achievable through less risky alternatives. We took evidence from a variety of witnesses and *none of them were able to give us a compelling reason for why the UK needed a central bank digital currency*. The concept seems to present a lot of risk for very little reward. We concluded that the idea was *a solution in search of a problem*. (quoted in Turton, 2022, my italics)

The Report's overall conclusion was that 'We have yet to hear a convincing case for why the UK needs a retail CBDC' (p. 2) and it noted that a CBDC 'would present significant challenges for financial stability and the protection of privacy' (p. 40). It then posed a series of questions for the Joint Taskforce, including, in particular, to what problem is a CBDC the answer? and asked that the Joint Taskforce's 'assessment should compare CBDCs against alternative means of achieving the same aims' (p. 40).

I now drill down into the Report's contents: The Report acknowledged that 'few central banks ... including the Bank of England' see a direct CBDC model as viable (p. 3). Thus, the focus was on indirect CBDCs.

On CBDCs' benefits to consumers, the Report stated that most witnesses were sceptical that a UK CBDC payments system would provide significant advantages to consumers over the existing payments system. It quoted Patrick Honohan, a former Governor of the Bank of Ireland, saying that the benefit of a CBDC to UK consumers, 'at present [would be] absolutely nothing'. Because the UK already has a 'reasonably efficient payment system ... just having a CBDC does not give you an advantage' (p. 11).

On the 'significant risks' posed by a CBDC, the Report stated that it had heard that: CBDCs have the potential to provide the government and the central bank with the power to monitor citizens' payment transactions, posing risks to individual *privacy*; that if a retail CBDC proved to be popular, people might transfer money out of their bank accounts into CBDC wallets, which could *disintermediate* the banking sector, increase the cost of credit and exacerbate financial instability during periods of economic stress; CBDCs could provide central banks with powerful *new monetary policy tools* with uncertain effects that might increase the role and influence of the central bank over the economy; and CBDCs could represent a vulnerable *single point of failure* in the payments system, serving as a target for cyber-attacks from criminals and hostile nation-state actors.

Elaborating now on these italicised points, on privacy, the Report stated that widespread adoption of any CBDC would depend on a high level of public trust. While there were design options that would provide some privacy safeguards, technical specifications alone may be insufficient to counter public concern that a government might use a CBDC as an instrument for state surveillance. The Bank risked being drawn into controversial debates on privacy, which could undermine its reputation for independence from the government (p. 41). Moreover, the Report gave no evidence that the high level of public trust required for widespread CBDC adoption actually existed.

On disintermediation, the Report stated that introducing a CBDC would lead 'inevitably' to some disintermediation of the banking sector, which would in turn likely lead to more expensive credit and tighter lending criteria. Without safeguards, CBDCs could exacerbate financial instability during periods of economic stress as people would likely seek to replace bank deposits with a CBDC (p. 41).

On new monetary policy tools, the Report stated that the Bank of England could 'program' a CBDC to have an expiry date by which it would need to be spent, or conditions could be placed on a CBDC so that it could be spent on certain goods only. However, no central bank was yet implementing an interest-bearing or programmable CBDC as a possible crisis-response measure and the Report said, 'these are theoretical concerns at best and are unlikely to be featured in any first phase CBDC project' (p. 26).

The Report also acknowledged that 'Most witnesses were sceptical that a CBDC should be remunerated' (p. 26) and concluded that monetary policy applications 'should not be a motivation for introducing a CBDC' (p. 27).

The Report highlighted two security problems. One was that individual accounts, managed by the private sector, could be compromised as a result of cyber-security weaknesses. The second was that a CBDC system, as a piece of critical national infrastructure, would be a target for attack from nation state or criminal actors, and such attacks would risk the exposure of sensitive payments data (p. 36).

On the threat posed by fintech firms setting up their own digital currency, the Report stated that some central banks were concerned that big tech companies would combine crypto asset technology and their vast network of users to launch a digital currency capable of rapid adoption by large numbers of people. While it agreed that this was a risk, the introduction of a CBDC may not be a necessary or complete response to it. Private entities of a size that can compete with the existing payments systems can and should be regulated (and not prohibited).

On cash and financial inclusion, the Report observed that cash continued to be widely accepted in the UK. If this were to change it is not obvious that the properties of CBDCs would satisfy any residual demand for cash, which is often valued for its physical properties and the privacy that it can provide. It noted that the Bank of England has said that it will continue to issue cash on demand and that the public need for money without default risk is covered for most savers by the availability of cash and deposit protection. Should cash acceptance decline significantly, a CBDC *could* be a way to ensure greater financial inclusion in that it would provide access to digital payment services that are like bank accounts. However, for some, not having a bank account was a choice and for others, the technological requirements for CBDC transactions may exclude them from accessing it. 'It is likely that there are more straightforward and targeted ways to support access to financial services than to launch a CBDC' (p. 40).

### 5.1.3 The 2023 Public Consultation on CBDCs

On 6 February 2023, the Bank of England and HM Treasury issued a joint paper announcing a 4-month public consultation on the subject of whether, and if so, how, to establish a CBDC. In response, the Bank received over 51,000 (!) comments from the public that primarily addressed concerns about privacy, programmability and the decline of cash. Those who commented on the consultation included Lord (Mervyn) King, the former Bank of England Governor, who pointed out that

> CBDCs are about ways of making payments; they are not a new currency. Whether a country needs a CBDC is really about the state of its current payments system. . . .
>
> There are no [payments system] problems to which a CBDC is the only, or even the most obvious, answer. Our payments system is more efficient than those in most other countries.

The UK payments system is no longer based on paper cheques, but on digital payments that clear more or less instantaneously. 'It would be somewhat odd to try to increase competition in this area by creating a state monopoly', he said.[1]

[1] King quotes are cited in Young (2023).

Another sceptic was Lord George Bridges, Chairman of the House of Lords Economic Affairs Committee, who said: 'We have to be very clear about what problem we are trying to solve before we get carried away with the technology and the idea. I am not convinced about some of the problems that we might be trying to solve' (New, 2023).

The lobby group UK Finance, which represents 300 financial services firms, warned that Britcoin was 'likely to trigger concerns about privacy and state interference' if it were widely adopted. It described initial limits by the Bank of between £10,000 to £20,000 as excessive, adding those figures would 'introduce significantly more risks to financial stability than benefits', particularly in times of crisis. It also questioned whether the public would be satisfied with Bank reassurances that it would not know users' identity (quoted in Chan, 2023).

The title of Szu Ping Chan's *Telegraph* article – 'Sunak's Britcoin Ambitions Hit by Huge Public Backlash' – captured the public mood perfectly. Some of the comments in the media were perceptive: Writing on *CapX*, economic commentator Peter Young observed that the focus of the Britcoin effort was not about whether there was a current need, but more about 'creating new possibilities'. 'In fact this "new possibility" has every prospect of becoming a major menace and the sooner that this little Bank of England and Treasury scheme is shut down the better.' He emphasised that there is no current need for a CBDC and nor is there ever likely to be.

However, it was the threat to privacy and the risk of greater government control that many people found most frightening about CBDCs. Every personal transaction involving a CBDC would be recorded, giving the tax authorities, using existing powers, unprecedented access to one's financial history. An inept Bank of England should stick to their knitting and try and do its basic job properly rather than 'foist upon us a dangerous and unneeded CBDC scheme' (Young, 2023).

Blogger Rusere Shoniwa commented that those who have observed the transition from the pretence of democracy to bare-faced authoritarianism over the last three years need no confirmation from the House of Lords that CBDCs are an evil to be avoided at all costs. But the fact that the Lords have poured cold water on the scheme ought to tell us that the BoE is on a hiding to nothing in terms of building credibility for this project. A 'payment system is being used to transform a key function of money from a medium of exchange into a medium of control' (Shoniwa, 2023).

Banking expert Bob Lyddon pointed out that the Bank engaged with vested interests in the Visa and Mastercard ecosystems and US big tech, and drew on a narrow evidence base from its trusted sources among international financial bodies. However, this 'investigative' process

> appears to be a smokescreen to disguise its pushing ahead with major alterations to national life regardless of counter-evidence and events in the real world... The [CBDC] project appears to have been hijacked by a 'concert party' of organizations who will benefit financially from its going ahead. The Bank allows these organizations to front-run the project because it establishes a plausible smokescreen for its own machinations: these organizations play back the Bank's own pre-baked opinion and supply the Bank with spurious and ostensibly market-based support for it. (Lyddon, 2023, pp. 1–3)

Never mind what the public want, the Bank seemed determined to proceed regardless. As David McGrogan points out, their objective is still that

> we, the *hoi polloi*, should come to view our money not as our own, but as the product merely of the tyrant's largesse – a benefit which he bestows upon us, rather than a store of our own wealth. We are of course well along the road to that destination already, but the 'digital pound' is really the finishing line. That is why the Bank of England keeps coming out with banal-looking documents saying things like 'we judge it likely that the digital pound will be needed in the future' and 'we are convinced preparatory work is justified'. Do you know a single living, breathing human being who has ever opined to you that they wish there was such a thing as a 'digital pound' or that they consider there to be a 'need' for one? Of course not. But in the fullness of time, they can be made to rely on its existence, and therefore on the existence of the State which backs it, all the same. (McGrogan, 2023)

The Bank published its response or, should I say, its non-response in January 2024. It talked repeatedly of a 'national conversation' about the digital pound, but the Bank's idea of a conversation appears to refer to a situation in which they talk and we listen. On this issue, McGrogan is again to the point:

> I hear people in positions of authority and decision-making power using words like 'conversation' and 'consultation'. It raises the interesting question as to which is more insulting: to not be consulted about a matter that affects you ... or to be consulted in such a way that it is made plainly evident your views do not matter.... The important point is that whatever is the outcome of this 'national conversation' we're having, it's going to mean the digital pound will be introduced. Why are they even pretending? (McGrogan, 2024b)

The Bank's response then quotes Deputy Governor Sarah Breeden – 'Trust in all forms of money is an absolute necessity. ... It is essential that we build that trust and have the support of the public and businesses who would be using it if introduced' (Bank of England, 2024) – which merely begs the key point at issue and confirms, once again, that the Bank is not listening.

It never seems to have occurred to the Bank that the 'trust' that it imagines it enjoys from the public on the Britcoin proposal does not exist and the fact that it does not exist was demonstrated by the huge public backlash against it – like what else could that backlash mean? As experienced Bank watchers well know, however, this is how the Bank always responds when it goes through the motions of 'consulting' the public but has no intention of listening to what the public actually have to say.

## 5.2 THE CBDC CONTROVERSY IN THE UNITED STATES

### 5.2.1 Outline of the US CBDC Controversy

Proposals for the Federal Reserve to establish a CBDC go back to blogs by J. P. Koning in 2013 and 2014. The idea then started to attract interest after David Andolfatto blogged about it in February 2015. However, there was relatively little interest from the Fed until the announcement of Facebook's Libra stablecoin in June 2019 made central bankers around the world suddenly more aware of the threats they faced from stablecoins. In May 2021, Fed Chair Jerome Powell announced plans to publish a discussion paper to stimulate a public conversation about the possible benefits and risks of a US CBDC.

The discussion paper 'Money and Payments: The U.S. Dollar in the Age of Digital Transformation' was published in January 2022. The paper stated that

> The introduction of a CBDC would represent a highly significant innovation in American money. Accordingly, broad consultation with the general public and key stakeholders is essential. This paper is the first step in such a conversation. It describes the economic context for a CBDC, key policy considerations, and the potential risks and benefits of a US CBDC. It also solicits feedback from all interested parties.
>
> The Federal Reserve does not intend to proceed with issuance of a CBDC without clear support from the executive branch and from Congress, ideally in the form of a specific authorizing law. (Board of Governors of the Federal Reserve System, 2022, p. 3)

The Fed's proposals unleashed a whirlwind of opposition. Most public commentary about CBDC was critical, some highly so – even much of that put out by the Fed itself – and an opinion poll published by the Cato Institute in May 2023 showed that a substantial majority of the American public were opposed to CBDCs (Michel, 2023c).

By 2024, CBDCs had become a highly politicised issue. The subject featured prominently even in the 2024 presidential campaign. Among the politicians, Ron DeSantis signed a bill in March to prohibit a national CBDC within Florida and said in July that 'If I am the president, on day one, we will nix central bank digital currency' (Sandor, 2023). Robert F. Kennedy, Jr, promised 'to end the efforts to move toward a CBDC' in January 2024 (Attlee, 2024) and the same month, Donald Trump said that he would never allow the use of a CBDC, as it would 'give the government absolute control over your money. This would be a dangerous threat to freedom – and I will stop it from coming to America' (Durden, 2024). Numerous other GOP and Libertarian politicians also spoke out against them, as have conservative media stars such as Joe Rogan and Tucker Carlson, and CBDCs have been banned or bills to ban them are going through legislatures in a number of states.

Then, on 23 January 2025, US President Donald Trump signed an Executive Order that effectively bans the Fed from issuing a CBDC. More specifically, the Executive Order takes 'measures to protect Americans from the risks of Central Bank Digital Currencies (CBDCs), which threaten the stability of the financial system, individual privacy, and the sovereignty of the United States, including by prohibiting the establishment, issuance, circulation, and use of a CBDC within the jurisdiction of the United States' (The White House, 2025).

### 5.2.2 Views of Fed Officials on CBDCs

For their part, the views of senior Fed officials about CBDCs range from somewhat positive at the one end to highly sceptical at the other. 'I am legitimately undecided on whether the benefits outweigh the costs or vice versa', Fed Chair *Jerome K. Powell* told the Senate Banking Committee in July 2021 (Reuters, 2021). The only top rank Fed official to come out in favour of a CBDC is former Fed Vice Chair *Lael Brainard*.[2] For example, she told the Aspen Institute in July 2021, 'The dollar is very dominant in international payments, and if you have the other major jurisdictions in the world with . . . a CBDC . . . and the US doesn't have one, I just, I can't

[2] Ms Brainard has since left the Fed to become Director of the US National Economic Council.

wrap my head around that. That just doesn't sound like a sustainable future to me' (Saphir, 2021).

Of particular interest are articles or talks by former St Louis Fed Vice President David Andolfatto, former Fed Chair for Supervision Randal K. Quarles and Fed Governor Christopher J. Waller and Minneapolis Fed President Neel Kashkari.

To quote *Andolfatto* from a 2021 blog posting:

> At a conceptual level, CBDC is a compelling idea. It envisions everyone having an account with the central bank consisting of a direct claim against digital fiat currency that can be used as a safe and efficient form of payment. . . .
>
> But more importantly, do we want to rely on the government sector to deliver high-performance customer service at the retail level and to keep up with technological advances in the space? A well-functioning government is essential for a well-functioning private sector (and vice-versa), but these two sectors should probably stick to their knitting. Let the central bank handle monetary policy, bank supervision, lender of last resort operations, and wholesale payments. Let the private sector handle servicing the vast, demanding and rapidly-evolving retail sector. It's a model that has proven to work best, in my view.
>
> As for financial inclusion, one should keep in mind that the most significant progress along this dimension in recent years has been the outcome of private initiatives, not state initiatives. Consider, for example, the hundreds of millions [of] people who now have access to digital payments thanks to M-Pesa, WeChat and AliPay. . . . [W]hat makes us think that retail-CBDC is essential? (Andolfatto, 2021d)

One might note, however, that his 'compelling idea' case for a CBDC envisages a direct CBDC in which everyone has a Fed account, a model that even most CBDC proponents reject because the Fed is not set up to do retail-facing activities. He concludes: 'While I see no reason why a CBDC could not work in principle, I also do not see why it is essential in practice' (Andolfatto, 2021c).

*Randal Quarles*'s 'parachute pants' speech of 28 June 2021 is sceptical of a number of claims made by CBDC advocates and is dismissive of claims that a foreign CBDC would pose a threat to the status of the dollar. He outlines the risks that stablecoins pose, particularly their financial stability risks, but argues that these are 'eminently addressable' and once they 'have been addressed, we should be saying yes to these products, rather than straining to find ways to say no. . . . [T]he combination of imminent improvements in the existing payments system . . . combined with the cross-border efficiency of properly structured stablecoins could well make superfluous any effort to develop a CBDC' (pp. 8–9).

He is sceptical that a CBDC would improve financial inclusion[3] or that a CBDC would spur and facilitate private sector innovation.[4]

*Christopher Waller*'s August 2021 speech, 'Central Bank Digital Currency – A Solution in Search of a Problem?', states:

> I think the first order of business is to ask whether there is compelling need for the Fed to create a digital currency. I am highly skeptical . . .
>
> In all the recent exuberance about CBDCs, advocates point to many potential benefits of a Federal Reserve digital currency, but they often fail to ask a simple question: What problem would [only] a CBDC solve? Alternatively, what market failure or inefficiency demands this specific intervention? After careful consideration, I am not convinced . . . that a CBDC would solve any existing problem that is not being addressed more promptly and efficiently by other initiatives. (p. 1)

Finally, in a Columbia seminar in March 2024, Minneapolis Fed President *Neel Kashkari* asked what problem a CBDC would solve:

> I keep asking anybody, at the Fed or outside of the Fed, to explain to me what problem this is solving. . . . I can see why China would do it. If they want to monitor every one of your transactions, you could do that with a central bank digital currency. If you want to directly tax customer accounts, you could do that with a central bank digital currency. So I get why China would be interested. Why would the American people be for that?[5]

One thing is certain: some of the most persuasive arguments against establishing a Fed CBDC come from senior officials at the Fed itself.

However, the US discussion is now moot, at least in the United States itself, now that President Trump has banned CBDCs in the US.

## 5.3 THE CBDC CONTROVERSY IN SWEDEN

The Swedish CBDC controversy is interesting because of the way that it highlighted how the prospect of a future cashless economy might justify the central bank issuing a CBDC, the e-krona. Sweden had long been

[3] "I am far from convinced that a CBDC is the best, or even an effective, method to increase financial inclusion" (Quarles, 2021, p. 9).

[4] "I am puzzled, however, as to how a Federal Reserve CBDC could promote innovation in a way that a private-sector stablecoin or other new payment mechanism could not. . . . the potential benefits of a Federal Reserve CBDC are unclear. Conversely, a Federal Reserve CBDC could pose significant and concrete risks" that could "expose the public to a host of unanticipated, and undesirable, consequences" (Quarles, 2021, p. 10).

[5] See https://twitter.com/wideawake_media/status/1771869647085683165. Accessed 4 February 2026.

regarded as leading the world in the trend towards a cashless economy, so it was natural that this issue should arise there first.

The connection between digital currency and a cashless economy was raised by Riksbank Deputy Governor Cecilia Skingsley in a speech in November 2016: 'In the future, will we have e-krona in an e-wallet, just as obviously as we now have a wallet with cash? The less we who live in Sweden use banknotes and coins, the clearer it becomes that the Riksbank needs to investigate whether we should issue electronic money as a supplement to the money we have today' (Skingsley, 2016). Moreover, she was adamant that even if the Riksbank eventually issued an e-krona, it would not be to replace cash but to supplement it. 'The Riksbank will continue to issue banknotes and coins as long as they are in demand in society. It is our statutory obligation and we will of course continue to live up to it', she concluded.

She begs a key question, however. Even if it makes sense for an e-krona to be issued, there is no reason why it should be issued by the central bank. It could also be issued by private payments providers, for example as a synthetic. Instead of issuing the e-krona itself, the central bank would simply set out the terms under which a synthetic e-krona could be issued and leave the private sector to issue it themselves. If the demand is there, one must presume that the private sector is able to meet that demand at least as well as the central bank could. Recall also that in the previous chapter we discussed how a suitably designed synthetic CBDC is always superior to a 'real' CBDC and has none of its disadvantages.

Going further, the government could also relax legal restrictions against the private issue of banknotes and see if the private sector can do a better job at issuing banknotes than the central bank. My historical sense is that any such relaxation would help improve the supply of banknotes and there was never any benefit from a note monopoly anyway. Jonung (2023) suggests that private note issue in Sweden worked well before the note issue was monopolised in 1904.[6]

A later government-sponsored enquiry into the Swedish payments system chaired by former politician Anna Kinberg-Batra issued its report in March 2023.[7] This report made a number of recommendations. First, that a new digital ID to give the estimated 1 million people with no, or

[6] The case studies in Dowd (2023) also suggest that this was the case among many other historical free banking systems.

[7] An English translation of the report is available at https://tinyurl.com/4w9nwxpf. Accessed 4 February 2026.

limited, access to digital payments better access to digital payments systems, and to help them overcome obstacles caused by AML and terror financing regulations. Second, it proposed that banks be encouraged to offer 'low-risk accounts' that provided limited service (e.g., limits on international payments) to increase financial inclusion. Third, it concluded that it was important to continue to keep cash as part of the Swedish payments system, otherwise Sweden might be vulnerable in a severe crisis, and called for government agencies, pharmacies and shops selling goods 'deemed essential to life', to be required under law to accept cash payments. Finally, the report concluded that there was no current need for the Riksbank to issue an e-krona, but also recommended that the Riksbank continue to monitor the situation.

Even so, I am not convinced that the debate in Sweden gets to the bottom of the cashlessness issue. So let me offer my stab at it as follows:

Recall that cash here can be thought of as Riksbank notes or coins. We then ask two key questions. The first is, why does cashless matter? The second is, does cashlessness imply a need for a CBDC?

We can answer the first question from each of three different perspectives. The first is a 'monetary determinacy' perspective. By 'monetary determinacy' we mean that the monetary system ensures that all monetary magnitudes have determinate values even if the demand for cash goes to zero.

Consider an economy with a positive demand for cash. In such an economy, the existence of a positive demand for cash ensures that the 1:1 exchange rate between deposits and cash is maintained. Remember that deposits are private bank money but in a fiat money system cash is money supplied by the state. Even if the demand for cash is low, the fact that people are converting deposits into cash and vice versa at that 1:1 exchange rate ensures that that conversion rate between bank money and state money is maintained.

Consider two distinct cashless scenarios. In the first scenario, the government abolishes cash by fiat: all cash is removed by state order. The banks can then no longer maintain the 1:1 exchange ratio between deposits and cash, because cash has disappeared. In this scenario, people might imagine there is some determinacy problem, because when depositors buy and sell deposits, then it is not clear what they are buying and selling them for, or with.

But so what? People can still exchange claims for bank money denominated in the local currency unit. They can continue making bank transfers to each other, but what they cannot do is enter cash into the system or take cash out of the system. But otherwise the system continues to function even without cash. There is still a determinate monetary base, but in this case the monetary base has only one component, bank reserves. The fact that the monetary base is determinate ensures that the price level is also determinate. The only requirement to ensure that the price level is determinate is that there is still a positive demand for the monetary base. These results follow from basic money multiplier analysis.

In the second scenario the government does not abolish cash but the demand to hold cash falls to zero. In this case, the banks would still be obliged to maintain a 1:1 exchange rate between deposits and cash *if requested*. Christopher Waller (2021, p. 121, note 8) puts it nicely: 'Physical currency can effectively disappear, and everything still works.[8] All the central bank needs to do is promise to provide the currency if requested.'

The upshot is that the monetary system continues to function without any serious problem under either cashless scenario.

The second perspective is a 'redemption medium' perspective. By 'redemption medium' we refer to the asset that a bank uses to redeem its deposits when a customer demands redemption of them. Under a fiat money system, this redemption medium is state money, namely, cash. But if cash is to disappear, then banks at some point must switch to another redemption medium, because a cashless system cannot then redeem with units of cash. The redemption medium would be some claim to a valuable asset. For example, it could be a claim to a pack of cigarettes, to certain units of gold of a certain fineness or so many kronas' worth of bitcoin. The valuable asset in question does not especially matter, but what does matter is that that asset should have exchange value into some asset whose value is determined in a market. Switching the redemption medium away from cash as the system approaches cashlessness enables the banking system to maintain the convertibility of bank money as cashlessness approaches.

The third perspective is a 'death of cash' perspective. As the demand for cash falls, merchants would find that offers to pay in cash would also fall, and at some point, they would fall to the level where it is no longer worth their while to accept cash at all – there would no longer be any point in

[8] As an aside, one might add that this conclusion should be especially obvious in a Swedish context. The work of Knut Wicksell (especially his 1898 *Interest and Prices*) had already established that cash could disappear from circulation and the monetary system would still work perfectly well.

replacing the cash machine and going through the (costly) cash management process that goes with it. They would lose a little bit of cash business, but they would take the view that such business is no longer worth catering for. Simultaneously, members of the public would find it increasingly difficult to find businesses that accept cash, and cash would lose first its generally-accepted-for-payment status and eventually perhaps be not accepted at all. Then cash would 'die'.

As this prospect approaches, the authorities would face a choice: they could either let it happen, or they could intervene to prop up the demand for cash. To do the latter, they could pass legal tender laws to compel people to accept cash payments, or they could introduce other measures such as putting pressure on banks to ensure that a sufficient number of cash machines are made available to the public. Such measures might impose costs on those who would prefer not to use cash, but would, however, also have the benefit of retaining cash which might become handy in an emergency, for example in the event of a natural disaster where the power goes out. This, in a nutshell, is the dilemma that societies across the world will face if the demand for cash continues to decline. However, Sweden has made its decision on this issue and decided to prop up cash usage to protect those who depend on it.

As to the second key question, does cashlessness imply a need for a CBDC? The answer is a clear no for reasons already explained. Also, as Waller explains in the US context:

> many central banks are considering adoption of a CBDC as their economies become 'cashless.' Eliminating currency is a policy choice, however, not an economic outcome, and Chair Powell has made clear that U.S. currency is not going to be replaced by a CBDC. Thus, a fear of imminently vanishing physical currency cannot be the reason for adopting a CBDC. (Waller, 2021)

The same would apply in Sweden, too.

An interesting postscript: in a 2018 blog, 'Swedish Betrayal', J. P. Koning suggests that the Swedish drift to cashlessness might not be all it first appears to be. He writes:

> While digital payments share some of the blame for the obsolescence of paper kronor, the Riksbank is also responsible. The Riksbank betrayed the Swedish cash-using public this decade by embarking on an aggressive note switch. Had it chosen a more customer friendly approach, Swedes would be holding a much larger stock of banknotes than they are now. As long as other countries don't enact the same policies as Sweden, they needn't worry about precipitous declines in cash demand. . . .

> Even Norway, which has probably proceeded further along the path of digital payments than Sweden, has experienced only a small decline in notes outstanding, nothing akin to Sweden's white-knuckled collapse. (Koning, 2018c)

Central banks periodically replace their currency with updated designs and anti-counterfeiting measures. Traditionally, such replacements have been carried out by having long periods in which old and new notes would circulate concurrently, to minimise inconvenience to note holders. However, in 2015, the Riksbank only allowed a very short one-year replacement window, and it appears that many Swedes responded by depositing large note holdings in their banks.

Koning continues:

> The timetable that ended up being adopted by the Riksbank in May 2012 was basically the same one proposed by industry. So there you go.
>
> The Riksbank introduced a shot-gun approach because *that's what Swedish bankers wanted*. But in designing the changeover to be convenient for banks, the Riksbank threw the Swedish public under the bus. (Koning, 2018c)

The Riksbank was perfectly aware that a short window would cause what it cheerfully called 'complications' for noteholders. However, the Riksbank considered that the interests of the banks were more important.

There is a big conflict of interest here between the banks and the public. The more people switch from cash to cards, the more fees banks would earn, and the more they switch from cash to deposits, the more the banks earn on the cost of funding.

Thus, the end of cash, like the demise of Mark Twain, would appear to be exaggerated.

## 5.4 A WORLD OVERVIEW OF CBDC SCHEMES

We end this chapter with a brief look around the rest of the world.[9]

Central banks around the world divide into the following categories in terms of their CBDC development: (a) CBDC schemes that have been implemented but then abandoned as failures; (b) CBDC schemes that have been abandoned before implementation; (c) CBDC schemes that are currently operating; (d) CBDC schemes that are currently in the pilot

[9] I gloss over here the influence of the big international organisations – the Bank for International Settlements, the International Monetary Fund, the United Nations, the World Bank and the World Economic Forum – which are all strongly promoting CBDCs on the time-honoured principle that the elite, who would benefit from CBDCs, always knows what is best for the hoi polloi, even though the latter do not want them.

stage of development; (e) CBDC schemes that are currently at the proof of concept or pre-pilot stage; and (f) CBDC schemes that are currently at the research stage where central banks are looking into them with a view to taking them further to the proof of concept stage.[10]

Some of these schemes are retail CBDCs, others are wholesale CBDCs and others are both retail and wholesale.

*(a) CBDC schemes that have been tried and abandoned as failures*

Central banks in Finland (in the early 1990s) and Ecuador.

We provide a more detailed evaluation of these two CBDC experiences in Chapter 6.

*(b) CBDC schemes that have been abandoned*

Central banks in Denmark and Kenya.

*(c) CBDC schemes that are currently being implemented*

Central banks in Bahamas, China, Jamaica, Nigeria and in the East Caribbean Currency Union.

Chapter 6 provides a more detailed evaluation of these CBDC experiences.

*(d) CBDC schemes that are currently at the pilot stage*

Central banks in France, Ghana, India, Kazakhstan, Russia, Saudi Arabia, Switzerland, Tunisia and Uruguay.

*(e) CBDC schemes that are currently at proof of concept stage*

Central banks in Brazil, Canada, Iran, Japan, Laos, Malaysia, New Zealand, Norway, Solomon Islands, South Korea, Sweden, Taiwan, Thailand, Turkey and Ukraine.

*(f) CBDC schemes that are currently at the research stage*

The *vast majority* of remaining central banks!

Thus, it would appear that we might – perhaps – have potentially many more future CBDC experiences to look forward to.

[10] Overviews of different CBDC schemes around the world are provided by the Atlantic Council CBDC Tracker (at https://cbdctracker.org/) and the Human Rights Foundation CBDC Tracker (at https://cbdctracker.hrf.org/home).

# 6

# CBDC Experiences to Date

**Main Point**

**Wherever CBDCs have been attempted, the empirical experience indicates that CBDC adoption rates by the public have been extremely low. The clear implication is that the public do not want CBDCs.**

This chapter examines CBDC experiences to date.[1] We consider both CBDC schemes that have already failed and those that are currently being implemented. In all cases, we give a brief historical discussion. Where a CBDC has already failed, we give an explanation for why that CBDC experience failed. In cases where the CBDC experience is still ongoing, however, we also need to set an assessment criterion. The main one I choose is the latest amount of CBDC that has been adopted per capita of the relevant population, the adoption rate being the ultimate criterion for success or failure. If the per capita holding of CBDCs is 'high' then we can say that that CBDC has been a success; and if the per capita holding of CBDC is 'low', then we can say that that CBDC has been a failure.

## 6.1 FINLAND

The world's first CBDC was the Avant smart card system created by the Bank of Finland in the early 1990s, long before the term 'CBDC' came into

[1] An earlier version of this chapter was published as "So Far, Central Bank Digital Currencies Have Failed" in *Economic Affairs*, 28 February 2024. https://doi.org/10.1111/ecaf.12621. I thank John Wiley & Sons for permission to reproduce this material. Lloyd (2023, pp. 129–134) gives an alternative overview of retail CBDC experiences.

use. Using modern CBDC terminology, it would be described as a 'token-based retail CBDC'.[2]

A key difference between Avant and contemporary CBDC systems is that for modern CBDC systems cards might be an additional feature, whereas in Avant, cards were the main component. Avant cards were based on smart card technology, which was nascent at the time, similar to that used in debit and credit cards today. It was intended that the new payment instrument should resemble cash as much as possible, and that paying with it should be easy and anonymous.

The Bank of Finland launched its Avant project in 1993. By 1995, the total number of outstanding cards reached 500,000. During its first three years, the business entity that issued Avant cards was fully owned by the central bank. Avant was then spun off to the private sector. Though it had been positioned as a low-value payment instrument to replace coins and small-denomination banknotes, it turned out to be similar in effect to pre-paid cards. Fees were later added for reloading, which dented demand, and over time debit cards became more popular. Avant was discontinued in 2006.

The Bank of Finland had expected that Avant would take over from coins for small purchases but Avant never really took off. Users were not happy about fees, merchant take-up was low and alternative debit and credit card networks were much more functional.

As David Gerard observes, Avant's lesson for future payment systems is that user convenience is king. He adds:

> The existing debit card systems are *really very good* – they have user take-up, they have merchant take-up, and they're actually displacing cash – and they give the typical user the reassurances they really want. Did you know that if you lose your card . . . your money is safe, and not lost? You can't say that about a £20 note.
>
> CBDC advocacy hasn't changed since Avant. CBDCs are the sort of thing the vendor loves – but I've yet to see the case for consumers.
>
> CBDCs will have to be *better* than debit cards – for the typical consumer. A technically exciting back end, that gets other vendors to sign on with you, is not enough – your market is users, not other vendors.
>
> You might think that's obvious – but it's a lesson that history keeps having to hit technology vendors over the head with, repeatedly. (Gerard, 2020a, his italics)

[2] This discussion is based on Gerard (2020a) and Grym (2020).

## 6.2 ECUADOR

In 2014 the Ecuadorian government announced to great fanfare that the Ecuadorian Central Bank would soon begin issuing an electronic money (dinero electrónico, or DE), a form of retail CBDC.[3] Users would keep account balances on the central bank's own balance sheet and transfer them using a mobile phone app. Enabling legislation was passed in September and accounts became spendable in February 2015. Ecuador becomes the first country in the world to roll out a CBDC, declared the media. The stated objectives of the new currency were to benefit the unbanked and to reduce reliance on physical cash. At the same time, private digital currencies and cryptos were banned.

The DE flopped.

When it was launched, the government was optimistic that the system would rapidly prove popular. The leading newspaper, *El Comercio*, reported on Christmas Day of 2014 that authorities expected some 500,000 people to use it in 2015. In the event, the number of accounts opened in 2015 turned out to be less than 1 per cent of this number. By the end of January 2016, the DE accounted for no more than 0.003 per cent of the monetary liabilities of the Ecuadorian financial system and the system peaked with DE balances of less than 0.05 per cent of the country's narrow money stock, M1. The impact on financial inclusion was undetectable.

A key reason the DE failed to be adopted was because after previous defaults, the public did not trust the government as much as they trusted private banks. So they preferred private sector alternatives to the DE and the authorities abandoned the scheme in early 2018. It also appears that the government could not even recover their own costs on the project. White (2018a) cites an Ecuadorian government accounting report that suggests that the scheme produced debt service savings of just over $900,000 but the government's expenditures on the project were apparently just under $8 million, more than eight times greater. The government could not even make money issuing its own digital currency.

This episode teaches an important lesson about the limits to a central bank's ability to introduce a new CBDC when the public lack trust in the central bank and prefer alternative payments media.

As Lawrence H. White explains:

[3] This discussion draws on White (2018a), Gerard (2020b) and Arauz et al. (2021).

The Ecuadorian case ... shows that implementation of a central bank electronic money system isn't so easy. It requires more than merely setting up a website ... and letting households and firms open deposits. A convenient point-of-sale deposit-transfer mechanism, requiring both hardware and software, must be provided to many thousands of merchants. Consumer service and marketing are part of the business of providing retail payments. There is no reason to think that central banks are or would be good at a commercial business operation. (White, 2018a)

It turns out that in Ecuador, they were not.

David Gerard offers this explanation:

One lesson that [this case] does teach us is to work hard on retail acceptance of your exciting new payment system. I keep finding all these whizz-bang payment system plans – and they all died of minor inconvenience. ... Serving customers at scale keeps turning out to be *quite difficult in practice.*

And ... don't try to back your system with a bank that your users don't trust ... (Gerard, 2020b, his italics)

However much the fanfare, if people do not trust it, then they will not use it.

Arauz et al. emphasise that the banks did not like it either:

Incumbent banks perceived DE to be a threat to their payment business. The perceived threats included loss of revenue from processing payments and a potential reduction in the size of their customer base. The incumbent banks were vociferous in calling out the possibility of an evolution of DE into a sovereign currency ... which implied a de facto de-dollarization that would bring inflation and instability to the Ecuadorian economy. This was the banks' main public criticism, as clearly stated by the BCE's general manager: '[they] wanted to mix the use of a payment system available in mobile phones with a de-dollarization process' ... Ultimately, the banking sector's opposition contributed significantly to DE's demise ...

The Ecuadorian experience suggests that the support or acquiescence of the private banking sector is crucial to the success of any CBDC initiative. (Arauz et al., 2021, pp. 7–8)

We next look at the schemes currently being deployed.

## 6.3 THE BAHAMAS

The Bahamas has one of the highest per capita incomes in the Americas. Its currency, the Bahamian dollar, is pegged to the US$, and over 94 per cent of adults have a bank account. Against this background, the central bank announced a retail CBDC in 2017 and launched it in October 2020. The Bahamian 'Sand Dollar' generated much interest and was widely praised around the world. An article published by the Official Monetary and Financial Institutions Forum hailed it as a 'ground-breaking innovation' and according to the Bahamian central bank itself, 'The Bahamas is considered a global leader in CBDC development' (quoted in Walker, 2022).

The Sand Dollar had the usual objectives: to modernise and streamline financial stability, reduce delivery costs, increase transactional efficiency and above all to increase financial inclusion, notwithstanding that the Bahamas already had a reasonably high degree of financial inclusion already.

The main feature of the project is a digital version of the Bahamian dollar. The CBDC can be used for all domestic transactions, does not pay interest and has low transaction fees. There is also an ecosystem of Authorized Financial Institutions (AFI) to provide AML/KYC checks, wallet services and custodial services for customers. There are two tiers of individual wallets available: (a) tier 1 holders can only hold $500 at a time and cannot spend more than $1,000 a month; these wallets do not require government identification but cannot be linked to a bank account; and (b) tier 2 holders can only hold $8,000 at a time and cannot spend more than $10,000 a month; these wallets require government identification and can be linked to a bank account.[4]

More than three years after the launch, Governor John Rolle gave a talk on progress thus far to an EU digital euro audience, its status as a CBDC pioneer meaning that its experience was being closely followed across the world. He talked a good talk. Efforts to encourage more adoption were 'still in very early stages', but he emphasised they were building a network of merchants that accept and encourage CBDC use and efforts are 'beginning to accelerate through direct outreach to the business community'; achieving interoperability with the traditional banking system; enlisting participation from the traditional banking sector and credit unions; and so on and so on, and 'messaging is being crafted to inspire user confidence' (quoted in Hall, 2022).

The data tell a different story, however. By January 2025, the volume of Sand Dollars in circulation was only $1.96 million or $4.7 per capita. This amount was about 0.034 per cent of notes in circulation or 6.7 per cent of coins in circulation. The Sand Dollar 'barely registers as a form of currency', as Walker (2022) put it.

[4] See www.sanddollar.bs/individual. Accessed 10 January 2026.

Despite gimmicks such as spending some $1 million on incentivising (i.e., bribing) people to adopt the Sand Dollar and sending out Sand Dollar 'Ambassadors' to encourage adoption, it was still acknowledged that with just 1,500 merchants (and even fewer businesses) having adopted it, the Sand Dollar was 'barely scratching the surface' when it came to adoption (Hartnell, 2023). Most people just do not seem to want it. And UK comedian Dominic Frisby (2024) reports a friend who lives in the Bahamas writing to him: 'LOL. I have never seen one person use it.'

Walker draws some pointed lessons:

> The lessons of the sand dollar (to-date) apply to all CBDC projects, if not fintech innovations in general. Firstly, they need to be aimed at real problems. Financial exclusion in the Bahamas does not seem to be a major problem by international standards. Secondly, the proposed solution needs to genuinely solve the problem (even if relatively small). The minimal impact of the sand dollar to date suggests it does not. Finally, 'pilots' of the type so frequently carried out in fintech, particularly by central banks, need to be re-considered as a form of proof [of concept]. Simply implementing something [and informally] judging whether it 'works' is not a good guide for either policy making or commercial investments, unless there is an objective evaluation of alternatives.

By late 2024, however, the take-up of CBDCs was in decline. However, rather than accept that the public was rejecting them despite the central bank's best efforts to make them attractive, Governor John Rolle was paraphrased as suggesting in an interview that the carrot was turning into stick and regulations were being prepared to force them to distribute the CBDC (reported in Anthony, 2024a). As Nick Anthony drily points out, 'As a general rule, central bankers (and all government officials) would be wise to remember that if something has to be forced, it is probably not a good idea in the first place. CBDCs are no exception to this rule' (Anthony, 2024a).

At the end of the day, the Sand Dollar was more like a sand castle than a world-shattering fintech innovation – and it is already starting to blow away.

## 6.4 EAST CARIBBEAN CURRENCY UNION

The East Caribbean Currency Union is a currency union among Anguilla, Antigua and Barbuda, Dominica, Grenada, Montserrat, St Kitts and Nevis, St Lucia and St Vincent and the Grenadines. Its currency is the East Caribbean dollar, which is pegged to the US dollar at a rate of EC$2.70 to US $1.

The East Caribbean Central Bank (ECCB) launched its CBDC, DCash, in March 2021. DCash was aimed at 'achieving three policy goals: payments system efficiency, financial inclusion of the unbanked and underbanked populations, and increased resilience and competitiveness in the ECCU', the central bank said (quoted in Anonymous, 2022). As ECCB Governor Timothy Antoine explained in an announcement just prior to the launch, 'DCash is a major innovation ... a faster, cheaper and safer alternative to physical cash and other payment options. A huge motivation and big benefit of DCash is the *significant reduction in the cost of financial transactions*' (Antoine, 2021, his italics). In his announcement statement Governor Antoine also stressed the 'careful attention [that] has been paid to the underlying infrastructure which supports the DCash ecosystem'.

However, the ECCB does not report any DCash data on its website and my email request to the ECCB itself for data did not get an answer.[5]

Failing to provide data is not the only instance of the ECCB's lack of professionalism, however. On 14 January 2022, the ECCB announced on its website that 'the DCash platform [had] experienced an interruption in service that has affected all users. This break in service has been caused by a technical issue ... Therefore, DCash transactions are not being processed at this time' (ECCB, 2022).

The system had gone down! So much for all that 'careful attention to the underlying infrastructure'. The problem, it turned out, was that the version of Hyperledger Fabric, the network that hosts DCash's distributed ledger, had a certificate expiry. As David Black comments:

> Did it go down for an hour? Bad. A day? REALLY bad. A week or more? A complete, unmitigated, no-excuses disaster.
>
> What if you were a user of DCash and you couldn't use it? It would be like having money in your bank account, but the bank claims it's unable to give you any! What are you supposed to do? To whom can you appeal? No one!
>
> It's worse than that. [At the time of] *writing at the end of February, a full six weeks after DCash D-Crashed, it's still down.* (Black, 2022, his italics)

Black concludes:

> ECCB seems to have done everything right. They carefully studied. They worked with an experienced vendor, who had experience doing CBDC. They used the

[5] However, the ECCB did report some DCash data in its 2022–2023 *Annual Report*. On p. 104, it reports that it issued EC$2,450,000 (or US $907,407) in 2023 up from EC$2,270,000 the previous year. This latter amount is equivalent to $1.46 per capita (ECCB, 2023).

leading blockchain fabric. They used Google for hosting. They did a limited trial, released it in one of their regions, and then made it more widely available. And then something went wrong. Very wrong. What it could possibly be that involves 'certificates expiring' is mysterious. How they could have built something that could be dead for over six weeks is beyond mysterious – it is extremely rare in software.

CBDC's are a terrible idea. We don't need them. They add nothing in terms of cost or speed to the digital fiat currency and associated software that we already have. How can any government guarantee that they won't have a DCash disaster when their own CBDC rolls out? So governments are suddenly wonderful [at] bringing out great software that works? I've got this bridge, by the way, and I can let you have it for a limited-time-only bargain price...

DCash service finally resumed on 9 March.

Three months later, the ECCB was awarded Central Banking Publications' FinTech and RegTech Global Award for – of all things! – CBDC Infrastructure! As David Gerard drily observed, 'There's no reason to presume that when a central bank puts a blockchain into place, it'll be any less clown-shoes than any other blockchain endeavour' (Gerard, 2022a).

This episode raises worrying questions both about the reliability of other CBDC projects and their vulnerability to single point of failure problems that can bring the whole system down.

The DCash experience reminds us that a CBDC is just another public sector IT project; as such, it would be unwise to expect too much of any of them.

## 6.5 JAMAICA

After a pilot scheme that started in August 2021, the Bank of Jamaica launched its Jamaica Digital Exchange or Jam-Dex[6] CBDC in July 2022. Its aims were to facilitate greater financial inclusion and provide a safe, convenient and secure means to make payments and transfers (*Jamaica Observer*, 2022). Jam-Dex operates on the *Lynk* e-money platform. Transactions are free.

[6] The name Jam-Dex was met with considerable criticism. Twitter (now X) users were quick to point out that Jam-Dex suggests a digital currency but the 'DEX' in crypto parlance refers to a decentralised exchange. This ambiguity caused considerable confusion. Jaymeon Jones wrote on Twitter on 18 February 2022: "Is it a CBDC or a DEX? ... this logo cannot work. It should have been put to a broader voting mechanism – the panelists let you down here big time." See https://x.com/Jaymeon_Jones/status/1494475878671302660. Accessed 4 February 2026.

As part of the launch the first 100,000 customers who signed up for Jam-Dex via the *Lynk* app were given an incentive bonus of $2,500 Jam-Dex (US $16) in their wallets by the government. By 16 July 2022, over 120,000 users and 2,300 merchants had signed up and the Bank of Jamaica and the *Lynk* team embarked on an island-wide public education programme about the benefits of using Jam-Dex on *Lynk*.

As of February 2023, the total number of Jam-Dex customers was 190,000, while total transactions for 2022 were valued at $357 million, less than 0.01 per cent of Jamaica's $4.7 trillion electronic retail transactions for that year and 0.1 per cent of currency in circulation.

Over 2024, there was also discontent brewing. In August 2024, the country's largest bank, the National Commercial Bank, which was the only bank offering a CBDC wallet, admitted that its clients were not interested in a CBDC. Its CEO Bruce Bowen revealed that its mobile app, *Lynk*, had recorded high adoption rates for the payments media that it was offering, but that its clients were not keen on the Jam-Dex offered by the central bank. As he explained:

> It is simpler for people to use Lynk today without converting to CBDC. And the question that we've certainly raised, and there is a dialogue going on, is it worth putting a lot of effort into eliminating the friction to use a CBDC? Or as an industry and a society, are we better off putting that investment into just building the ecosystem? (quoted in Kaaru, 2024)

Meanwhile, the country's second bank, the Jamaica National Bank, was still giving no indication of when it would launch its CBDC wallet.

By January 2025, the amount of Jam-Dex in circulation was $258.5 million or US$1.65 million, equivalent to US$0.59 per capita or roughly a tenth of the level in the Bahamas, or 0.09 per cent of notes and coins in circulation!

As we will see at the end of the chapter, the Jam-Dex has the distinction of being the most unpopular CBDC of all.

### Box 6.1 Thailand's Quasi-CBDC

In July 2024, the Thai government announced an interesting one-off monetary experiment: it was launching a digital wallet programme to distribute $15.6 billion in 10,000 baht ($281) portions to each of 50 million Thai citizens aged 16 or more with incomes under 840,000 baht ($23,710, almost 80 per cent above Bangkok average

**Box 6.1 (cont.)**

income) and savings under 500,000 baht ($14,072). The app that hosts the digital wallet was run by government agencies rather than the central bank so the payments media it issued were not a CBDC as such. Nonetheless, this payments system had many features of a CBDC, including the government taking greater control of individual payments and the financial system.

Applicants were required to verify their identity using digital verification and had to be approved by authorities. Once approved, they were also required to spend the distributed money in the districts in which they live and do so within 6 months of receipt, so the money expires. They are also under restrictions on what they can spend the money on (e.g., no booze, tobacco, lottery tickets, etc.) and the outlets where they could spend it. Registration for the wallet opened on 1 August 2024 and the system soon crashed as millions of applications came in.

Professor Eswar Prasad observed that

> These limitations seem entirely defensible but also show how easily digital money can be subverted for social engineering purposes. The Thai government has decided that only worthy individuals can benefit from the programme, must spend the funds in specific areas and cannot purchase products deemed undesirable. It is not hard to envision a future in which CBDC usage is restricted to 'good' citizens and 'acceptable' expenditures, as deemed by the government. . . .
>
> The Thai experiment will teach us a lot about what the future holds and serves as a warning about how technology might push us towards a dystopian world. (Prasad, 2024)

## 6.6 China

'In the early age of digital money, before smartphones, the machine learning and AI algorithms necessary to make sense of hundreds of millions of transactions did not exist', writes Alex Gladstein.

> But today, governments and corporations can understand the language of global payments. Within moments of buying something online with a tap or swipe, your identity is revealed to authorities and data markets that share and trade your personal information. The end of cash and the insta-analysis of financial

transactions enable surveillance, state control, and, eventually, social engineering on a scale never thought possible.

In China, this is unfolding with alarming rapidity and existential social impact. Real-time linking of all payments to identities has allowed for the beginnings of a vast social credit system that – though more Kafkaesque than Orwellian and seemingly patchwork for the time being – lays the foundation for eventual financial omniscience ... When the government can take financial privileges away for posting the wrong word on social media, saying the wrong thing in a call to parents, or sending the wrong photo to relatives, individuals self-censor and exercise extreme caution. In this way, control over money can create a social chilling effect. (Gladstein, 2021, pp. 280–281)

### 6.6.1 Chinese Social Credit

The first point that we need to appreciate is that the e-yuan is a means to reinforce the Chinese Social Credit System, that is, to control the Chinese population.

This system, first announced in 2014, aims to reinforce the idea that 'keeping trust is glorious and breaking trust is disgraceful', as the government likes to put it. The idea is to impose standards of behaviour by rewarding good and penalising poor behaviour, but the government decides which is which and how good or bad the behaviour might be. You get surveilled when you go out and you get points added to or subtracted from your social credit score depending on how you behave. If your social credit score falls low enough, you get penalised. There is no single Social Credit System yet, but a patchwork of different systems across the country. Participation is mandatory.

Infractions include, for example, bad driving, smoking in non-smoking zones or buying too many video games. They also include numerous political offences, such as circulating pictures of Winnie the Pooh, posting fake news and criticising the Social Credit System. Punishments include not being allowed to buy a train or plane ticket, having your dog taken away, having your child denied a good school or a good job and having your internet connection slowed.

A couple of examples show how damaging this system can be:

Liu Hu is a journalist in China, writing about censorship and government corruption. Because of his work, Liu has been arrested and fined – and blacklisted. Liu found he was named on a List of Dishonest Persons Subject to Enforcement by the Supreme People's Court as 'not qualified' to buy a plane ticket, and banned from travelling some train lines, buying property, or taking out a loan.

> 'There was no file, no police warrant, no official advance notification. They just cut me off from the things I was once entitled to. What's really scary is there's nothing you can do about it. You can report to no one. You are stuck in the middle of nowhere'. (Kobie, 2019)

A low social credit rating also leaves the victim exposed to the danger of a downward spiral involving extra paperwork or fees reminiscent of the Stasi's practice of *Zersetzung*. The threat of having one's life turned upside down by the Stasi's successors often suffices to ensure compliance.

As another example, in April 2018, the Civil Aviation Administration of China sent letters to international airlines demanding that they show Taiwan as part of China, stating that the government would 'make a record of your company's serious dishonesty and take disciplinary actions' against any that did not comply. They all eventually did (Kobie, 2019).

'It's all about building trust', said the Chinese government.

But this claim is false: the Social Credit System is about enhancing government control. 'China's social credit system is a state-driven program designed to do one thing, to uphold and expand the Chinese Communist Party's power', writes Australian academic Samantha Hoffman (quoted in Kobie, 2019). As the *Washington Post* put it in 2016, China's Social Credit System

> uses omnipresent cameras, smartphone apps and more to sort people into categories, track their movements and even take preemptive action against those considered threats. This strategy is fully realized in Xinjiang as part of China's cultural genocide of the Uighur minority, but the expansion of the nation's Social Credit System promises a wider rollout. China infamously censors its Internet with its Great Firewall, and a new cybersecurity law allows the government legal cover to snoop on civilians' online activity even within this restricted space.
>
> China is trying to convince the world . . . that closed is better than open and that controlled is better than free. . . .
>
> China's system of digital authoritarianism is a great danger to those living within that country's borders. It's also a danger to the rest of the world. (Editorial Board, 2020)

### 6.6.2 Origin of the e-Yuan

The PBOC had started researching a centralised CBDC in 2014 that it initially called the Digital Currency Electronic Payment, but also goes by the names digital yuan, e-yuan or e-CNY. It then launched a Digital

Currency Research Institute[7] devoted to the subject in January 2017. In 2019, Facebook announced its new Libra digital currency; PBOC officials expressed concerns that the Libra might undermine the monetary sovereignty of the yuan and announced they were stepping up their CBDC project in response. 'Internal tests' were then carried out across four cities – Shenzu, Suzhou, Chengdu and Xiong'an – over 2020 and, in October 2020, the PBOC launched its pilot CBDC project, the e-yuan, which is technically ongoing. The e-yuan was to bear a zero interest rate but could be used to make payments without charge. This project has since progressed to an undeclared launch phase and involved the Shenzhen government giving out 10 million yuan (about $1.5 million) in digital currency in a lottery with 50,000 winners. The winners would download an app to receive a 'red packet', a traditional form of gift giving, worth 200 yuan (about $30) each, which they could spend at any designated retailer. The scheme was then rolled out to further cities in subsequent years and is still expanding. The initial idea was to test the technology while also boosting spending in the wake of the Covid pandemic. More fundamentally, the goal underlying the e-yuan and China's other social control programmes was to create a 'programmable society' firmly under the control of the Chinese Communist Party (CCP).

### 6.6.3 Key Features of the e-Yuan

The Chinese were already very familiar with the benefits of digital currencies even before the e-yuan. However, the e-yuan is not coming into being as a result of strong demand from the public, but is being imposed top down by the PBOC acting on behalf of the government. It also comes with significant additional features. It 'looks like a potential macroeconomic dream tool for the issuing government, usable to track people's spending in real time, speed relief to disaster victims or flag criminal activity' (Areddy, 2021). It offers Beijing vast new powers to tighten its authoritarian rule. The money itself is programmable and has been tested with expiration dates to encourage users to spend it quickly, for times when the economy needs a jump start. It's also trackable, adding another tool to China's heavy state surveillance. The government deploys hundreds of millions of facial-recognition cameras to

[7] Its first director, Yao Qian, was later accused of corruption on a large scale including 'us[ing] virtual currency to trade power for money and was removed from office and expelled from the Chinese Communist Party in November 2024' (Central Commission for Discipline Inspection and National Supervisory Commission, 2024).

monitor its population, sometimes using them to levy fines for activities such as jaywalking. The e-yuan also makes it possible to both mete out and collect fines as soon as an infraction is detected (Areddy, 2021).

Such a system is also highly weaponisable and can be deployed against anyone who incurs the displeasure of those in authority, for any reason whatever:

> China's control and surveillance-based CBDC system is also an increasingly inspirational and attractive proposition for authoritarian governments from Cambodia to Cuba to Cameroon. Even if a few hundred million people in North America and Europe enjoy enough civil liberties and democratic rights to push back against a digital panopticon, more than 4 billion people lack those same rights and have no way to fight back.
>
> ... in a fully implemented CBDC system, governments could financially exclude individuals or entire groups of people with the press of a button, leaving them with nothing. Governments like the CCP could target dissidents, sexual minorities, ethnic minorities, or religious minorities. If banknotes don't exist and access to government-issued digital cash is revoked, then they are truly helpless. (Gladstein, 2021, p. 283)

There is also the question of privacy, or rather, the lack of it. From the government's point of view, this issue is a no-brainer. Gathering transaction data may be the most perfect surveillance system possible. By merely observing what a person buys, a government can get an intimate look at their whereabouts, habits, personality, health and relationship statuses, aspirations, finances and even their fertility. The best part about financial surveillance is that it is practically invisible. No street cameras or microphones are needed. The data are gathered as a necessary component of the service. From the government's perspective, formally creating a state-run digital currency is merely the next logical step in China's progression towards omnipotent financial digitisation (O'Sullivan, 2020).

The PBOC's assurances about protecting privacy therefore need to be treated sceptically. The fact is, as Alex Gladstein (2021, p. 281) points out, 'Though marketed as offering privacy for users, DCEP will offer the PBOC *total* surveillance capabilities, augmented by big data analysis and AI systems' (my italics).

### 6.6.4 Limited Usage of the e-Yuan

The root problem with the e-yuan, however, is that there is no obvious use for a new digital currency that offers an inferior service to those already available from existing private providers.

The e-CNY boasts a large registered user base of 261 million (as of January 2022) with an outstanding circulation of approximately $14 billion (Srivastava, 2023). However, the actual usage of e-yuan remains very low. Reports also suggested that average balances in those wallets were tiny: $0.47 for individual wallets and $4.90 for corporate ones (Kumar, 2022). These figures indicate that few wallets were being used for transacting or holding e-yuan and raise the suspicion that most wallet holders had downloaded wallets only to obtain the free gifts being handed out with them but did not use them again.

It was then no wonder that even a former PBOC research director was quoted (see Coghlan, 2022) as saying that a circulation of $14 billion two years after launch was 'not ideal ... usage has been low, highly inactive'. Private sector firms have 'met needs for daily consumption ... People are used to [using private exchange media and getting them to change] is difficult', he conceded.

The latest available number for the amount of e-yuan issued is 1.361 billion for December 2022. This number is equivalent to 5.21 e-yuan per capita or $0.73 per capita (see Table 9.1): the total amount of e-yuan is merely a rounding error compared to the amount of actual currency issued. Tyler Durden (2021a) would appear to have been correct when he breezily wrote that 'China's digital yuan is turning into a giant flop' thanks to low public demand to hold it.

Observers believed that the government underestimated how difficult it would be to create a new retail payments network given that existing private ones are so good. 'A lot of the ambition for this project has proven more difficult to achieve than they thought', remarked China fintech expert Martin Chorzempa (quoted in Orcutt, 2023). It was especially difficult to sign up enough merchants to create a rich enough ecosystem to enable the e-yuan to compete against existing payment systems. 'The e-CNY has to be as useful as Alipay and WeChat Pay for it actually to have a user base, and right now there really is not a use case. People just get a red envelope, they spend it, and they generally don't open the e-CNY app again' (Orcutt, 2023).

These issues are similar to those we have encountered with other countries: demand for the CBDC is promoted by artificial gimmicks and propaganda, but the scheme does not work because the underlying demand is not really there. In essence, you can create the CBDC but creating demand for it is much more difficult.

Those who have used the e-yuan are also unimpressed with it:

After interviewing users of China's digital currency, Bloomberg noted that they showed little interest in switching from mobile payment systems run by Ant Group and Tencent that have already replaced cash in much of the country, with some openly balking [rejecting] the digital yuan – which recall is programmable and comes with an ad hoc expiration date – and which gives authorities access to real-time data on their financial lives. ...

Meanwhile, as Bloomberg notes, it was concerns about privacy – or lack thereof – that were among the biggest turnoffs for Jan Chen, a 33-year-old civil servant. It's 'a little scary' that authorities might be able to trace every payment, she said. In a country where compliance with tax laws is often patchy, some merchants may also be wary of their transactions flowing directly into a government database.

The PBOC has tried to quell those concerns by making the digital yuan free to use for merchants – which currently pay service fees of around 0.6% for transactions on Alipay and WePay – and by pledging that most payments will remain anonymous. Not that anyone actually believes that. (Durden, 2021b)

Other participants had similar views, which boil down to the fact that Alipay and WeChat Pay are highly competitive and already offer them all the services they want:

'For end users, using the e-CNY wallet is like you have to manage an extra bank account. It doesn't give [users] many benefits nor convenience.'

'The only incentive that would make me use the e-CNY would be coupons and benefits, but the promotions have yet to be attractive enough for me to register an account right away.'

'I downloaded the e-CNY app initially for some sort of discount coupons or giveaways, but I really didn't use it because I found it more convenient to use WeChat Pay and Alipay.'[8]

Once again, we have the familiar story that central banks are ill-equipped to interface with retail users, because they lack the business experience and acumen of private payments providers.

Finally, a trial involving state employees being paid in e-yuan also reported lacklustre results. Most of the early recipients immediately transfer the digital yuan balances to their bank accounts to spend as cash, it was reported. 'I prefer not to keep the money in the e-CNY app, because there's no interest if I leave it there', said one participant in the pilot. 'There are also not so many places, online or offline, where I can use the e-yuan' (quoted in Crawley, 2024).

In short, the e-yuan is not popular among the Chinese public.[9]

[8] The quotes are from Shen and Zuo (2023).

[9] One also wonders how popular it will be among Chinese merchants, not least because, being legal tender, no merchant can refuse to accept it. Merchants will then be obliged to

### 6.6.5 The PBOC Competes Against the Private Issuers Whose Support It Needs

There is also the further problem that the PBOC is actively competing against the interests of the private banks on whose support the success of the e-yuan depends. The PBOC is then in a fundamentally contradictory position with respect to the private institutions, who have no interest in promoting the e-yuan and good reason not to, because they lose the return they could have earned on the deposit.

To compound matters further, at about the same time as they launched their e-yuan pilot, Chinese authorities launched a crackdown on the country's technology giants, including Alibaba and Tencent, the owners of Alipay and WeChat Pay. This crackdown was interpreted as CCP leaders becoming concerned about the growing influence of the technology conglomerates and wiped billions of dollars from their market valuations.

The CCP position would seem to be that it can take such actions against the big tech companies and still expect their (full?) support in helping to integrate e-yuan wallets with WeChat Pay and Alipay applications. The CCP would also seem unconcerned about payment providers being asked to forgo the benefits of deposits when people switch deposits into e-yuan wallets and to be unconcerned about taking international consumers and businesses for granted given worries about the country's capital controls, its Communist Party-dominated legal system and the country's state surveillance apparatus.

### 6.6.6 The e-Yuan Will Not Achieve Widespread Public Adoption

My main conclusion is that the e-yuan will not achieve the widespread adoption that its promoters had hoped for. Yes, they could continue to push the experiment out in more cities and more applications, they could continue to promote it with more red packet programmes and similar gimmicks, they could continue to promote it among more merchants, they could continue to promote it among banks and the big payment firms, they could continue to expand the ways in which people could use it to make payments to the state, for example to pay taxes or fines, and, in the limit, they could make the e-yuan the only means to make payments to or

install e-yuan terminals and payment systems once the e-yuan is formally launched. The same does not apply to Alipay or WeChat Pay, which merchants are allowed to refuse.

receive payments from the state. Such measures would increase adoption, but I suspect they would not be enough to induce people to use it for everyday transactions while the private providers that the state is competing against have the advantages of much greater retail experience, a superior product and continued public support. More to the point, it is difficult to see how any measures to promote an inferior state digital currency would make the highly efficient Chinese payments system work much better than it already does.

If they choose to, they could quietly accept that the e-yuan adds nothing of value to the Chinese payments system, because central bankers are ill-suited to providing retail payments and will realistically never be able to beat professional private payments providers at their own game. If they wished for the best outcome for the Chinese economy, they could abandon the experiment – quietly if they wished to save face and leave the private sector to provide all the retail digital currency that the people want. I would strongly recommend that Chinese authorities follow this route.[10]

## 6.7 NIGERIA

We turn now to CBDCs in Nigeria, a classic story of how *not* to introduce a CBDC. Nigeria has a population of about 225 million people with a median age of 17. Over 60 per cent of transactions are cash and about 55 per cent of the population do not have a bank account. At the same time, parts of the country are financially sophisticated and more than half of the population are said to have used cryptos.

### 6.7.1 Launch of the eNaira

On 25 October 2021, the Central Bank of Nigeria (CBN) launched its CBDC, the eNaira. The eNaira is a retail CBDC programme based on a permissioned Hyperledger Fabric platform with a zero interest rate and no provision for transactions anonymity. It was initially targeted to people

[10] Alternatively, they could take a leaf from the Great Leap Forward and axe the private system that is fundamentally sound and doing its job well. If they do enough damage to it, people might then turn to the e-yuan for want of something better – i.e. they could degrade private Chinese digital payment systems to make the e-yuan more attractive in comparison. To anyone tempted to recommend such a policy, I would simply say that if a system is working well as it is, then it is best to leave it alone.

with bank accounts, but further updates allowed for it to be used on phones and to those without bank accounts.

The Governor of the Central Bank of Nigeria, Godwin Emefiele, explained the reasons for introducing it: 'The e-Naira is expected to enhance financial inclusion, support poverty reduction, enable direct welfare payments to citizens, support a resilient payment ecosystem, improve availability and usability of central bank money, facilitate diaspora remittances [and] reduce the cost of processing cash' (quoted in Ujah, 2022). But critics objected that the eNaira was pointless. 'The issue is that all of this can already be adequately addressed using the existing financial payments system', said one analyst. 'Nigeria is the fintech capital of Africa, so there are just so many options, so many ways to pay somebody, and pay them fast, already' (Munshi, 2021). Victor Asemota, a tech investor, wrote on Twitter (now X) on 27 October 2021: 'I am still at a loss on what eNaira is meant to solve other than helping the government print money.'[11] Others pointed out that the real-time nature and speedy transfer features of the eNaira are moot, since the Nigerian financial system has had instant digital payments for a decade already. 'How is it superior to the existing money and payments system?' asked the CEO of a leading Nigerian bank (Idris, 2021).

There were also issues of trust or, rather, the lack of it. 'The only reason to use the eNaira over cryptocurrency would be trust in the government, and that trust has been eroded for many', said the CEO of a blockchain consultancy (Idris, 2021). Most Nigerians trusted cryptocurrency far more than they trusted the government and their mistrust of government was well founded in the recent historical record. Introducing a CBDC that gave them no rights of financial privacy was unlikely to promote the trust that the CBDC needed if it was to be accepted.

And there was the problem that a key advantage that a digital currency might have had for moving funds in and out of Nigeria is undermined with the eNaira by the multi-rate foreign exchange system managed by the central bank, which causes major problems for international cash flows and especially remittances. Indeed, it was precisely these problems that had led Nigerians to rely so heavily on cryptocurrencies in the first place.

[11] See https://twitter.com/asemota/status/1453140948905496578. Accessed 4 February 2026.

### 6.7.2 Slow Uptake

Uptake of the new e-currency was slow. A media report of 31 May 2022 stated that there had been 764,000 eNaira app downloads, but almost half have never used the app (*Ledger Insights*, 2022). Just 18,460 have funded wallets, and only 80 merchants' wallets were active, because demand was so low. 'The eNaira is also yet to have very many *recurring* users. It's averaging 1.35 transactions per active wallet', observed David Gerard (2022b) in late August.

As one merchant observed, 'Majority of the transfers are done using bank apps, not eNaira. There are also channels like PoS, which the customers prefer. So the eNaira does not come into the discussion' (*Ledger Insights*, 2022).

The eNaira was unpopular among the banks too:

> For banks, the issue with the eNaira is that it lacks a business case. Many bank sources say operators in the financial services industry want the CBN's approval to layer their services on the eNaira technology, however, the apex bank's total control of the eNaira entire process makes their request not feasible. In the absence of a viable business case, the majority of the banks are unable to push the publicity of the eNaira.
>
> 'If they won't let banks layer their services on the eNaira technology, the CBN should pay banks to market the eNaira,' a bank source who would like to remain anonymous said.
>
> There is also thinking among the banks that the eNaira is a competition [sic] as it is offering nearly all the services that banks have already solved through their digital banking channels. (Eleanya, 2022)

The reader will recall that these concerns are *exactly* those raised earlier in Chapter 2, namely, no one would pay the banks' costs to host a CBDC product that was competing against them.

On 18 August 2022, Governor Emefiele said that the eNaira had reached ₦4 billion or $9.5 million in transaction volume (Ujah, 2022). He failed, however, to mention that this $9.5 million figure translates into a ratio of CBDC transactions volume to total e-transactions volume of just 0.013 per cent,[12] that is, the take-up was negligible.

By 25 October 2022, an IMF working paper reported:

[12] The CBDC transactions volume is $9.5 million, total e-transactions volume was ₦29.3 trillion and the exchange rate was ₦415 to $1. The ratio of eNaira to total transactions was then 9.5 million multiplied by 415/ ₦29.3 trillion = 0.013%. Data sources: Steward (2022), Nigeria Inter-Bank Settlement Systems (2022).

> The average number of eNaira transactions since its inception amounts to about 14,000 per week – only 1.5 percent of the number of wallets out there. This means that 98.5 percent of wallets, for any given week, have not been used even once. The average value of eNaira transaction[s] has been 923 million naira per week – 0.0018 percent of the average amount of M3 during this period. (Ree, 2023, p. 14)

By this time, Emefiele had revealed his true intentions, which were to establish a cashless economy by force, *whatever the cost*. He clarified that, 'The destination, as far as I am concerned, is to achieve a 100% cashless economy in Nigeria' (quoted in Osae-Brown et al., 2022). His Deputy Governor in charge of economic policy, Kingsley Obiora, added that people just needed 'a little push from the government' and they would 'embrace' the eNaira (quoted in Dietz, 2022).

### 6.7.3 The Nigerian War on Cash

That 'little push' came on 23 November 2022, when the CBN announced a new currency 'redesign notes' policy. Existing notes in denominations of ₦200 ($0.45), ₦500 ($1.125) and ₦1000 ($2.25) were to cease to be legal tender on 31 January 2023. (The deadline was later extended to 20 February, and for ₦200 notes again to 10 April, as measures to alleviate the subsequent shortage of cash.) New notes would be issued from 15 December and the public would be obliged to go to banks to have their notes exchanged. However, ATM withdrawals were limited to ₦20,000 ($45) per day or ₦100,000 ($225) per week, citizens wishing to take out larger sums were subject to a processing fee between 5 per cent and 10 per cent and only ₦200 ($0.45) notes or lower denominations were available in the machines.

The policy triggered chaos as people rushed to their banks to convert their notes. They queued for long hours and often overnight. The banks often failed to meet demands for redemption because they had not been provided with sufficient amounts of new notes. Stories about people struggling with cash restrictions quickly spread on Twitter (now X), TikTok and other social media. 'It seems like Nigeria wants to eradicate half the population ... No cash, bank transfers not working, people can't access basic needs', wrote one observer on Twitter.[13] The scarcity of cash drove people to bank and electronic transfers, but these often broke down under the strain as people struggled with failed transactions or a poor

[13] See https://twitter.com/BukolaOyebodeW/status/1628372151056142336. Accessed 22 January 2026.

internet. Mobile phone and Bitcoin transactions skyrocketed. Commuters were left stranded for want of cash. Many small businesses, which represented the lion's share of the economy and which predominantly relied on cash payments, had to shut because their customers did not have the cash to pay. Protesters attacked bank ATMs and blocked streets, and demonstrations turned violent in some cities. Economic activity plunged.

To give one vivid example of the resulting suffering:

> No one in Godgift Inemesit's family of eight is sure when they will eat each day – except for her three kids, two of whom have malaria. She can't pay for the drugs they need or feed the rest of her family regularly.
>
> Like most Nigerians, the family's savings are trapped in the bank. ... There aren't enough new banknotes in a country reliant on cash. ...
>
> 'We usually eat three square meals, but now we eat once sometimes because there is no money to use', Inemesit said. (Corbishley, 2023b)

But even as ordinary people's lives were plunged into chaos, Governor Emefiele hailed it as a success, because most of the cash previously held by the private sector had been deposited with financial institutions. Finance Minister Zainab Ahmed agreed. 'The only sore point is the pain it has caused to citizens', she said (Bloomberg, 2023) as if that was but a small price to pay.

Heritage Falodun, a Bitcoin consultant, gives a particularly vivid picture of the situation on the ground as of 11 February 2023:

> In [Emefiele's] view, Nigerians should have found that the CBDC is the solution to their financial predicaments ... Not surprisingly, the reverse has been the case, as the situation on the ground in Nigeria right now is gradually moving from 'banking the unbanked' to 'un-banking the banked.' ...
>
> ... the well-informed ... youth, which happens to be about 70% of Nigeria's population, understand that these regulations are mostly about financial control. They are about pushing a cashless policy in which the government has complete control over all citizens while having the luxury of tracking every single transaction. ...
>
> [But] the Nigerians disposition [for cryptos] is visible to the blind and audible to the deaf ... (Falodun, 2023)

To learn more about the balance between Bitcoin adoption and being forced towards the eNaira, he had spoken with a few business owners. One told him:

> The cash swap policy has been ridiculous, to say the least. Today, February 4, 2023, alone, you could not get any physical cash in the entire Garki ultra modern market in Abuja, Nigeria. People are unable to take care of little business deals, like cash for services, transportation, etc. It's so bad because even the traditional

banking applications seem to be overwhelmed by the sudden surge in transactions and cannot cope.

Even so, Emefiele was adamant, 'Nigeria must go cashless', he declared in mid-February (quoted in Corbishley, 2023a).

### 6.7.4 The Supreme Court Overrules the Cash Redesign Policy

In the meantime, a number of state governors had filed a lawsuit at the Supreme Court to challenge the cash redesign policy. On 3 March 2023, the Nigerian Supreme Court ruled that the demonetisation policy was illegal and unconstitutional: the old notes were still legal tender and should remain in circulation until 23 December 2023.

By this time, supply of cash in circulation had fallen to 29.8 per cent of its 22 October value. There had been a big switch towards cryptos and mobile banking[14] and the ratio of CBDC transactions volume to total e-transactions volume around the same time had barely moved to 0.016 per cent.[15] Thus, the policy had delivered a massive reduction to the note supply, which in turn had a devastating impact on the real economy and led to a big jump in crypto and online banking, and a negligible impact on the demand for CBDCs.

### 6.7.5 Economic Cost

The economic cost of the redesign policy was enormous. On 12 March 2023, the Centre for the Promotion of Private Enterprise in Lagos released a report that estimated that CBN's demonetisation policy had cost the Nigerian economy an estimated ₦20 trillion ($43.3 billion, about 10 per cent of GDP). Its CEO Dr Mada Yusuf said that the policy had crippled economic activity and

> Millions of citizens have slipped into penury and destitution as a result of the disruptions and tribulations perpetrated by the currency redesign policy, especially the mopping up of over 70 percent of cash in the economy. Nigerians have not been this traumatised in recent history.

[14] By March, mobile banking transactions had jumped by more than five times to 183.8 million (Adamoleikun, 2023).

[15] The CBDC transactions volume was ₦22 billion and total e-transactions volume was ₦135.5 trillion. ₦22 billion divided by ₦135.5 trillion = 0.016%. Data sources: Nwite (2023), *Ledger Insights* (2022).

> The economy is gradually grinding to a halt because of the collapse of payment systems across all platforms. Digital platforms are performing sub-optimally because of congestion; physical cash is unavailable ... and the expected relief from the supreme court judgement has not materialised. The citizens are consequently left in a quandary. (Yusuf, 2023, quoted in *Rate Captain*, 2023)

These losses arose from the deceleration of economic activities, the crippling of trading activities, the stifling of the informal economy, contraction in the agricultural sector and the paralysis of the rural economy. There were hundreds of thousands of job losses. 'We again plead with the president to immediately intervene to put an end to the devastating and traumatic outcomes of a repressive, poorly conceptualised and badly implemented currency redesign policy', wrote Dr Yusuf.

The supply of cash had reached its nadir at the end of February. In an editorial in mid-March, the newspaper *Premium Times* called for Emefiele's arrest and prosecution, arguing that the monetary redesign policy was an infringement on the rights of the people. For his part, the President received a stinging rebuke from the president of the Nigerian Bar Association:

> This is the greatest test or challenge to our constitutional democracy and the Executive cannot afford to disregard the ORDERS of the Supreme Court made for the benefit of the people that elected it to power. I therefore, on behalf of all Nigerians, call on the President to immediately direct compliance with the terms of the orders made by the Supreme Court in its judgement delivered on 3 March 2023. (quoted in *Rate Captain*, 2023)

President Buhari then apologised for the redesign policy and started to dismantle it.

On 29 May 2023, Bola Tinubu took office as the new President after winning the presidential election on 25 February. On 9 June, Tinubu suspended Emefiele as Governor with immediate effect and investigations were started into his activities. The next day Emefiele was arrested and then accused of a string of offences relating to the abuse of his office, stealing public funds, sabotage and so on. He was also accused of having 593 unauthorised foreign bank accounts totalling £543 million in the UK alone.

Meanwhile Emefiele's influential overseas supporters from the IMF, the Fed and elsewhere, who had enthusiastically cheered his pioneering policies, now remained conspicuous by their silence.

We can safely assume that the Nigerian War on Cash is over.

The CBDC experiment continues but by February 2024, the amount of eNaira held by the public was equivalent to $13.2 per capita.[16]

### 6.7.6 Conclusions about the Nigerian CBDC Experiment

The Nigerian experience shows that the Nigerian public are not interested in CBDCs and much prefer cash or private sector digital alternatives such as mobile banking or cryptocurrencies. To quote a Bloomberg report, 'Nigerians' passion for cryptocurrencies does not extend to the central bank offering … [Nigerians view the eNaira as] "a symbol of distrust in the ruling elite" [and view the government as] hostile to them and therefore have no interest in anything it introduces' (Giambruno, 2022). Nigeria's experience suggests that the typical citizen sees through the pro-CBDC propaganda and understands that CBDCs bring no benefit except to the elite.

## 6.8 CONCLUSIONS

Every single CBDC experiment tried so far has been a failure.

Table 6.1 summarises our headline results for CBDC adoption rates expressed in terms of average amounts held per capita.

TABLE 6.1 *CBDC adoption rates*

| CBDC | Amount Issued (US $ Per Capita) |
|---|---|
| Sand Dollar | 4.7 |
| DCash | 1.46 |
| Jam-Dex | 0.59 |
| e-yuan | 0.73 |
| eNaira | 13.2 |
| Population-weighted average | 4.6 |

*Notes* to Table 6.1: Adoption rates are taken to equal CBDC in circulation divided by the national population, except for China where it is assumed that the rollout has now reached 261 million people.

[16] Assuming an exchange rate of $1 =₦1025.

TABLE 6.2 *CBDC issues as a percentage of total central bank liabilities*

| CBDC | CBDC Issues as % of Total Central Bank Liabilities |
|---|---|
| Sand Dollar | 0.034 |
| DCash | 0.024 |
| Jam-Dex | 0.019 |
| e-yuan | 0.003 |
| eNaira | 0.06 |

*Notes* to Table 6.2: Based on publicly available data on central banks' websites.

CBDC adoption rates have been very low in Nigeria, and lower still everywhere else. The amounts of CBDC adopted vary from an average holding of $13.2 per capita for the eNaira down to an average holding of $0.59 per capita for the Jam-Dex. The population-weighted average CBDC holding across all countries is a mere $4.6, enough to buy a few items from your local dollar store.

To give another perspective, Table 6.2 shows CBDC issues as a percentage of total central bank liabilities, and a not too dissimilar picture emerges: CBDC issues are very low for all countries, and especially China.

# 7

# CBDCs and Macroeconomic Policy

Main Points

This chapter examines a variety of claimed macroeconomic uses of CBDCs.

CBDCs could be used to carry out helicopter money drops. However, such drops can already be carried out in other ways, and the obstacle to using them is not implementing the helicopter drop, but the time needed to plan the distribution.

CBDCs could be used to implement a digital version of an 'expiring money' policy of the type first proposed by Silvio Gesell. This is a potentially promising policy in a depressive environment and evidence from the 1930s suggests that applied locally it has locally stimulative effects.

CBDCs could be used alongside the abolition of cash to help implement negative interest rate policies (NIRP). However, a NIRP is a tax in sheep's clothing and empirical evidence to date suggests that such policies do not stimulate the economy.

CBDCs could be used to end fractional reserve banking, but there are other ways to end fractional reserve banking that do not involve CBDCs, and such a policy is questionable anyway.

Recent discussions of CBDCs have made a number of claims about how CBDCs might be used to implement exciting new macroeconomic policies. However, these innovative policies are overrated – just because one *could* implement a new type of macroeconomic policy does not mean one *should*!

## 7.1 CBDCS COULD BE USED TO IMPLEMENT HELICOPTER MONEY DROPS

It is sometimes claimed that CBDCs could be used to implement helicopter money drops:

> Monetary policy could ... be implemented through 'helicopter drops' of money, once seen as just a theoretical possibility of increasing cash holdings in an economy in a nondistortionary fashion by making lumpsum transfers to all households. This would be easy to implement if all citizens in an economy had official electronic wallets and the government could transfer central bank money into (or out of) those wallets. Channels for injecting outside money into an economy quickly and efficiently become important in circumstances of weak economic activity or looming crises, when banks might slow down or even terminate the creation of outside money. (Prasad, 2021b, p. 3)

I am not convinced.

CBDCs *could* be used to implement helicopter money drops, but the government already has a number of other distribution channels that could be used for the same purpose. The tax-benefit system could be used to make payments to everyone registered for tax purposes, and transfers could be made directly to everyone with a bank account. Distributions could also be made the old-fashioned way by sending bank account holders cheques through the post. So even if everyone already had a CBDC wallet, CBDCs would merely provide another distribution channel and there is not much to choose between them.

The question to be established is not whether CBDCs offer a(nother) distribution channel, but whether they offer a distribution channel that is superior to existing channels and sufficiently so as to make a real difference.

The answer to that question is surely 'No'. Even if CBDCs did provide a superior distribution channel, distributions still take time to plan, and the planning takes much longer than the time needed to make the distribution itself.[1]

[1] Conversely, CBDCs could also be used to implement *reverse helicopter money drops*. Instead of boosting the amount of CBDC money in circulation, the central bank could cancel some (or even all of) the CBDCs already in circulation. Such a policy might be used in a situation where policymakers were concerned that prices were too high or were increasing too fast. Unlike traditional disinflationary policies, such a policy would be exceptionally easy to implement, but the mere *possibility* that such a policy might be implemented in the future gives potential CBDC holders another reason to be reluctant to hold them.

## 7.2 USE OF EXPIRY DATES ON CBDCS TO BOOST AGGREGATE DEMAND

It is sometimes claimed that CBDCs with expiry dates could be a useful macroeconomic policy tool. If the central bank wanted to discourage money 'hoarding' and boost spending, it could announce that on some specified future date holdings of CBDCs would expire. The expiry could be full ('we will cancel all your CBDC holdings') or partial ('we will cancel some of your CBDC holdings'). The message to money holders: spend it or lose it.

Indeed, it was reported in 2021 that the PBOC has already tested digital currency with expiration dates, for times when the economy needs a jump start (Areddy, 2021). 'And there you have it', commented 'Tyler Durden' on *ZeroHedge*, 'the Keynesian wet dream to boost the velocity of money finally comes true. For the past decade, we have joked that it is only a matter of time before central banks slap on an expiration date on every monetary unit in circulation' (Durden, 2021a).

Such a policy is reminiscent of Silvio Gesell's 'stamped money' proposal. 'Stamped money' lends itself to digitisation because the practical difficulties of implementing the original scheme – taking currency to an office every month to be stamped etc. – disappear when the scheme is implemented digitally, because the implementation is now done by algorithm rather than human effort.

The idea underlying expiring money is an old one. The original idea, stamped money, had been suggested by the German social reformer Silvio Gesell (1862–1930) in 1891 as a proposed solution to end the depression of the time in Argentina where he then lived. He set it out in his book *Die Reformation des Münzwesens als Brücke zum sozialen Staat* (*The Reformation of the Monetary System as a Bridge to a Social State*, 1891) and developed it further in his later writings. Gesell died in 1930 having never seen his system implemented.

The idea was that currency should bear a cost to encourage holders to spend it quickly. He set out a scheme in which paper currency would automatically expire unless notes were regularly stamped for a monthly fee of 1 per cent of face value.

Stamped money was implemented locally in 1932 in the Austrian town of Wörgl, where it worked with success during the Great Depression to help restore prosperity to the local economy. The scheme attracted considerable notice as the 'miracle of Wörgl'. Similar schemes were implemented in other Austrian towns and in Hawarden, Iowa, and Anaheim,

California. Stamped money received positive endorsements from both Irving Fisher and John Maynard Keynes. The scheme ended in 1933 when the Austrian central bank prohibited it, and then the depression returned to Wörgl.

In a recent World Bank blog posting, Biagio Bossone and Ahmed Faragallah write of the monetary policy possibilities of

> [e]xpiring money, one whose value falls to zero after a specific date, [a]s a potential monetary policy tool. 'Programmability,' a technical feature made possible by digitalization, can accelerate decisions to spend it, making it a very effective means for stimulating consumption.
>
> This could be very useful for central banks and governments distributing aid to people during severe recessions or events like pandemics or calamities, when higher uncertainty makes people spend less. (Bossone and Faragallah, 2022a)

The idea is that expiring money would encourage people to spend money instead of holding onto it, and so increase the velocity of money and hence overall spending and economic activity.

Bossone and Faragallah explain how the policy might be implemented:

> In the case of expiring money, … the money would keep its full value for a predetermined interval after issuance and would decline in value from then onwards. This form of programmable money would set in motion a sequence of spending decisions – since no holder would have reasons to hold it beyond expiration – and would thus raise aggregate demand permanently (all else being equal).
>
> For this money to be acceptable, however, the expiration mechanism should be designed on a 'resettable timer' basis, so that while the interval to expiration is fixed for each holder, the clock is set back to zero anytime money passes hands. This would give its new holders the full time interval before the new expiration date sets in. An automated alert system could advise holders of the approaching expiration dates. (Bossone and Faragallah, 2022a)

They then describe expiring money as 'a most powerful policy tool', 'a form of "hyperbolic" helicopter money' that would offset the incentive to hoard and, 'once injected into the economy, would support a permanently higher velocity of money' (Bossone and Faragallah, 2022b).

One might respond by wondering (1) how printing money might create sustainable spending opportunities and (2) whether Bossone and Faragallah might be conflating saving with money holding. However, the big question is, under what conditions would people willingly accept expiring money? The obvious answer is that they would accept it as a gift, for example as part of a helicopter drop or as winnings from a lottery, but it is not clear why they would accept it otherwise. Why would shopkeepers accept the money with the expiry clauses, when they could insist on regular money without expiry clauses instead?

A *possible* answer, which might also explain the success of the Wörgl experiment, is that shopkeepers might accept currency with expiry clauses in cases where they were *not* able to insist on being paid with conventional currency, as appears to have been the case in the depths of the Great Depreciation when currency seemed to be disappearing from circulation because people were hoarding it.

## 7.3 USING CBDCS TO IMPLEMENT NEGATIVE INTEREST RATE POLICY

It is sometimes claimed that CBDCs could be used to stimulate the economy by implementing NIRP. For example, 'CBDC *would* ... *overcome* the zero-lower bound ("ZLB") of monetary policy and therefore allow for ... unconstrained [NIRP and allow] *strong monetary stimulus* in a sharp recession and/or financial crisis' (Bindseil, 2022, p. 4, my italics).[2]

Such claims need to be qualified, however. One reason is that such policies require that CBDCs have already become widely accepted and that cash has disappeared from use. Otherwise, if cash were still in use, an attempt to implement unconstrained NIRP would trigger a flight to cash that would prevent interest rates from going too far into negative territory.

A second consideration is that there are good reasons why interest rates had been positive over the past 5,000 years or so. Positive interest rates reflect positive time preference, the expectation that the future productivity of capital will be positive and compensate for default risk. Alasdair Macleod (2015) is to the point here: 'NIRP is a preposterous concept. It contravenes the laws of time preference, commanding by diktat that cash is worth less than credit.' If negative interest rates seem unnatural, that is because they are. My wife once put this idea to the test with our two-year-old grandson on a visit to the countryside. 'Would you like your ice cream now or after our walk?' 'Now!' was the adamant answer. Two-year olds have an impeccable understanding of time preference.

[2] Leaving CBDCs aside, promoting NIRP to improve the effectiveness of monetary policy in a low or zero interest rate environment is a common theme among Keynesian economists, such as Haldane (2015) or Rogoff (2016).

A third reason is that NIRP would not actually stimulate the economy. The key feature of NIRP is a negative central bank rate that pushes down other bank rates and bond coupons. In 2009 NIRP was first implemented when the Swedish Riksbank imposed a negative deposit rate for commercial bank holdings (i.e., reserves) held with the Riksbank[3] – the first negative interest rate since at least Hammurabi. Denmark, the Eurozone, Japan and Switzerland subsequently implemented their own versions of NIRP. The last remaining NIRP experiment – that in Japan – came to an end in March 2024. The amount of negative yielding bonds rose to a peak of over $16 trillion in 2019 before falling back (Milne and Arnold, 2020), by which time negative yielding bonds had risen to 30 per cent of the market (Durden, 2019). These NIRP experiments were modest, however; rates only went as low as minus 75 basis points and central banks could not push interest rates much lower because doing so would have triggered a flight to cash.

Empirical evidence suggests that NIRP has been a failure. It led to greater rather than lower savings rates (Kantchev et al., 2016; Blackstone, 2019), reduced bank lending and credit creation, and to declines in banks' net interest margins and profitability (Molyneux et al., 2019, 2020). Negative Interest Policy also had adverse impacts on savers, not just because it lowered their yields, often to below zero, but also because it reduced their investment opportunities (Stoller, 2019) and pushed them to take on more risk in their search for positive yields. Likewise, negative yields made it more difficult for pension funds and insurance companies to meet their obligations and pressured them also to take on more risk. NIRP was introduced because policymakers wanted to give their economies a short-term stimulus jolt, but central banks then experienced difficulties weaning their economies off the policy. 'Overall, we are on a painkiller', one observer noted, 'and it's very hard to get off it' (Blackstone, 2019).

Then, in 2019, the central bank that had pioneered negative interest rates, the Riksbank, ended them. The main reasons it gave were concerns about the long-term impacts if NIRP were to be continued – namely, that negative rates would weaken banks, discourage lending, encourage cash hoarding and lead to further increases in already high levels of household debt (Milne and Arnold, 2020). Two prominent Swedish economists, Frederik Andersson and Lars Jonung (2020), also expressed other

[3] The Riksbank, however, did not make its main policy rate – the repo rate – negative until 2015.

concerns about NIRP, including its impact on the housing market, its ineffectiveness in helping to achieve inflation targets and its weakening the exchange rate. They gave a blunt assessment of the policy: 'It is evident that the policy's effect on the inflation rate was modest, and that it contributed to increased financial vulnerabilities. The lesson from the experiment is clear: Do not do it again.'

Most of all, negative rates cannot stimulate the economy because they are a tax on money and no tax is ever stimulative. Christopher Waller puts it beautifully:

a negative interest rate is just a tax on the banks' reserves. The tax has to be borne by someone:

- The banks can choose not to pass it on and just have lower after-tax profits. This will depress the share price of banks and weaken their balance sheets by having lower equity values.
- The banks can pass the tax onto depositors by paying a lower interest rate on deposits or charging them fees for holding the deposits. In either case, depositors have less income to spend on goods and services.
- The bank can pass the tax onto borrowers by charging them a higher interest rate on a loan or higher fees for processing the loan. In either case, it is more costly to finance purchases of goods and services by borrowing.

None of this sounds very 'stimulative' for consumer spending. But then, no tax ever is.... At the end of the day, negative interest rates are taxes in sheep's clothing. Few economists would ever claim that raising taxes on households will stimulate spending. So why would they think negative interest rates will? (Waller, 2016)

## 7.4 USING CBDCS TO ABOLISH FRACTIONAL RESERVE BANKING

It is sometimes claimed that CBDCs could be used to abolish fractional reserve banking. In his posting, 'Which Fedcoin?' on 5 February 2015, Robert Sams writes:

it's the economic implications [CBDCs], which are radical: *it would cause the demise of fractional reserve banking.* A central bank that went down this path would effectively bring about something dubbed the 'Chicago Plan', an early 20th century proposal that banks hold 100% reserves and the CB [central bank] compensate for the destruction of privately-created 'endogenous money' with a dramatic expansion of base money. (my italics)

We will come to the Chicago Plan in a moment. Sams goes on:

> the problem (or opportunity, depending upon your perspective) with Fedcoin ... is that it will compete with bank deposits in a big way. Unlike your bank deposit, which is an *unsecured loan* to a highly leveraged deposit-taking institution, Fedcoin is *central bank money*. It cannot default, by definition. ...
>
> The reason why Fedcoin is so radical is that, for the first time, central bank money would be available to everyone in electronic form. *Electronic payments would finally be divorced from bank deposit.*

More precisely, the idea is to separate the issuing of money from the lending process. 'Who said payment systems were boring! The whole edifice of fractional reserve banking is held up by the union of electronic payments and bank deposit (along with LLR, depo insurance, etc.). Break that union and, I conjecture, the union of fiat money and fractional reserve breaks too' (Sams, 2015).

The Chicago Plan was a monetary and banking reform programme suggested in the wake of the Great Depression by a group of prominent Chicago economists. Its main provision was to require 100 per cent reserves on deposits, so that fractional reserve banking would be eliminated and the creation and destruction of money through private lending operations would become impossible. The plan was designed to prevent the money supply from cyclically varying as bank loans were expanded or contracted. The payment system would become perfectly safe and no great monetary contraction like that of 1929–1933 could ever occur again. Various versions of this plan have been put forward over the years, and interest in it revived after the Great Financial Crisis (see, e.g., Benes and Kumhof, 2012, or Vollgeld Initiative, 2018).

The main issue with this plan and others like it is how lending is to be carried out if fractional reserve banking is abolished. Broadly speaking, one can imagine two alternative lending models in such circumstances.

The first is that as the central bank monopolises the money supply, it also takes over the lending that had previously been done by banks – that is, it monopolises bank lending too. Leaving aside the difficulties of the transition process, the replacement of a competitive lending process by a state monopoly has obvious drawbacks, including the inherent inefficiencies of a monopoly and the dangers and corruption possibilities associated with state interference in lending.

The second model is for lending to be carried out by the private sector. For example, lending could be carried out by banks that provide loans that are not financed by bank deposits subject to chequing, or lending could be carried out by equity-funded investment trusts. However, lending would then be more restricted and more expensive than it currently is.

In short, we *could* abolish fractional reserve banking, but we *cannot* replace it with an alternative banking system that is equally efficient, a point that Sams does not address. But in any case, none of these issues have much to do with CBDCs, because such policies could have been introduced many decades before CBDCs were even conceived.

## 7.5 CONCLUSIONS

Various suggestions have been made for innovative macroeconomic uses of CBDCs but these usually offer slim pickings for CBDC enthusiasts. Yes, CBDCs *could* be used to implement helicopter money drops, but we could implement similar policies already even without CBDCs. The same applies to suggestions to use CBDCs to abolish fractional reserve banking. CBDCs *could* be used to implement expiring money schemes. Such schemes are promising, but more work needs to be done on them because questions remain about how expiring money would be passed on after being introduced into the economy. CBDCs *could* also be used to implement NIRP, but recent experience suggests that NIRP fails to generate the stimulus that its proponents have hoped for. Admittedly, those recent NIRP experiments were constrained by the ZLB, which itself derives from the ability of currency holders to run to cash. But even if cash were abolished so that the ZLB no longer applied, it is not at all obvious that the impact of a more powerful NIRP would be stimulative.

In short, the argument that CBDCs have convincing macroeconomic uses is a weak one. However, digital versions of stamped money schemes are worth exploring further.

# 8

# A CBDC Could Disintermediate the Banking System

## Main Points

CBDCs have the potential to disintermediate deposits from the banking system and move them into CBDC accounts held at the central bank. Such disintermediation could lead to a less productive financial system because previously stable bank credit is undermined by CBDC issue. The banking system would also be more prone to crisis, which could erupt suddenly too.

In the event of a major market shock, there may be no CBDC interest rate sufficient to prevent fund holders moving large amounts into CBDCs, and this problem could be aggravated further by administrative 'fixity' in CBDC rates of return. We would then get a situation similar to what happened with the US Postal Service system in the 1930s when administrative fixity in Post Office interest rates sucked deposits out of the banking system.

CBDC policymakers would also have to grapple with a clear contradiction between a central bank's commitment to maintain a fixed rate of exchange between commercial and central bank money, and a central bank considering the use of quantitative restrictions on the issue of CBDCs. Should the demand for CBDCs surge, then it may become impossible to maintain parity between CBDCs and conventional central bank money. Such an occurrence would threaten the 'singleness' of central bank money, which is a bedrock principle of central banking.

Imagine that the central bank introduces a retail CBDC and is willing to issue whatever amount of CBDCs the market demands. If the return on CBDC is appreciably higher than the return on deposits, then we might expect bank depositors to convert their holdings to CBDCs and banks would face a run on their deposits.

This thought exercise suggests that, unless the amount of CBDC issued is constrained, we cannot have the return on CBDCs be appreciably higher than the return on deposits.

## 8.1 CBDCS COULD DISINTERMEDIATE BANK DEPOSITS

However, even if the return on CBDCs were not appreciably higher than the return on deposits, it is still possible that CBDCs could disintermediate deposits.[1] Will Luther explains:

> If people are holding more money in government-issued CBDC accounts, they are holding less money in private financial accounts [or cash, but let's assume the former for the moment, KD]. That's a big deal. Private financial institutions use deposits to support their lending activities. The conventional view is that financial depth (that is, more people with more funds in the private financial system) promotes economic growth. The logic is straightforward: more deposits mean more financial intermediation, and more financial intermediation means entrepreneurs can take on more productive ventures.
>
> A CBDC risks disintermediating the private financial system. Unless one thinks that the government will channel loanable funds into valuable investment projects at least as well as the private financial system, the shift of funds from private financial accounts to government-issued CBDC accounts will result in less productive investment and, hence, lower economic growth. (Luther, 2022)

Or, as the American Bankers Association explained, a CBDC would 'serve as an advantaged competitor' to retail bank deposits that will move money away from banks and into accounts at the Fed. Losing this critical funding source would undermine the economics of the banking business model, restricting credit availability, reducing investment, making loans more costly and causing a slowdown of the economy (quoted in Callahan, 2023).

Thus, to the extent that CBDCs replace bank deposits, they also deprive banks of their most reliable source of income, that is, interest on loans,

[1] It is also conceivable that banks could offset the loss in deposits by increasing their deposit rates and that the net result could be even higher deposits and higher bank lending overall. One finds such results in some of the simulations in Barrdear and Kumhof (2016) and in the models of, e.g., Chiu et al. (2020) and Andolfatto (2021a).

and disintermediate the financial system.[2] The more successful CBDCs are at replacing bank deposits, the bigger this disintermediation problem becomes.

Indeed, if CBDCs proved sufficiently popular, they could in the extreme suck all deposits and similar instruments out of the financial system and the consequences could be potentially catastrophic. In the US, such an event could stretch the central bank's balance sheet from $8 trillion to $21.5 trillion. Who, then, would provide the $15 trillion in loans that US banks currently provide to the American economy?[3]

The banks could then find themselves in a situation where the deposit base they used to finance their lending has fallen. The issue is then how the banks could finance their lending in circumstances where they had lost the underlying asset to the central bank, but the central bank would not have the expertise, employees or scale to manage it nearly so well. In the most extreme case, we would have the scenario outlined earlier in which deposits go to zero and the banks fail. In less extreme scenarios, banks would lose some deposits and many lending customers would face the dire prospect of their financing drying up with no obvious alternatives for replacement. The supply of loans would fall and their cost would rise, and there would be no policy response to this problem that could undo the damage and get the economy back to where it would have been before CBDCs were introduced.[4]

The question then arises as to who would take on the specialist, information-intensive and relationship-based role of allocating credit

[2] Holding CBDC wallets for retail customers brings the bank itself no benefit. The bank loses the return it would have made on bank deposits and now has a costly-to-manage asset that must be monitored, e.g. for AML purposes, which brings it no pecuniary benefit. We have here one good reason why banks might oppose a CBDC. A commercial bank would then have to charge either the central bank or the customer to hold the CBDC wallets.

[3] It is sometimes suggested (e.g., by Bordo and Levin, 2019) that the central bank might address this problem by holding an auction to loan back the funds it collects to the commercial banks for them to lend out. However, it is highly likely that such an auction would become politicised and reflect political rather than purely commercial priorities, with some parties (e.g., real estate) being favoured over others.

[4] Bank of Canada et al. (2021) examine the financial stability implications of bank disintermediation and suggest possible responses by banks that would likely have a negative impact on their profitability. These include 'switching to alternative market-based funding sources which could be more expensive and less stable' (p. 6), deleveraging, increased risk-taking, increased lending rates and of course reduced bank lending. Even so, the report concludes that a 'material shift from bank deposits to CBDC ... could have a non-trivial, long-term impact on bank lending and intermediation ... [and] could increase the risk of systemic bank runs and make money market funds or instruments more susceptible to abrupt outflows' (pp. 17–18).

that banks previously fulfilled, a serious problem because no one else such as the central bank or the financial markets could do that task nearly as well. The central bank is not set up to be a commercial bank or to compete against the commercial banks. It does not have the size, the retail branch network or the large staff of personnel with the training and experience in managing retail credit risk to carry out that task itself. For their part, bank loans are not suited to be held by money market participants because they require investments in relationships, regular monitoring and credit risk management expertise that money market participants cannot easily provide. For example, with regular commercial banking, a potential (and often small) bank loan customer can simply call their bank to request a loan, but what would they do if their bank was credit-constrained because its depositors had fled to CBDCs? We discussed these issues in Chapter 3.

Dirk Niepelt, however, offers an interesting counterargument.[5] He proposes a world in which

> [i]n principle, a central bank can completely neutralise the effects of CBDC on bank balance sheets and macroeconomic conditions when certain conditions are met. The main element of the neutral central bank policy is a refinancing operation in which the central bank funds banks at terms that keep both their financing and their incentives unchanged. (Niepelt, 2021, p. 39)

The key words here are '[i]n principle . . . when certain conditions are met', to which the response is that these conditions are not and cannot ever be met. The reason is it would require the central bank to manage loans with the same expertise as commercial banks have, but without their expertise or their being set up to manage a retail business. As we have emphasised already, central banks are not set up to do retail. Therefore the case Niepelt considers, known as one of costless central bank pass-through funding, does not apply.

We are then back to the situation already considered in Chapter 3. Imagine, for example, the possibility that the central bank could recycle its higher CBDC liabilities by acquiring more assets from the banking system. It could do so by expanding its existing quantitative easing (QE) programmes to the banks to buy some of their assets and/or it could set up a new lending programme to the banks that goes beyond its traditional lender of last resort function and makes it more of a lender of first resort.[6]

[5] A more formal (i.e., mathematical) treatment of this issue is offered in Niepelt (2021).

[6] The central bank would be taking on a lot of credit risk to the banks unless it could differentiate their credit quality, but it does not have the means to differentiate credit

Either way, the central bank thereby assumes a more active role in credit allocation to the banks despite its well-known limitations as a retail credit allocator. The efficiency of credit allocation is then weakened, all the more so because the central bank involvement (a) introduces a new element of centralisation in credit allocation; (b) makes the central bank more conflicted, as it is now competing with private sector parties in the market for loans to banks, as well as regulating them; and (c) increases possibilities for further state involvement in banks' investment decisions, leading to more inefficiency and greater corruption. These possibilities include the imposition of conditionality requirements that limit the set of borrowers and the terms on which the banks are allowed to lend. We must then expect that the central bank would use its regulatory powers to benefit itself and/or its political masters at the expense of the firms it regulates, that is, the regulatory playing field would become more distorted in the central bank's favour. Lastly, (d) a formerly highly reliable source of funds, bank deposits, becomes less stable, which would increase banks' cost of funding. In short, the central bank attempting to acquire more assets from the banking system could lead to a significant weakening and even politicisation in the credit allocation process throughout the economy as the central bank became more of a lender of first resort.

To paraphrase Selgin on this same issue, tens of thousands of bureaucrats would take the place of the tens of thousands of bankers who now decide where bank credit goes (Selgin, 2021b).

Disintermediation from CBDCs can be especially severe in a crisis, which can erupt suddenly[7] too:

> As every money and banking student learns, in a fractional-reserve system, every dollar of paper currency withdrawn from the banking system can lead to a much larger reduction in bank deposits and, hence, the total money stock. In principle, aggressive central bank expansion can keep the money stock from shrinking. But because central banks generally don't lend to private-sector borrowers, the

quality. Longer term, the central bank might build up its own credit risk management capability, but there would still be the problems of centralisation and conflicts of interest discussed in the text.

[7] A bank customer could switch their deposit holding into a CBDC holding merely at the push of an electronic switch, constrained only by the settings in their online bank account. But as Jens Weidmann warned years ago, 'what might be a boon for savers in search of safety might be a banc for banks as this makes a bank run potentially even easier' (quoted in Durden, 2017). Much has been made of this CBDC hyper-fast e-bank run issue and the idea that we can electronically run on our banks in seconds without the need to physically queue up outside them like we used to have to do. However, as the run on Silicon Valley Bank in March 2023 illustrated, we can have such bank runs already even without CBDCs.

substitution of central-bank-supplied paper money for bank deposits can't preserve the private credit that collapses along with the stock of commercial bank deposits. A serious 'credit channel' bust can still occur. (Selgin, 2021a, p. 334)

## 8.2 DISINTERMEDIATION COULD BE ESPECIALLY SEVERE IN A CRISIS

In the event of a major market shock like a repeat of 2008–2009 or 2020, there may be nothing to prevent corporate treasurers and investors from moving large amounts of money to CBDC. Even if that move was very short, say for a day or a week, the impact on the economy could be devastating, and a CBDC could transform deposits from a stable source of funding under stress to an unstable one (Baer and Nelson, 2021, p. 7). The result would be an immediate disruption to the flow of credit to the real economy, thereby aggravating the impact of any underlying stress event. To quote the Board of Governors' own discussion paper:

> Because central bank money is the safest form of money, a widely accessible CBDC would be particularly attractive to risk-averse users, especially during times of stress in the financial system. The ability to quickly convert other forms of money—including deposits at commercial banks—into CBDC could make runs on financial firms more likely or more severe. Traditional measures such as prudential supervision, government deposit insurance, and access to central bank liquidity may be insufficient to stave off large outflows of commercial bank deposits into CBDC in the event of financial panic. (Board of Governors of the Federal Reserve System, 2022, p. 17)

As Baer and Paridon (2022, pp. 8–9) observe, a 'major takeaway from this discussion paper is that it proposes no design solution that would eliminate or even mitigate this concern', which remains 'a grievous flaw' with a CBDC, and no one else has done so.

Now Selgin (2021a) envisages that a CBDC is then introduced that pays interest roughly in line with the Fed's interest on bank reserves. Since CBDCs could be attractive investment assets, it is then easy to imagine circumstances in which administrative 'fixity' in CBDC rates and falls in market rates might combine to produce a run to CBDCs not just from bank deposits, but also from alternatives such as shares in money market mutual funds. One could imagine, too, that some such run scenario would be especially likely in a financial crisis, when people might be more inclined than usual to run to the safest asset.[8]

[8] One might add that such a crisis could be *more severe* than a traditional bank run crisis in at least one important respect. In a traditional crisis there is not a run from deposits as

Some of these concerns have a historical precedent in the experience of the US Postal Service system during the Great Depression. In their recent working paper, Jaremski, Fleitus and Schuster (2020) report that the relatively high, bureaucratically set rates on postal savings accounts during the 1930s drew desperately needed funds away from private lenders and so prolonged the effects of the Depression. They conclude that a positive shock to postal savings led to a semi-permanent decline in Building and Loan (B&L) share values, because the existence of a federally insured deposit alternative for small deposits was drawing funds away from them. In the absence of postal savings banks, B&Ls would have maintained a significantly larger number of deposits and may even have been able to expand lending (Jaremski et al., 2020, p. 8). The problem was that a low rate of interest set in stone by bureaucrats became a high return when market rates fell during the Great Depression and the amount of money deposited in the US postal system increased eightfold from $154 million to $1.2 billion over the period 1929 to 1933.[9]

## 8.3 NO EASY POLICY RESPONSES TO DISINTERMEDIATION

Unfortunately, there are no easy policy responses to these disintermediation problems short of avoiding CBDCs in the first place. Consider the following passage from an important BIS policy document, 'Central Bank Digital Currencies: Foundational Principles and Core Features', published by a group of major central banks in 2020:

> For the central banks contributing to this report, the common motivation for exploring a general purpose CBDC is its use as a means of payment. . . . this report advances the foundational international work by outlining common principles and the key features a CBDC and supporting infrastructure would need in order to contribute to central bank public policy objectives. The principles emphasise that: (i) a central bank should not compromise monetary or financial stability by issuing a CBDC; (ii) a CBDC would need to coexist with and complement existing forms of money; and (iii) a CBDC should promote innovation and efficiency. The possible adverse impact of a CBDC on bank funding and financial intermediation, including the potential for destabilising runs into central bank money, has been a concern of central banks. Any decision to launch a CBDC would depend on an informed judgment that these risks can be managed, likely through some combination of safeguards incorporated in the design of a CBDC and financial system

a whole, as here, but a run from deposits at weaker banks into deposits at stronger banks – i.e., there is merely a recycling of deposits.

[9] The figures quoted are drawn from Anthony (2023b).

policies more generally. Understanding the potential market structure effects of CBDC, their implications for financial stability, and any potential mitigants is a further area of work for this group.

A CBDC robustly meeting these criteria and delivering the features set out by this group could be an important instrument for central banks to deliver their public policy objectives. (BIS, 2020)

Whatever are we to make of this statement?

The first 'principle' ('fantasy' would be a more appropriate description) emphasises that '(i) a central bank should not compromise monetary or financial stability by issuing a CBDC'. However, we have repeatedly emphasised that a CBDC *does* compromise monetary/financial stability and no feasible solutions to that problem have yet been proposed. And there the matter should have ended, and the committee may as well have gone to the pub to drown their sorrows. Principle (iii) states that 'a CBDC should promote innovation and efficiency', but how does it do that? We have already established that a CBDC is inefficient relative to alternatives such as stablecoins, so how does an intrinsically inefficient central bank monopoly promote efficiency? Or innovation for that matter? The next sentence notes that 'the potential for destabilising runs into central bank money' has been a concern of central banks, and thereby undermines principle (i), as if acknowledging the problem suffices to exorcise it. The sentence after that ('Any decision to launch …') begs the questions of who is qualified to make the 'informed judgment that these risks can be managed' and to design the 'safeguards' to be incorporated into the design of the CBDC. Again the committee helpfully set out the problem but overlooked to explain how it should be resolved. The last sentence then adds that the CBDC must not only meet these 'criteria' but do so 'robustly' too, as if that solves anything either. This is what happens when committees write policy documents with the luxury of kicking all the contentious issues into the long grass for someone else to sort out later.

But this is just a mockery of serious discussion, a game of 'let's pretend' we have solved the problem when everyone knows that all we have done is pulled a rabbit from a hat instead. Who do these people think they are kidding?

Another potential response to the prospect of CBDC-induced disintermediation is to limit the amount of CBDCs issued. Broadly speaking, such limits could be price-based and/or quantity-based.

Price-based limits might take the form of a lowered and maybe negative CBDC interest rate to discourage a run to CBDC, but no one knows how to set such rates in the heat of a crisis. The remuneration on CBDC might also be single-tier or two-tier. In the former, remuneration would be at a single rate regardless of the size of the CBDC holding. In the latter, remuneration would be at one rate up to some threshold level, then at a lower rate beyond that threshold. However, as Nick Anthony has pointed out, the argument being made here amounts to the strange one of making CBDC intentionally bad to discourage their use.

Quantity-based limits would involve restrictions on transfers and/or holdings of CBDC. Quantity limits could differentiate by type of holder, for example business or household, and could either be stock-based (with restrictions limiting the amount of CBDC held by account holders) or flow-based (with restrictions on the amount of CBDC that can be transferred within a given time period). However, we could imagine rationing problems if not enough CBDCs are created to meet demand, arbitrage problems if CBDC returns are out of line with returns on other assets and political problems if different investors lobby for preferential returns. CBDC limits might also undermine commercial applications if they prevent large payments. These are not trivial problems.[10]

Moreover, Sam Callahan reports simulations by the American Bankers Association that suggest that even a CBDC-holding ceiling as low as $2,500 dollars could produce a deposit loss of almost half a trillion dollars. As he concludes, 'a CBDC would drain a significant amount of funding from private banks by cannibalizing bank deposits. This could impact lending in the economy and increase financial instability, regardless of limits placed on CBDCs by central banks' (Callahan, 2023, p. 21).

But that might not be the worst of it. Reliance on these limits, whether price-based or quantity-based, potentially threatens a core principle on which the entire financial system is based. As Waller observes, a key feature of the financial system is that

> banks peg the exchange rate between commercial bank money and the U.S. dollar at one-to-one. Due to substantial regulatory and supervisory oversight and federal deposit insurance, households and firms reasonably view this fixed exchange rate as *perfectly credible*. Consequently, they treat commercial bank money and central bank money as *perfect substitutes*—they are interchangeable as a means of payment. The *credibility* of this fixed exchange rate between commercial and

[10] These problems would also appear to undermine Bindseil's (2019, p. 7) claims that 'central banks have ample experience with tiered remuneration systems' (referring to the ECB's experience of tiering the deposits of European public sector organisations) and that this experience 'could be readily applied to deposit-based CBDC'.

central bank money is what allows our payment system to be stable and efficient. (Waller, 2021, p. 2, my italics)

However, there is a clear contradiction between a central bank's *commitment* to maintain a fixed rate of exchange between commercial and central bank money come what may, and its use (or its even considering the use) of quantitative restrictions on the issue of CBDC for whatever other reasons. As is well known from other contexts, a central bank can either fix a quantity or it can fix a price, but it cannot credibly promise to do both at the same time. Should a crisis occur, the central bank would have to decide – possibly quickly and under unfavourable conditions – which objective to keep and which to sacrifice. Moreover, the known existence of this contradiction at the heart of its banking policy undermines its credibility and invites speculative attack at the very point and time where the system would be most vulnerable to such attack.

To see how this situation might play out, imagine that the central bank issues CBDCs but subjects the amount issued to some arbitrary upper limit. However, though it can limit the amount of CBDCs it supplies, the central bank cannot similarly limit the amount demanded. If the demand should exceed the supply, the market for CBDCs could only then clear if the price of CBDCs should rise: the price of CBDCs would then rise above its 'par' value. The central bank currency would then have two different values: its conventional 'par', say, cash or, the value of the CBDC, which would exceed par. Thus, a central bank might issue two different currencies of the same face value – cash and CBDCs – which would have different market values, the former worth, say, £1 and the latter worth something more than £1. Such an outcome would break one of the key principles underlying the integrity of the entire financial system – the idea that a central bank currency should have a unique market value whatever the form that currency might take. The consequences for the central bank are so severe that they give themselves nightmares worrying about the prospect.

Or put it this way, if central banks are so worried about 'breaking their buck', then why are they so keen to promote CBDC scenarios where such an outcome is most likely to occur? All I can say to that, is that if the BIS really want to make themselves a laughing stock by breaking their central bank digital buck then by all means be my guest.

I repeat, if a central bank is to issue a CBDC, the only prudent way to do so would be to issue the amount of CBDC the market might demand.

# 9

# CBDCs and Financial Inclusion

Main Points

The most commonly cited argument for CBDCs is that they would help promote financial inclusion. However, this claim is a myth that is devoid of any empirical support.

CBDCs do not address the causes of financial exclusion, and alternative methods (e.g., reducing regulatory barriers that discourage financial innovation) would better promote financial inclusion.

To the extent that financial inclusion is even an issue in the developed world, it is only the case in the US. Even there, many people are financially excluded because they wish to be or because government regulations make bank accounts unattractive. Financial inclusion is a more important issue in the developing world, but even there, there are much better ways to achieve financial inclusion than establishing a CBDC. Recent developments there suggest that non-CBDC digital currencies, in particular innovations driven by the spread of quick response (QR) transactions technology and market competition, are already drastically increasing financial inclusion and will likely eliminate the problem before CBDCs make any impact on it.

## 9.1 WOULD CBDCS PROMOTE FINANCIAL INCLUSION?

Advocates of CBDCs like to claim that CBDCs would help increase financial inclusion, which typically means that they would help to bank the unbanked.[1] To give some examples:

[1] This is a dated definition of financial inclusion, however: it is dated because the spread of mobile payments technology means that people can have access to mobile payments technology even without a bank account. But I do not want to argue the toss too much here.

'Too many Americans don't have access to easy payments systems and banking accounts, and I think this is something that a digital dollar, a central bank digital currency, could help with.' (Yellen, quoted in Kempe, 2021)

'Financial inclusion should be a prominent consideration in CBDC design.' (Mutton, 2021)

'CBDCs can increase financial inclusion ... A well-designed CBDC is uniquely positioned to address barriers to inclusion, including by offering the unbanked alternative pathways to open transactional accounts and participate in the digital economy ...' (Fingerhut et al., 2022)

One can find any number of similar quotes, especially in BIS or IMF reports on CBDCs, and the claim has been entertained in high places. Indeed, every report put out on the subject by these organisations repeats the claim like a mantra.

To give just two high-profile examples out of many of this literary genre, consider 'Central Bank Digital Currencies: A New Tool in the Financial Inclusion Toolkit?' published by the BIS and World Bank and in 2022 (Auer et al., 2022) and 'Central Bank Digital Currency's Role in Promoting Financial Inclusion' published by the IMF in 2023 (Lannquist and Tan, 2023). Despite having spent much of my life reading the guff that central banks regularly put out, these reports nevertheless deserve a special place in the infernal regions. They provide long-winded discussions of CBDCs and financial inclusion that amount to no more than trite statements of the obvious or else just plain nonsense, and I will not go through the pointless effort of quoting from them. Meanwhile, as central bankers continue to spout reams of silliness on the subject, market forces are well on the way to resolving the problem without any assistance whatever from central banks. Indeed, one wonders if they will still be telling us that CBDCs can solve this problem well after that problem has already been solved. The World Bank, BIS and IMF should be ashamed of themselves for publishing reports that are no more than make-work projects for those involved. Their arguments boil down to the shallow assertion that, as David McGrogan puts it, 'It would be good to get these [financially excluded] people "included" ... and wouldn't a CBDC be a brilliant wheeze for achieving that [end]?' (McGrogan, 2024c).

We have to remind ourselves that endlessly repeating a false claim does not make it any more true.

We can also say that this claim is certainly not supported by the Nigerian experience with CBDCs. On the contrary, that experience suggests that the attempt to introduce CBDCs with a war on cash backfired badly. To give a typical example, recall the quote from the Bitcoin consultant Heritage Falodun from Chapter 6 above:

> In [Governor Emefiele's] view, Nigerians should have found that the CBDC is the solution to their financial predicaments … Not surprisingly, the reverse has been the case, as the situation on the ground in Nigeria right now is gradually moving from 'banking the unbanked' to 'un-banking the banked.' (Falodun, 2023)

This sounds more like CBDCs decrease financial inclusion rather than increase it.

According to the World Bank, the proportion of adults with a bank account in the United States in 2021 was 94.3 per cent.[2] The corresponding proportions were 99.6 per cent for Canada, 99.8 per cent for the UK, 99.3 per cent for France, 99.98 per cent for Germany, 99.3 per cent for Sweden, 98.59 per cent for Japan, 99.3 per cent for Australia and 98.8 per cent for New Zealand.[3]

Among these countries, financial inclusion is an issue only in the US.

## 9.2 CBDCS AND FINANCIAL INCLUSION IN THE US

But does the financial inclusion argument even apply within the US?

### 9.2.1 FDIC Evidence

According to the FDIC's own measure, the proportion of unbanked Americans was 4.6 per cent in 2021, equivalent to 95.4 per cent banked, down from 8.2 per cent in 2011.

These people are often described as 'financially excluded'. In truth, they are often not so much excluded from the banking system as actively avoiding it. From their perspective, their being 'financially excluded' is often not even a problem.

### 9.2.2 Why Are Unbanked People Unbanked?

We need to understand why unbanked people are unbanked in the first place, however. FDIC (2021) asked unbanked households about their

[2] The survey covers adults who 'had an account at a bank or regulated institution such as a credit union, microfinance institution, or a mobile money service provider'. www.worldbank.org/en/publication/globalfindex. Accessed 4 February 2026.

[3] See www.worldbank.org/en/publication/globalfindex/Data. Except for New Zealand, these proportions have all risen since 2011.

reasons for being unbanked. 'Don't have enough money to meet minimum balance requirements' was the most cited main reason. 'Don't trust banks', 'Avoiding a bank gives more privacy' and 'Bank account fees are too high' were the second, third and fourth most cited main reasons. Overall, almost 73 per cent of respondents without a bank account said they were not interested in holding one.

### 9.2.3 A CBDC Does Not Address These Concerns

Introducing a CBDC would do nothing to address any of these concerns, however. Therefore, introducing a CBDC would be unlikely to encourage much greater financial inclusion. For people who currently choose not to have a bank account because they do not trust banks or prefer to maintain their own financial privacy, then a CBDC is hardly a solution, because merely *issuing* a CBDC would do nothing to make those people trust banks or abandon their financial privacy.

There are also other considerations. If the issue is that someone lacks the money to meet minimum balance requirements or to cover fees, then a government might subsidise accounts to eliminate those costs on the front end, but if such subsidies are to occur, they could be done using any consumer payment method, for example a pre-paid card. There is no need to make that subsidy specifically by issuing a CBDC. Also, access to a CBDC is not the same as access to a bank account. Where a bank account opens the door to receiving loans, lines of credit and other financial services, a CBDC does little more than offer access to digital payments.

Put it this way: you have a bunch of people who currently choose not to bank because they do not like banks and do not trust them, like their own financial privacy, and/or do not have the money to meet minimum account requirements or pay bank fees. They choose to remain unbanked despite a proliferation of basic bank accounts and other means of making payments already being made available to them, so it is not obvious why introducing yet another would make much difference. Anecdotal evidence suggests that many of these avoid engagement with banks because they are undocumented or get paid in cash, and fear that a bank would report their status or suspicious transactions to the government, which banks are *required* to do. Many would also be financially illiterate, so would struggle to handle a CBDC even if they wanted to. The Fed then introduces a CBDC that requires them to establish an account at a bank or other financial company, go through a full KYC process under existing AML and sanctions rules, upload a digital wallet to a phone or computer and then have their transactions monitored by their bank and possibly by the government too. Explain again why you think they would sign up.

The issue is not to provide the unbanked with bank accounts, but to provide them with bank accounts they actually *want to hold*. A CBDC does not address this issue, let alone resolve it.

### 9.2.4 Financial Inclusion Problem Resolving Anyway without CBDCs

In any case, it would appear that the financial inclusion problem is already well on the way to being resolved without any need for contrived 'assistance' from a CBDC. Recent improvements in access and cost cutting have been remarkable. One of these is the Bank On movement. The non-profit Cities for Financial Empowerment Fund has created the Bank On basic banking account, which is targeted at unbanked and underbanked customers and is now offered by over 375 banks and credit unions around the country representing over 60 per cent of the domestic deposit market; more than half (53%) of all US bank branches offer a Bank On certified account. These accounts generally cap monthly fees at $5, have no overdraft fees, offer a debit card and have low minimum deposit requirements; and 95.5 per cent of low- and moderate-income Americans live near at least one bank branch that offers a Bank On certified account.[4] Mobile banking has experienced similar success: mobile banking was the main way to access one's bank account for only 9.5 per cent of households in 2015, but 43.5 per cent by 2021 (FDIC, 2020, 2021). Developments like these help to explain the recent increase in financial inclusion and why it is likely to increase further in future.

### 9.2.5 More Direct Methods of Promoting Financial Inclusion Are More Effective

If central bankers want to promote financial inclusion, there are more direct and effective methods than a CBDC. These include deregulation and measures to promote competition, especially reducing regulatory

[4] See CFE (https://cfefund.org) and Bank On (https://joinbankon.org/about/), and BPI staff (2020). The latter also suggests that the Community Reinvestment Act currently gives Bank On accounts an unclear regulatory treatment. Establishing greater clarity would make these accounts more attractive to issuing banks and should increase their uptake.

barriers to market entry and not requiring gratuitous permission for innovations in mobile and other payment systems. The objective should be to provide a regulatory playing field in which all forms of payments systems are permitted to compete on comparable fair terms. Within this context, the challenge is then to encourage the growth of bank accounts that *actually* appeal to the unbanked, as opposed to merely paying lip service to the idea.

They could also get rid of regulations that undermine financial inclusion. A case in point is the 2010 Durbin Amendment (Section 1075 of the 2010 Dodd-Frank Act) that established payment card price caps that shifted nearly all debit card processing costs from retailers to consumers. This measure had the unintended side effect of making free checking accounts unfeasible for many low-income consumers and led to around a million of them leaving the banking system (Zywicki et al., 2014). Policymakers could also take another look at the 1970 Bank Secrecy Act, which legally requires banks to collect and report the personal information of customers to the government. This Act cost US financial institutions an estimated $45.9 billion in financial crime compliance costs in 2022 (LexisNexis Risk Solutions, 2022, p. 9) and these costs are then passed on to bank consumers. Getting rid of such regulations would not only make customers better off, but would also promote greater financial inclusion.

Arguments claiming that CBDCs would increase financial inclusion often overlook the point that if policymakers can think of using CBDCs to achieve some specific purpose, then private sector parties could also think of ways to achieve that same purpose themselves, for example by creating synthetics, and would do so if they believed they could make a profit from it. They also often overlook the point that the private sector has much more expertise and experience in customer-facing activities.[5] So if the private sector does not do it, policymakers' instinct is to think that they have identified a 'gap in the market' that their preferred policy would fill, when all they have achieved is to identify yet another way for policymakers to waste more public money on some vanity project that they have not thought through. Policymakers also often overlook the true costs of whatever it is that they are proposing and overestimate the expected

[5] '[Central bankers] spend comparatively little time on ... customer-facing ... Yet, far from [being] a trivial sideshow, this aspect of CBDC development is all-important, if CBDCs are indeed to promote financial inclusion. And in this regard, private-sector players have a leg up on central banks because many of them interact with customers daily, online and offline. Some even operate their own digital wallets' (Zuluaga, 2021, p. 417).

benefits, because it is not their money they are playing with. They also show little awareness of the tendency of public sector projects to often overshoot on their costs. None of the proposals that we have seen to use CBDCs to increase financial inclusion come even close to addressing these concerns.

Let us also not forget that CBDCs seek to address a problem that the private sector has already resolved in most developed countries and is close to resolving in the United States as well: as far as financial inclusion is concerned, CBDCs in the developed world are a non-solution to a non-problem.

## 9.3 CBDCS AND FINANCIAL INCLUSION IN THE DEVELOPING WORLD

Then there is the issue of financial inclusion in the developing world.

Table 9.1 shows the World Bank's estimates of the proportions of the populations in emerging countries that have a bank account.

These proportions are much lower than for developed economies, but they have also risen much faster between 2011 and 2021. For the world as a whole, the proportion rises from just over 50 per cent to just over 76 per cent.

These figures show a remarkable increase in financial inclusion across the developing world. Writing in 2018, Schoenholtz and Cecchetti observe:

> Six years ago, the World Bank estimated that roughly 2.5 billion adults (aged 15 or older) had no bank deposit, no formal credit, and no means of payment other than

TABLE 9.1 *Proportions of banked populations in emerging countries*

| Year | 2011 | 2021 |
|---|---|---|
| Developing World | 41.7% | 71.4% |
| Latin America and Caribbean | 34.5% | 73.6% |
| Middle East and N. Africa | 37.8% | 52.8% |
| Sub-Saharan Africa | 23.3% | 55.0% |
| South Asia | 32.3% | 67.9% |
| World | 50.6% | 76.2% |

*Source:* https://databank.worldbank.org/source/global-findex-database.

cash or barter. Stunningly, in its new Global Findex Database 2017, the Bank now estimates that the number of unbanked adults has plummeted to 1.7 billion. Over the past six years, more than 1.2 billion adults have gained at least basic financial access through a financial institution or their mobile phone.

Few consumer products have ever diffused so rapidly, especially among the world's poor. The rise of financial inclusion rivals the remarkable diffusion of mobile phone subscriptions ... (Schoenholtz and Cecchetti, 2018)

These figures suggest that the problem of financial inclusion is already being resolved in the developing world with no assistance at all from CBDCs. The reasons for this reduction in financial inclusion will be apparent already from Chapter 4, and recall especially Figure 4.1: financial inclusion is rising rapidly thanks to brisk progress in banking and payment systems, especially progress in private digital systems and *most of all* thanks to the spread of mobile phones.

We can also point to specific payment programs that have done much to improve financial inclusion in particular regions.

### 9.3.1 Pix in Brazil

The first is the Pix digital payments programme in Brazil, which was fully operational by November 2020. Its main motivation was to help the economy to switch away from cash, promote the efficiencies of digital currency and increase financial inclusion.

The Pix system allows the user to pay in local currency through a QR code linked to a digital wallet or payment processor, while businesses receive their payments instantly in domestic currency, USD or a stablecoin. Connection to the system is via a mobile phone. A user selects a phone number, email address or some alphanumeric alias, user data is maintained in a central database held at the central bank and no fees are charged to individual users. As Maria Capurro (2024) explains 'The platform allows customers to transfer money instantly to a bank account or digital wallet, around the clock and without fees. The app became ubiquitous in the country within months, with its rapid take-up surprising even its own creators.' The rapid growth in the use of Pix in its first year alone is apparent from Figure 9.1.

By 2023, it was reported that Pix had become the biggest payment system in Brazil, with 42 billion transactions (Almeida, 2024). The next year, it was reported that 76.4 per cent of the population had used Pix (Banco Central Do Brazil, 2024) and Pix was expected to expand its

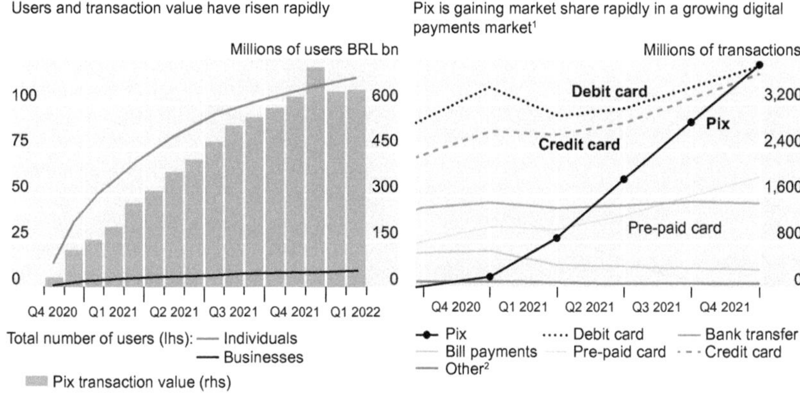


¹ Number of transactions for each payment instrument, excluding recurrent utility payments.
² Includes cheques.

FIGURE 9.1 In just over a year, Pix has witnessed dramatic growth
Source: Central Bank of Brazil, J. P. Koning (2022).

share of the online shopping market to more than 40 per cent by 2026 (Frontini, 2024).[6]

The adoption of Pix in subsequent years is apparent in Figure 9.2, where the numbers refer to the number of payments.

As Capurro (2024) further observes

> Brazil's central bank chief Roberto Campos Neto said the technology can help build a more efficient and inclusive financial system in a country where around 30% of the population didn't have bank accounts prior to Pix. After its launch, over 70 million customers made their first digital transfer, and now only 16% don't have a bank account. 'Pix played a pivotal role in the financial inclusion of millions of Brazilians,' he said in December 2023.

Pix is now attracting considerable interest from other countries as a potential role model.

### 9.3.2 Bakong in Cambodia

The second example is the Bakong digital payments system in Cambodia. The National Bank of Cambodia first launched the Bakong payment

[6] For more on Pix, see also, e.g., Pooler (2023) or abundant information on the website of the Brazilian central bank.

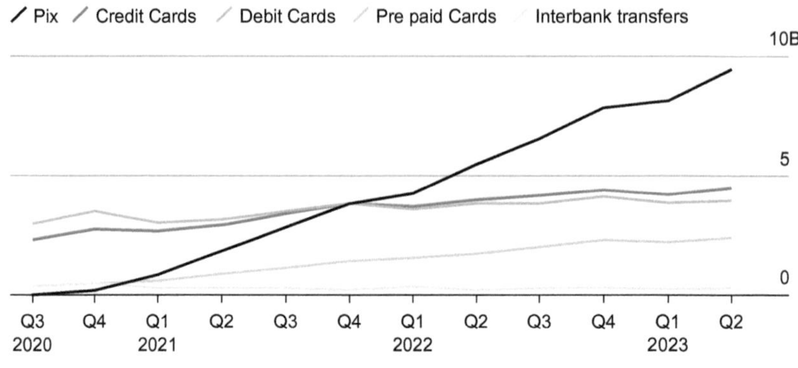


FIGURE 9.2 Brazilians mostly pay with Pix
Source: Capurro (2024).

system in October 2020. The National Bank of Cambodia Assistant Governor and Director General Chea Serey has said

> we don't refer to it as a central bank digital currency, because many of its elements don't fit that definition. We call it a backbone payment system, because it provides the backbone for all the players to connect to one platform. (quoted in Patel, 2020)
>
> I never described this project as a central bank, digital currency. I always described in many of my interviews that ... it is a backbone payment system, using the DLT technology. I mean, technology wise, because it's peer to peer, and is issued by the central bank, therefore people think [it] is central bank digital currency. It is quasi and it's not exactly what a central bank digital currency [is] supposed to be. (quoted in Daniel, 2020)

She is also explicit that there is no existing case for a Cambodian CBDC as such: 'It is too early to gauge the need for a central bank digital currency in Cambodia, there is no existing use case for one' (quoted in Daniel, 2020).

The Bakong system is built on a permissioned DLT. It is a mobile app-enabled payment system that facilitates peer-to-peer and QR code transactions in real time and round the clock, through open application programming interfaces (APIs). Citizens and tourists can access the system through a mobile app, but users must also choose a bank within the network to cash-in and out of the system. The banks and the payment service provider deposit fiat money at the central bank in exchange for digital currency, which they can then store in their wallet. They store this digitised fiat money either in the local currency – the riel – or dollars. The banks and tech companies hold the wallet on the same platform, so they then can communicate and exchange money in real time. They can also store their money in their bank's Bakong-embedded mobile wallet. They can then send money to customers of their bank, a different bank or a payment services provider.

The Bakong system exploits the fact that though many people are unbanked, there is a high degree of mobile phone penetration among the population so mobile apps are a good medium to provide affordable and inclusive financial services.

The Bakong payments system was rapidly adopted and highly successful in bringing banking services to the unbanked. By the end of 2022, the National Bank of Cambodia's Annual Report stated (2024, p. 49) that 19.5 million accounts had been opened in total – clear evidence of widespread adoption given a population of about 17 million people. The rapid growth in the numbers of customers is illustrated in Figure 9.3.

These two cases – Pix and Bakong – are rare examples where central bank-led programmes have successfully improved financial inclusion, but neither of them involved a CBDC. If central banks really wished to do something to promote financial inclusion, I would recommend that they study these two cases in particular.

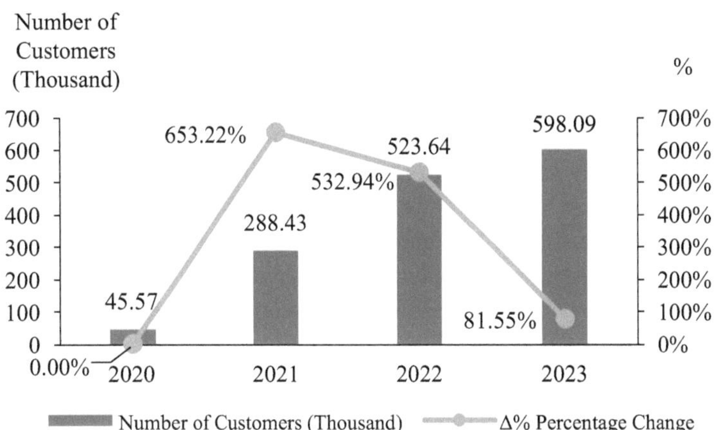


FIGURE 9.3 Number of registered customers via Bakong and percentage change, 2019–2023
Source: Graph 97 in National Bank of Cambodia (2024) 'Annual Report 2023 and Target for 2024', p. 50.

## 9.4 THE CRITICAL QUESTION FOR CBDC ADVOCATES

The critical question for CBDC advocates is the following. As the IMF observes:

> The decision-making process starts with understanding thoroughly the problem to be solved and the full array of solutions. In some instances, deploying fast payments would offer enhanced control over essential payment systems without issuing CBDC. ... [O]ther options could include promoting mobile money or incentivizing private-sector financial institutions to improve their product offerings. A *solid use case and rationale* for retail CBDC issuance is critical ... (Kiff et al., 2020, p. 47, my italics)

But such a case is virtually *impossible to make*, however.

First, you would need to show that CBDCs would provide a better-quality or lower-cost alternative to *whatever* payments systems the market would provide and to any other payment systems, including government-subsidised ones, that a government might provide. To meet this requirement, you would have to explain why the market solution was less attractive than the CBDC, even though the latter would have the common monopolistic drawbacks of reducing competition, increasing costs, stifling innovation and so forth. Moreover, achieving this task would also require demonstrating that a CBDC system was more attractive than a synthetic CBDC system, even though our comparison of these two systems in Chapter 4 suggested that synthetic CBDC systems were superior in every respect.

Let us give some examples. In the US, you would need to demonstrate why a CBDC would be superior, say, to the Bank On initiative. In Kenya, you would need to demonstrate why a CBDC would be superior to mobile phone alternatives such as MPesa. In India, you would need to demonstrate why a CBDC would be superior to mobile money such as PayTM and to the highly successful Pradhan Mantri Jan Dhan Yojana banking system, which has led to over 300 million new bank accounts (Cecchetti and Schoenholtz, 2017). In Nigeria, you would have to demonstrate why the eNaira is superior to the plethora of private sector alternatives available there. In every single country, you would have to demonstrate the superiority of a CBDC to all the alternatives available and potentially available in that country. No case for a CBDC that meets these requirements has ever been made.

Therefore, I can conclude that though CBDC advocates often *claim* that CBDCs would promote financial inclusion, they have *never made a remotely credible case to support their claims.*

The financial inclusion argument is perhaps the most common argument put forward by supporters of CBDCs. Yet it is also extremely weak and most obviously so: people are financially excluded either because they want to be or because they have no choice for one reason or another. A CBDC would address neither of these and would likely only increase financial exclusion. David McGrogan then observes:

> All of this is obvious. And serious advocates of CBDCs understand it perfectly well. . . . The[ir] idea . . . is that the CBDC is the umbrella under which, magically, the problems of financial exclusion will be somehow solved. [He then asks why] 'enabling access to the digital money infrastructure [and enabling] user education' [etc.] aren't working now to boost financial inclusion . . . *If it is open to us to act to improve financial inclusion, and if we are convinced that would be a good thing . . . well, let's do it now then. Why are we waiting for the invention of a CBDC?*
>
> The truth, of course, is that increasing 'financial inclusion' is a platitude. It sounds nice. It is mentioned as a benefit of CBDCs by enthusiasts because it makes their project seem benign, and because they perceive that talk of stablecoins and monetary policy and 'programmable currency' and negative interest rates gives ordinary people the heebie-jeebies. If it can also be claimed that CBDCs would be good for little old ladies in benighted rural communities . . . this goes some way to scraping off some of the bleak, authoritarian veneer that has already coated itself all over the entire project. It is nonsense, but it is vaguely plausible-sounding nonsense that has a pleasant ring to it at first blush. And that's really all there is to it. (McGrogan, 2024c, my italics)

# 10

# On the Importance of Financial Privacy

## Main Point

**The protection of financial privacy was traditionally regarded as a key principle of a free society and is a foundation of free exchange. However, in recent decades the right to financial privacy has gradually been downgraded in importance and a CBDC would severely downgrade it further.**

The purposes of this chapter are to highlight the importance of financial privacy, discuss its erosion in recent decades and to explain why more needs to be done to protect it: financial privacy is a fundamental principle of a free-market economy. However, a CBDC would further undermine what little financial privacy still exists.

Leading central bankers – including Fed Chair Jerome Powell, former BIS General Manager Agustín Carstens, ECB President Christine Lagarde and Bank of England Governor Andrew Bailey – have openly and repeatedly said that anonymity and complete privacy would not be an option with a CBDC. To share just one example, in 2024 Lagarde said, 'When we surveyed Europeans, the first concern that they had … was privacy. Privacy is first and foremost on their mind when we develop the digital euro. [But] there would not be complete anonymity as there is with [cash.]'[1] To spell it out, Lagarde is well aware that Europeans want to protect their financial privacy, but openly acknowledges that for her it is more important to promote CBDCs than it is to listen to their wishes on

[1] See www.youtube.com/watch?v=HYLRaEMEjh8. Accessed 22 January 2026.

the issue they are most concerned about. She may as well have told them to eat cake.

Instead of promoting CBDCs, it would be much better to restore older notions of financial privacy, which considered it not only to be important but to be sacrosanct.

## 10.1 DEFINITION OF PRIVACY

We can think of 'privacy' in terms of matters one prefers not to disclose to others. The Merriam-Webster's dictionary defines 'privacy' as 'freedom from unauthorized intrusion' and gives examples such as 'not known or intended to be known publicly' and 'preferring to keep personal affairs to oneself'.

The 'freedom from unauthorized intrusion' is a variant of the 'right to exclude others' from your private domain. There is an important connection between privacy and property rights and the larger question is: which is more important, civil rights (which include the right to privacy) or property rights? The answer is that property rights come first as they are the guardian of every other right.[2] For example, a right to privacy has no meaning if you do not own property upon which you can build a structure and enter it to be private and exclude others therefrom. The notion of private property here has, however, to be understood as including private property over one's own person. Hence, we all have a right to privacy, which follows from our rights over our own selves.

The right to privacy is thus fundamental to a free society.

## 10.2 WHY PRIVACY IS IMPORTANT

I first offer some defences of privacy as a matter of principle. In his article 'The Eternal Value of Privacy', Bruce Schneier wrote:

> The most common retort against privacy advocates – by those in favor of ID checks, cameras, databases, data mining and other wholesale surveillance measures – is this line: 'If you aren't doing anything wrong, what do you have to hide?'
>
> Some clever answers: 'If I'm not doing anything wrong, then you have no cause to watch me.' 'Because the government gets to define what's wrong, and they keep changing the definition.' 'Because you might do something wrong with my information.' My problem with quips like these – as right as they are – is that they accept the premise that privacy is about hiding a wrong. It's not. Privacy is an

[2] For more on this important topic, see Ely (2007).

inherent human right, and a requirement for maintaining the human condition with dignity and respect. . . .

Cardinal Richelieu understood the value of surveillance when he famously said, 'If one would give me six lines written by the hand of the most honest man, I would find something in them to have him hanged.' . . . Privacy is important because without it, surveillance information will be abused: to peep, to sell to marketers and to spy on political enemies – whoever they happen to be at the time.

Privacy protects us from abuses by those in power, even if we're doing nothing wrong at the time of surveillance. . . .

Too many wrongly characterize the debate as 'security versus privacy.' The real choice is liberty versus control. . . . And that's why we should champion privacy even when we have nothing to hide. (Schneier, 2006)

A second example is from Ed Snowden. 'Privacy isn't about something to hide', he said. 'Privacy is about something to protect. That's who you are . . . *Privacy is the fountainhead of all other rights*' (Snowden, quoted in Schrodt, 2016, my italics).

The final set of comments is from *A Cypherpunk's Manifesto*:

Privacy is necessary for an open society in the electronic age. Privacy is not secrecy. A private matter is something one doesn't want the whole world to know, but a secret matter is something one doesn't want anybody to know. Privacy is the power to selectively reveal oneself to the world. . . .

We must defend our own privacy if we expect to have any. We must come together and create systems which allow anonymous transactions to take place. People have been defending their own privacy for centuries with whispers, darkness, envelopes, closed doors, secret handshakes, and couriers. The technologies of the past did not allow for strong privacy, but electronic technologies do. . . .

We the Cypherpunks are dedicated to building anonymous systems. We are defending our privacy with cryptography, with anonymous mail forwarding systems, with digital signatures, and with *electronic money*.

Cypherpunks write code. We know that someone has to write software to defend privacy, and since we can't get privacy unless we all do, we're going to write it. We publish our code so that our fellow Cypherpunks may practice and play with it. Our code is free for all to use, worldwide. . . . We know that software can't be destroyed and that a widely dispersed system can't be shut down. (Hughes, 1993, my italics)

Thus, the cypherpunk agenda was to get the coding completed and into the public domain before governments could censor or control it.

*Financial* privacy refers to the protection of one's *financial information* from unauthorised access or intrusion. It entails safeguarding one's financial data, transactions and assets from unwanted scrutiny or disclosure.

A fortiori, what applies to the importance of privacy carries over to privacy in financial matters too. Three Federal Reserve economists – Charles Kahn, James McAndrews and William Roberds – have been publishing on the topic of financial privacy for almost two decades. Referring to this work, J. P. Koning (2018b) writes:

> A general theme of these papers is that cash isn't just a means for criminals to cloak their activity but also a way for regular people to conceal vital personal information, say their identities and addresses. If the information provided by transactions can be exploited – the seller might secretly plan to pawn off the data to annoying telemarketers, or identity thieves might desire the data to run a scam – then consumers will prefer to forgo some transactions, opting to protect themselves instead. The existence of cash empowers consumers by allowing them to retain the sole right to their information.

The buyer or seller might desire privacy from the other parties to the transaction or might desire privacy from the operator of the payments system.

One can even make plausible arguments for the authorities sometimes turning a blind eye to criminal activity. First, there is an argument that there is no point attempting to enforce the taxation of small-scale activities that could be paid for under the counter with cash, such as paying a cleaner or gardener with cash that is then unreported for tax purposes. We all know that such activities are common, but it is almost impossible to enforce tax collection on such activities and the amounts to be gained from doing so would be small.

A more radical argument still is that regulators should consider permitting third-party anonymous transactions – *precisely because* criminals would use them. These might take the form of transactions with high-denomination banknotes. A reason for not shying away from criminal embracement of such transactions is because it may be better than the alternative: the criminal takeover of legitimate business to make anonymous payments. If legitimate means of making anonymous payments are prohibited, there is more pressure on the mafia to find alternatives – taking over legitimate businesses, bribing police and engaging in violence or threats of violence – and society is worse off as a result. This argument is similar to the one for providing sterile needles for illegal-drug users. Even though free needles may increase the usage of drugs, they significantly decrease the dangers of usage, in turn reducing net costs to society. Allowing high-denomination transactions also makes it easier for law enforcement to keep track of potentially illegal transactions.

## 10.3 TRADITIONAL ATTITUDES TO FINANCIAL PRIVACY AND BANK SECRECY

Turning to traditional attitudes to financial privacy, the London banks of the nineteenth century are a good starting point. They took customer confidentiality extremely seriously:

> Numerous dissidents such as Louis Napoleon (the future Napoleon III) and Lajos Kossuth, the Hungarian revolutionary, could keep their money in London entirely without fear of expropriation ... As for Britain itself, with income tax at less than 5% for most of the nineteenth century there was no great incentive for tax evasion, although accounts were occasionally seized in fraud cases. ... Thus, banking secrecy [which is to be understood here as referring to as the financial privacy of a bank's customers] in 19th century London was in practice regarded as sacrosanct, yet was protected by banking ethics and practices, not directly by legislation. (Hutchinson, 2013)

We can regard nineteenth-century London as representing a 'gold standard in financial privacy', which I define to be a situation in which banks regard the financial privacy of their customers as sacrosanct, subject to the exception that they would divulge such information only if presented with a court order requiring them to do so, and a court order would only be granted as part of an ongoing criminal investigation. Underlying financial privacy is the principle that a customer's financial data are owned by that customer, but could be shared if (and only if) the customer gives the bank informed permission to do so.

I shall argue below that a gold standard in financial privacy was not only the ideal that operated in nineteenth-century London, but should be the ideal standard in modern financial systems too.

Post-World War I, a combination of high taxes, exchange controls and repressive governments created a demand for financial secrecy that led to the first bank secrecy law passed by Switzerland in 1934. This law played a vital role in enabling at least some German Jewish people to preserve their lives and their assets during the horrors of the Holocaust. In such a world, bank secrecy is a key civil liberty. As Hutchinson continued

> Switzerland had a tradition of neutrality and a solid banking system which ... had not been affected by World War I; hence it naturally became a haven for flight capital. ... The 'key civil liberty' aspect of bank secrecy laws thus cannot be dismissed. ... there are plenty of regimes around the world that oppress their subjects, and those subjects need an asset bolt-hole where they can preserve their wealth while they emigrate or simply decide to wait for better times. (Hutchinson, 2013)

After World War II exchange controls and financial repression continued, and so did the resulting demand for a safe bolt-hole. In Britain, people found ways to get their money into the safe hands of a Channel Islands or Swiss bank. High tax rates were also common in Europe and therefore it is

> not surprising that many perfectly respectable wealthy [European] citizens saw Switzerland, Luxembourg, or in the U.S. case the tax havens of the Caribbean as sensible places to park their money. The eurobond market, in which investments took the form of untraceable bearer bonds denominated in hard currencies, grew up from 1963, with Luxembourg a favorite place to deposit the bonds concerned. …
>
> [And] even in the 1970s morning trains from Brussels to Luxembourg were full of comfortable burghers (proverbially 'Belgian dentists') with bearer bonds tightly wrapped around their upper bodies, going to clip coupons. Then … Austria passed bank secrecy legislation … in 1978, in an attempt to get some of Switzerland's business. It was said to be tighter than Swiss legislation, because you never needed to give your real name, merely show the nationality of your passport. If you said your name was Mickey Mouse the bank staff would accept this, and when you visited the bank cheerfully greet you with 'Gruss Gott, Doktor Maus!' (Hutchinson, 2013)

## 10.4 EROSION OF FINANCIAL PRIVACY IN MODERN BANKING

### 10.4.1 Erosion of Financial Privacy in the United States

In the United States, financial privacy was traditionally considered to be protected by the Constitution, especially by the Fourth Amendment: 'The right of the people to be secure in their persons, houses, papers, and effects, against unreasonable searches and seizures, shall not be violated, and no Warrants shall issue, but upon probable cause'.[3]

However, concerns over the use of secret foreign bank accounts led to the Bank Secrecy Act of 1970 (BSA), which required that US financial institutions report certain financial transactions to the US Department of the Treasury. This Act forced financial institutions to report information that the government would otherwise need a warrant to obtain and was in breach of the Fourth Amendment. However, when the issue of financial privacy reached the Supreme Court in 1976 with *United States* v. *Miller*, the Court ruled that Americans do not have a right to privacy when they

[3] See https://constitution.congress.gov/constitution/amendment-4/. Accessed 22 January 2026. The discussion in this section draws on Anthony (2022b).

share information with a third party (e.g., a bank or other financial institution), a view that came to be known as the 'third-party doctrine'.

In 1978, Congress then passed the Right to Financial Privacy Act in an attempt to reverse *Miller*. This Act established a process for notifying the public when the government requests their financial information and providing them the opportunity to challenge such requests. However, this Act was littered with so many exemptions in which it did not apply, as to render it almost useless in protecting financial privacy.

The years since then have seen further erosions of financial privacy due to legislated expansions of financial surveillance, regulatory pressure to take advantage of loopholes, and the impact of inflation on thresholds.[4] In 1992, the Annunzio-Wylie Anti-Money Laundering Act entailed a major expansion of the Bank Secrecy Act. It gave the secretary of the Treasury the authority to require financial institutions to 'report any suspicious transaction relevant to a possible violation of law or regulation', a form of wording so vague that it could cover almost any transaction at all.[5] It also barred financial institutions from notifying the public when a report was filed. As Nick Anthony observed, 'instead of protecting the privacy of their depositors, financial institutions are forced to protect the secrecy of government investigations into the financial activity of Americans, whether those investigations have a legitimate criminal predicate or not' (Anthony, 2023a, p. 7). In 1994, the Money Laundering Suppression Act authorised the secretary of the Treasury to designate the Financial Crimes Enforcement Network (FinCEN) as the agency responsible for supervising Suspicious Activity Reports (SARs). In 2001, the USA PATRIOT Act dramatically reduced financial privacy further. This Act expanded requirements for financial institutions to file SARs and introduced 'Know Your Customer' rules that required financial institutions to collect identifying information and run checks on potential customers. Other bills before Congress call for further expansions of AML procedures and there have been various government initiatives – such as Operations

[4] When the Bank Secrecy Act was first passed in 1970, the reporting threshold for Currency Transaction Reports (CTRs) was $10,000. This was a high threshold and meant that most transactions were exempt. However, this threshold has never been revised and falls in real terms as inflation erodes the value of money. Thus, merely by doing nothing, more and more transactions fall under this threshold over time and the surveillance becomes more burdensome. According to the US Bureau of Labor Statistics' Consumer Price Index Inflation Calculator (www.bls.gov/data/inflation_calculator.htm), had the threshold been raised in line with inflation, it would now (December 2025) stand at over $85,000.

[5] See the Bank Secrecy Act, https://tinyurl.com/sv3rm8jv. Accessed 4 February 2026.

Choke Point I[6] and II[7] and others of dubious legality – that impinge on people's ability to go about their own affairs free from illegal government harassment.

We should also be concerned about the stealth with which financial surveillance is being expanded. As Howard Anglin observed when the Canadian government began to freeze the bank accounts of protesters in 2022:

> The government's action is troubling enough, but what should really disturb us is the ease and invisibility with which it is being done. When we can't see the consequences of government conduct, the risks of government misconduct increases. A government that sends in riot troops to dispel a crowd will rightly pay a price if the police commit abuses. But the diffuse and anonymous nature of financial enforcement mean that sweeping repression can easily go undetected. It is the political equivalent of using drone strikes instead of boots on the ground. (Anglin, 2022)

It is also clear that even if the public is not fully aware of the impact of creeping surveillance, they still think it reasonable to expect financial privacy in their own financial dealings. The Cato Institute surveyed Americans in August 2022 and found that 83 per cent of respondents thought that the government should need a warrant to access their financial record.[8] When asked if it is unreasonable for their bank to share their records with the federal government, 79 per cent said yes. The American public still overwhelmingly support the right to financial privacy.

Astonishingly, this immense surveillance system is almost totally ineffective. In the fiscal year 2019, over 20 million BSA reports were filed by US financial institutions, providing what FinCEN described as a 'wealth of potentially useful information'.[9] However, no information was provided on how much of this information was actually useful. A recent survey by the Bank Policy Institute (BPI) in 2018 found that only a median of

[6] Operation Choke Point I was an initiative led by the US Justice Department starting in 2013 to choke off (hence the name) access to bank credit by firms or industries (e.g., gun retailers, payday lenders and pornographers) that the Obama administration did not like. Its methods were sometimes questionable and critics pointed out that it discriminated against legitimate businesses. It ended after litigation compelled the Justice Department to call it off (Guida, 2017).

[7] Operation Choke Point II was a Biden-era initiative which used similar extra-legal measures to shut down cryptocurrency (and some porn) activities that senior officials disliked.

[8] See Cato Institute 2022 Financial Privacy National Survey, https://tinyurl.com/53txswc8. Accessed 4 February 2026.

[9] See Financial Crimes Enforcement Network, www.fincen.gov/what-bsa-data. Accessed 10 January 2026.

4 per cent of suspicious activity reports (SARs) and an average of 0.44 per cent of Currency Transaction Reports (CTRs) even warranted additional review from law enforcement. These low ratios suggest that the regime generates a flood of almost totally useless reports. Given that the available data suggest that the AML regime costs between $4.8 to $8 billion annually,[10] then FinCEN should openly report its success rates with data that explicitly note how many SARs and CTRs led to a conviction, how many were tacked onto ongoing criminal cases, how many were ultimately useless, etc. Yet regulators are reluctant to provide even this information, presumably because they do not want the public to realise how useless these regulations actually are.[11]

As David Burton and Norbert Michel point out:

> The current system's mind-numbing complexity and ad hoc nature impedes the effectiveness of governments' efforts to combat terrorism, enforce the laws, and collect taxes, and it imposes substantial costs on the private sector. For instance, the current framework requires financial firms to file millions of reports each year even though records show that there are only approximately 2,000 AML investigations per year. Similarly, the wide discretion given to FinCEN to change reporting thresholds and requirements predisposes financial institutions to err on the side of filing too many reports rather than risk legal liability.
>
> ... even though BSA/AML rules have been expanded consistently throughout the past four decades, it remains difficult to discern *any net* benefit of the overall BSA/AML regulatory framework. (Burton and Michel, 2016, pp. 3, 8–9, my italics)

### 10.4.2 The International Anti-Money Laundering Regulatory Regime

Turning to the international level, in 1989 the G7 summit sought to extend efforts to combat organised crime, particularly drug trafficking. To do so, they established the Financial Action Task Force (FATF) to help standardise anti-money laundering (and later, anti-terrorist financing) practices across national authorities. It soon established its 'best practice' standards and disseminated these globally. In practical terms, laws based on FATF standards require millions of financial institutions and other

[10] Burton and Michel (2016, p. 2) also report a back-of-the-envelope estimate that each conviction obtained costs $7 million and potentially much more in compliance costs alone.

[11] Levi and Reuter (2006) reports how the US GAO (then General Accounting Office, now Government Accountability Office) made several unsuccessful attempts to study SAR-based referrals in terms of their resulting prosecutions and convictions, but were frustrated by – of all things! – lack of data.

businesses to meet detailed and burdensome compliance obligations, verify their customers' identities and sources of funds, monitor financial transactions and report specified types of transactions and 'suspicious' activities to authorities.

Yet evidence indicates that this (almost) worldwide AML regulatory regime is arguably the world's least effective policy. A remarkable recent study found that:

> the anti-money laundering policy intervention has less than 0.1 percent impact on criminal finances, compliance costs exceed recovered criminal funds [far] more than a hundred times over, and banks, taxpayers and ordinary citizens are penalized more than criminal enterprises.
>
> A worldwide policy paradigm enforcing complex anti-money laundering laws gives the comfort of activity and feeling of security but does not make us safe from crime. Letting criminal enterprises retain up to 99.95 percent of criminal proceeds, the modern anti-money laundering experiment unwittingly enables, protects and supports terrorists, drug, human, arms and wildlife traffickers, sex and labor exploiters, and corrupt officials, fraudsters and tax evaders on a global scale. (Pol, 2020, p. 73)

Even Rob Wainwright, the outgoing director of Europol, admitted in 2018:

> Professional money launderers – and we have identified 400 at the top, top level in Europe – are running billions of illegal drug and other criminal profits through the banking system with a 99 percent success rate. . . . We have created a whole ton of regulations . . . the banks are spending $20 billion a year to run the compliance regime . . . and we are seizing 1 percent of criminal assets every year in Europe. (quoted in Paravacini, 2018)

Mr Wainwright appears to attribute this low success rate to inadequate international co-ordination between national law enforcement authorities, that is, he advocates a version of 'it would work if only we did it better'. One wonders whether it ever occurred to him that the entire exercise might be deluded.

As to why this failed regime persists, and specifically why evidence of policy failure has not led to a serious review of core policy design, Pol suggests:

> Groupthink is one possibility. Policymakers, regulators and practitioners may reject perceived criticism unreflectively. . . . If their efforts produce [occasional perceived] successes, and other experts 'just like them' agree, any talk of failure 'must' be wrong. Rather than prompt reconsideration, derogation and marginalization of out-group critical thinking, and constant repetition of in-group assumptions, may serve instead to amplify and reinforce a common narrative. (Pol, 2020, p. 76)

One can also speculate on the incentives that support this system. Many stakeholders have incentives to repeat (or not openly question), rather than rigorously test, the official narrative. Hundreds of thousands of businesses and professionals form an ecosystem that is dependent on the current paradigm. Also, in a compliance-oriented intervention model, it does not matter if such laws achieve their policy objective or not. Those involved must comply or risk ruinous reputational damage and financial penalties. Even sovereign nations are pressured to comply and FATF freely admits that governments must gain its tick of approval to ensure uninterrupted access to international financial markets (Pol, 2020, p. 76).

Moreover, the trivial confiscation of 0.1 per cent of criminal funds potentially overstates the policy impact of money laundering controls for two reasons. The first is that the costs of the policy are underestimated. Compliance cost estimates typically include only private sector operational costs, but the operational costs of thousands of enforcement agencies in 205 countries are unknown. The second is that estimates of the success rate of money laundering controls implicitly assume that all forfeitures are due to AML, which ignores those forfeitures coming from traditional police work.

Pol finishes by suggesting that

> if the impact of three decades of money laundering controls barely registers as a rounding error in criminal accounts and 'Criminals, Inc' keep up to 99.95 [or more] percent of the earnings from misery … the harsh reality is that the current policy prescription inadvertently protects, supports and enables much of the serious profit-motivated crime that it seeks to counter. In any event, the anti-money laundering experiment remains a viable candidate for the title of least effective policy initiative, ever, anywhere. (Pol, 2020, p. 89)

Put another way, regulatory authorities across most of the world have largely trashed the fundamentally important right to financial privacy to establish a hugely costly regulatory regime that gives the appearance of combatting money laundering but is in reality almost totally ineffective. This regime is, however, no more than anti-money laundering theatre.

If you thought it could not get any worse, the 2020 FinCEN Files leak suggests that the AML regulatory regime has been captured by the very people whose activities it was meant to stop. In a stunning exposé of the true nature of this system, BuzzFeed reported that

> Today, the FinCEN Files – thousands of 'suspicious activity reports' and other US government documents – offer an unprecedented view of global financial

> corruption, the banks enabling it, and the government agencies that watch as it flourishes. . . .
>
> These documents, compiled by banks, shared with the government, but kept from public view, expose the hollowness of banking safeguards, and the ease with which criminals have exploited them. Profits from deadly drug wars, fortunes embezzled from developing countries, and hard-earned savings stolen in a Ponzi scheme were all allowed to flow into and out of these financial institutions, despite warnings from the banks' own employees. . . .
>
> 'Some of these people in those crisp white shirts in their sharp suits are feeding off the tragedy of people dying all over the world,' said Martin Woods, a former suspicious transactions investigator . . . (Leopold et al., 2020)

Laws that were meant to stop financial crime instead allowed it to flourish. So long as a bank files a notice that it may be facilitating criminal activity, it all but immunises itself and its executives from criminal prosecution. The suspicious activity alert gives them a free pass to keep moving the money and collecting the fees. It does not, however, force the banks to shut the money laundering down, and in those rare cases where the government does crack down on banks, it often relies on sweetheart deals which include fines but no high-level arrests (Leopold et al., 2020).

Most of this money 'ends up in the coffers of the Davos elite, at the expense of the average citizen, with virtually none of the money launderers going to prison . . . Even in democracies, financial actors at the top of the food chain have immunity, while lower- or middle-class people face a proliferation of financial restrictions'(Gladstein, 2021, pp. 272–273). And so, thanks to AML regulations, we now have an outcome that can reasonably be described as the worst of all possible worlds. The system is hugely costly and almost completely ineffective. The question then arises why policymakers have sacrificed *our* financial freedom to achieve... nothing. That question should answer itself: we should reassert our rights to our own financial freedom and never mind that money launderers and other 'bad guys' would get an easier ride than they already do. We cannot prevent them doing what they are doing anyway. But what we *can* do is make it much easier and much less costly for the rest of us to go about our business, and it seems to me that the argument for abandoning a massively costly policy that delivers nothing is quite a difficult one to resist.

## 10.5 GREATER LEGAL PROTECTIONS TO BUTTRESS FINANCIAL PRIVACY

It is clear that much greater legal protections are needed to maintain customers' financial privacy. In the US, a good place to start would be to abolish the Bank Secrecy Act in its entirety. Congress should also reform the Right to Financial Privacy Act to remove the exceptions to its provisions to protect financial privacy. It should go back to the situation that existed in the late 1960s in which the government could only obtain citizens' financial information by convincing a judge there is probable cause. It should also reject the 'third-party doctrine' and reaffirm the old principle that financial institutions have a duty to protect bank secrecy. FinCEN and the entire AML regulatory apparatus should be dismantled.

Norbert Michel hit the nail on the head when he wrote:

> the United States has spent decades leading most developed nations down the ... path [of] discounting fundamental principles in the name of preventing money laundering, tax evasion, and terrorist financing. Central bank digital currencies (CBDCs) could very well end up the crowning achievement of those efforts ...
>
> [But] control over people is incompatible with a free society, and the United States should be leading the charge in the opposite dirxection.
>
> Fortunately, it's not too late to renounce launching a retail-based [central bank] digital currency, or to make up for past mistakes that infringed on law-abiding citizens' privacy. The United States should never have led the way in criminalizing the use of money, or in designating private companies as law enforcement. It should have done all that was necessary to strengthen the protections guaranteed by the Fourth Amendment to the Constitution, and to foster strength and diversity through competition in private financial markets. (Michel, 2022a)

The United States and many other western governments used to have a comparative advantage in protecting individuals' rights against government overreach. They can – and should – reaffirm that traditional value by abandoning modern control agendas, including those based on CBDCs, for a renewed emphasis on establishing strong standards for individuals' financial privacy.

To obtain maximum effect, these should be buttressed by radically different approaches to law enforcement, especially those based on AML regulations, and also by a major rethink about the merits, or rather demerits, of prohibition laws. Such reforms could bring enormous gains in terms of, for example, reduced compliance costs, smaller prison populations and reduced illegal activity.

## 10.6 CRYPTOCURRENCIES CAN ALSO HELP PROTECT FINANCIAL PRIVACY

Users can also help protect their own financial privacy by using privacy-enhancing technology that cannot be abused by governments. To this end, cryptographers have developed a large amount of open source code that cannot be stopped or easily regulated. This work led to the development of Public-Key Encryption, which enables strong encryption, and to the development of cryptocurrencies. With such tools, anyone anywhere can download software from the internet and send any amount of crypto to anyone else within minutes, without needing to provide personal information and without asking permission from any government.

Cryptos also offer many opportunities to operate with some degree of privacy. Those who use them are only visible by their pseudonyms, not by their real identities.[12] Crypto holdings can be made difficult to seize if users keep their keys hidden or memorised. In practice, cryptos usually have to be purchased in the first place and normally from a recognised exchange such as Coinbase. However, due to regulatory pressure such exchanges collect identifying information from purchasers so great care needs to be taken if one uses cryptos for illegal purposes.

Even in the worst-case scenario where financial regulators manage to drive financial privacy to extinction in the regulated space, there can be little doubt that financial privacy will continue and will thrive in the unregulated anarcho-capitalist hinterland beyond. Indeed, for many people trapped under authoritarian regimes, operating on the Dark Web may be their only route to financial privacy. My advice to them is to make the best of it and Godspeed. To quote *A Cypherpunk's Manifesto*, 'We cannot expect governments, corporations, or other large, faceless organizations to grant us privacy out of their beneficence' (Hughes, 1993). Instead, if we want financial privacy, we must make it for ourselves as best we can.

## 10.7 BEWARE THE ILLUSION OF 'PRIVACY-MINDED CBDCS'!

We should also avoid being fooled by the illusion of 'privacy-minded CBDCs', so-called. CBDC proponents argue that concerns that they would lead to greater surveillance could be met by designing them 'right' or having a 'CBDC bill of rights'. They fail, however, to explain why anyone could reasonably expect the government to respect any such new bill of rights when it has been trampling on the old one for

[12] For more on how true identities can be recovered from bitcoin trades, see Meiklejohn et al. (2013).

decades and has largely destroyed the privacy protections that existed in the past.

A CBDC would give the government even greater opportunity to infringe people's financial privacy than it already has. It would potentially provide a direct line into everyone's financial activity at a key stroke and in real time. It could put an end to the government having to carry out lengthy data searches and give it the information it wants with much less inconvenience than at present. It would give the government direct access to everyone's spending information by default. It would also allow it more means and greater opportunity than it already has to target opposition groups, political enemies and other disfavoured groups.

There is also the danger once a CBDC system has been set up that its objectives could later be subverted for darker ends in the event, say, of a war or major terrorist attack.

Central bankers naturally offer assurances that CBDCs would not abuse people's financial privacy. For example, speaking to a Senate Committee on 8 March 2024, Chair Powell raised the 'concern' that CBDCs would allow 'the government [to] see all your transactions'. To this, he responded 'That's something that we would not stand for, do or propose here in the United States. That is how it works in China, for example' (quoted in *Ledger Insights*, 2024). One could give examples of similar reassurances from other Fed officials and other western central banks.

I do not doubt Mr Powell's sincerity, but he can speak only as the Fed's current chair, and he does not speak for the US government. Anyone inclined to believe such assurances might wish to consider how that government's security agencies have respected people's financial privacy in the past. Consider a couple of examples.

When Ed Snowden leaked classified information in 2013, he revealed how extensive domestic surveillance had become after 9/11. It also transpired that a second whistleblower, Thomas A. Drake, had proposed a system at the National Security Agency (NSA) that would have afforded US citizens better protection of their privacy. His proposal was that even though surveillance would be sweeping, any identifying information should be anonymous by default. However, if actionable information was discovered, then a warrant could be secured to de-anonymise it. Drake took this proposal to the NSA leadership, but was told that the NSA was not interested in it.

It later emerged that the programme Drake proposed *was* used, but the features that would have protected citizens' privacy had been stripped out.

Thus, the team that worked to create a limited surveillance system that attempted to respect Americans' privacy had inadvertently created one of the largest surveillance systems ever.

A second example is the ostensibly private messaging service ANOM. However, ANOM was actually the centrepiece of the FBI's Operation Trojan Shield and messages sent on ANOM were not only delivered to recipients, but also to the FBI. As Will Luther (2024) observes:

> The FBI maintains that it did not technically violate the fourth amendment by using a backdoor in the messaging app to snoop on US citizens, because it transferred the data to Lithuania, where foreigners would snoop on US citizens and then tip off the FBI when illegal activity was suspected. Think about that. The FBI developed the ability to spy on US citizens, promoted the use of the enabling technology, and then handed the data collected by this technology over to foreign nationals in order to circumvent the Constitutional constraints designed to safeguard US citizens from such activities. These efforts not only undermined the due process afforded to criminals – though that would be bad enough. It also facilitated the snooping on perfectly lawful messages. Some of these messages involved intimate details shared between romantic partners. Others involved protected conversations between attorneys and their clients.

In short, the FBI ran a horse and coaches over the protections granted by the Fourth Amendment.

These experiences should provide a warning for those who would have us put our trust in privacy-minded CBDCs. As comedian George Carlin might have put it, 'privacy-minded' CBDCs are like 'military intelligence' or 'business ethics', an oxymoron.

## 10.8 CONCLUSIONS

It is clear that CBDCs would further undermine what little financial privacy still exists. The initial impact of CBDCs would be minimal as central bankers would at first seek merely to get CBDCs accepted by the public. However, if CBDCs became established, the temptation to expand their control possibilities would prove irresistible, especially to governments of a paternalistic mindset. We could anticipate that they would then be weaponised against the population, and especially against dissidents who opposed the ruling elites, and a weaponised CBDC would be complemented by similar weaponisation to the same ends of private payments also.

By contrast to a CBDC agenda, a reform agenda based on a renewed focus on financial privacy – ideally, a 'gold standard in financial privacy' –

would generate potentially *huge* benefits for all concerned, except for those with a stake in the current AML regulatory system, such as the Davos elite. Indeed, one would have thought that the case for reform of the world's least effective regulatory policy and its replacement by a renewed commitment to financial freedom was overwhelming.

# 11

# CBDCs as Weaponised Currency

Main Points

- There is an important distinction between traditional permissionless money that anyone can use without permission from the issuer and permissioned money that allows the issuer to control who, how and when that money can be used.
- We saw clearly during the Covid period that governments already have many ways to use access to bank deposits as a means of social control.
- Governments can use CBDCs to weaponise currency even further, however. A suitably weaponised CBDC would give the central bank total control over all purchases made by everyone. The key is to control the public's access to alternative payments media: forcing the public to use a suitably weaponised CBDC would then give the central bank total control over all purchases made by everyone. The governing elite would then be able to punish at will those of whom it disapproved and impose their own agendas without being held accountable for how they exercise the arbitrary power that CBDCs give them. The resulting scope for social control has the potential to go well beyond the tyranny achievable by existing Chinese-style Social Credit System.

## 11.1 PERMISSIONLESS VS PERMISSIONED MONEY

A key feature of traditional money is that it is permissionless, meaning that people can use it without seeking others' permission to do so.[1] The ability to carry out permissionless transactions is a key principle of a free society and is what makes our money truly ours. However, some writers envisage 'permissioned' systems or programmable currency that would embed rules that can be defined by the creator or distributor to set limits and controls over its use. The result is that even 'a currently innocuous programmable digital currency may, over time, morph into nothing less than weaponizable money' (Earle, 2021). It is this permissioned feature of CBDCs that makes them dangerous and '"dark side" applications ... should not be considered as purely hypothetical' (Adams, 2021).

Consider the following passage, which discusses one of the 'huge potential gains' arising from CBDCs, namely that they could be used to impose restrictions on less desirable purchases: 'You could have ... a potentially better – or some people might say a darker world – where the government decides that units of central bank money can be used to purchase some things, but not other things that it deems less desirable like, say ammunition, or drugs, or pornography, or something of the sort'(Eswar Prasad, quoted in Moran, 2023). The first point that jumps out from this passage is that it is the *government* that decides what can be purchased and what cannot. This point raises deep concerns. If one believes that giving the government control over how people should spend their own money is a good idea, then one risks giving sanction to authoritarian regimes that control how money is to be spent. The issue here is not what is good or bad, but *who should decide what is good or bad*. The importance of this question cannot be overstated, for it goes to the central issue in western political thinking: the freedom (or not) of the individual.

One thinks of the Chinese Social Credit System discussed in Chapter 6. It is programmed to allow only people of good standing to spend it, where good standing refers to people who have an acceptable social credit score. Those not in good standing would be designated as 'Dishonest Persons Subject to Enforcement' and their ability to buy and sell, travel, buy property or borrow money would be restricted. In the Social Credit System, you only live at the pleasure of those who determine how much social credit you have.

## 11.2 PAYMENT SYSTEM MECHANICS

We first consider how much power governments already have (i.e., without CBDCs) to use their control over the monetary or payments system to oppress people. To do that, we must examine how payment systems work.

[1] Except, of course, for purchases of 'controlled substances' and so forth.

While writers on CBDCs often claim that CBDC would enable the central bank to track and potentially block each transaction, the fact is that existing payments technology does not actually work that way. This is because payments systems are built to economise on the data transferred and the only data transferred is that which is necessary for the transaction to take place. Otherwise, the system slows down and yet speed is essential if the system is to function effectively at a required rate of, say, at least 30,000 transactions a second.

Suppose I make a payment with bank money (e.g., a debit card). The payment machine contacts my bank and approves the payment if the bank authorises it, and otherwise declines. The bank's automated response checks only if funds or an overdraft facility permit the transaction. The payment machine might give me a receipt that itemises my purchase but the bank does not have a record of that receipt or of the transactions made. The only information available to the bank is my name, card details, place and time of transaction, and the amount and payee, that is, the information it gives me on my bank statement.

One expert explains the process this way:

> The problem is that Visa, Mastercard or whichever card schemes you and the merchant use to process your payment do not know what you have purchased. They do not know because they do not need to know. As far as payment is concerned, what you bought is irrelevant. All that matters is that the correct amount is reliably transferred from the payer to the payee. When the till instructs the card machine to initiate a payment it only has to give it the amount, and possibly a transaction code, but no product information. There is nowhere in the payment systems to handle that information. That is why you do not see your shopping list replicated on your credit card statement, only where you shopped. It is also why it can be hard to identify items on your credit card bill, or at least exactly what it was that you bought. This commonly happens with online purchases where the merchant is some blandly named holding company whose name is not related to their products. You can try calling the credit card company, but they cannot help because they do not know what was purchased. The data is just not there. (Anonymous IT reporter, 2023)

So even if it wished to, and even if the payment was made using a CBDC, the bank is unable to provide the central bank with details of what I purchased. Therefore, the central bank could not use the CBDC to track details of what I purchased; still less could it stop the purchase when I attempt to make it.

One could then imagine a case where the police contact my bank to give them a list of people whose bank accounts are to be blocked. My name is on that list so the bank puts a block on my account. The blocking of my account may or may not be a legitimate act – I may be under investigation for a crime and the police might present the bank with a court order – but the legitimacy of the block is an entirely separate issue from the mechanics of how the block would work.

Or one could imagine that there is a social credit system in place, as in China. When the payment machine contacts my bank, the bank not only checks that I have the funds to permit the payment, but also automatically checks my social credit score. If that score is too low, it might reject the payment.

## 11.3 WEAPONISED CURRENCY

Now consider the notion of *weaponised currency*, defined as the central bank enabling itself to block a user from making a payment on grounds other than his or her financial capacity to make that payment. Several points about weaponised currency will be apparent.

First, using weaponised currency is not necessarily illegal or wrong, because it may be used as part of a legitimate law enforcement activity in which, for example, police need court orders to obtain private bank information. However, we are not concerned here with bona fide uses of state power, but with its use to target specific individuals based mainly on politicisation of their observable characteristics.

Second, these characteristics would be revealed by a social credit score or comparable (e.g., police) check that would be carried out as part of a payment process. This check might reveal characteristics such as age, gender, ethnicity and so forth. These revealed characteristics could be acted upon during the credit check. Other characteristics of the proposed transaction are not revealed and therefore cannot be acted upon during the check. These include, most particularly, the nature of the proposed purchases.

## 11.4 LESSONS FROM LOCKDOWN

Experiences of lockdown provide many illustrations of how governments – even democratic ones in so-called 'rule of law' societies – used whatever powers they had, including weaponisable currency, as a lockdown enforcement tool. Governments across the world used lockdown powers to go after their own citizens in highly aggressive ways, often pushing their existing powers beyond their legal limits, operating under regulations with flimsy or no legislative approval, almost no legislative oversight, checks or balances and with virtually no regard for people's established legal rights.

Those they targeted were mostly ordinary people who protested against lockdowns or the abuse of lockdown powers, those who supported those protesters (e.g., by making donations to them), those who expressed views that authorities did not like, those who promoted alleged 'disinformation' (i.e., offered opinions that conflicted with the prevailing official narrative) or just the most ordinary people who were unlucky enough to get caught up in the government's dragnet.

We now examine three cases from the lockdown period. These illustrate the enormous powers governments already have to oppress their citizens, even without a CBDC.

### 11.4.1 Canadian Truckers

This story begins with an announcement by Canadian prime minister Justin Trudeau on 19 November 2021 that all cross-border truck drivers were to be subject to mandatory vaccine and quarantine requirements from 15 January the next year. Coming in a context of increasing dissatisfaction with the country's Covid policies, this announcement set off a protest movement that led truckers to block crucial US–Canada border crossings and to sit-down protests in major Canadian cities, most notably in the country's capital, Ottawa. On 28 January 2022 a convoy largely consisting of thousands of individuals and hundreds of trucks under the banner of 'The Freedom Convoy' started to arrive in Ottawa from across Canada to oppose the vaccine mandate and set themselves up in the city centre close to Parliament.

Trudeau's response to the protesters was not to engage them in meaningful debate, but to abuse them with one defamation after another. In truth, the protesters spanned the demographic diversity of Canada, including young and old, people of colour and new immigrants. They were just ordinary people who objected to his policies.[2]

By 14 February, the sit-in in Ottawa had gone on for about three weeks and the government announced that it intended to end (i.e., stamp out) the protest by invoking the Emergencies Act for the first time ever. Parliament

[2] As evidence, journalist Rupa Subramanya reported that she spoke to close to 100 protesters. She did not find a single insurrectionist, white supremacist, racist or misogynist among them. What she did find was a diverse group of decent people who had had enough of government tyranny (Subramanya, 2022).

then had up to seven days to approve the measures. The invocation of the Act gave authorities sweeping temporary powers, including the power to freeze the bank accounts and credit cards of protesters and cancel their vehicle insurance. Supporters of protesters could be targeted too. Attending any event deemed an unlawful assembly, such as the Ottawa convoy protest, also became illegal.

The measure was passed by the House of Commons on 20 February by a modest margin but was widely condemned, at home and abroad. Political opponents decried it as government overreach. Conservative MP Mark Strahl wrote, 'The Emergencies Act orders that allow for the bank accounts of Canadian citizens to be impacted without a court order and without legal recourse against the government or the banks is an outrageous overreach.'[3]

The Canadian Civil Liberties Association said the government had not met the standard for invoking the Emergencies Act, which is intended to deal with threats to 'sovereignty, security and territorial integrity'. It also noted that the Act was unnecessary because the protests were not a legitimate national emergency (Scherer et al., 2022). Many others agreed.

Another critic was Jonathan Turley:

> The vote [to approve the emergency powers legislation] is chilling given the fact that the protest has ended and the roads have been cleared. Nevertheless, the Trudeau government still wants to wield the excessive and unnecessary powers claimed under the Act. The vote shows how easily many drift into more and more draconian measures against their political opponents. …
>
> It is an ignoble and troubling moment for civil liberties in Canada. (Turley, 2022)

'Ottawa is now freezing bank accounts as if the truckers are terrorists', wrote the editorial board of the *Wall Street Journal* (Editorial Board, 2022).

A key point in the controversy was the government's claim that the convoy was being funded by terrorist financiers. In response, Finance Minister Chrystia Freeland expanded the AML and terrorist financing role of the Financial Transactions and Reports Analysis Centre of Canada (FINTRAC) to target donors to GoFundMe and GiveSendGo, in order to freeze bank accounts of convoy supporters. However, FINTRAC's own Deputy Director of Intelligence Barry MacKillop flatly contradicted her in

[3] See https://twitter.com/markstrahl/status/1495472037438967808. Accessed 4 February 2026.

evidence to a parliamentary committee: FINTRAC had not seen *any* uptick in reporting on suspicious transactions related to the Ottawa protests, he said (Bexte, 2022).

The casual arbitrariness of the application of the new rules also swept up victims who were innocent of any wrongdoing. In one case, the Communications Director for the Ontario ministry for law enforcement was fired after a $100 donation was revealed in a hack of donors to a GiveSendGo campaign. 'Marion Isabeau-Ringuette was one of several government staffers whose donations drew the eye of Sauron after the list of some 100,000 donors was leaked', explained *ZeroHedge* (Durden, 2022). In another, a single mother with a minimum wage job allegedly had her bank account frozen after she made a small donation to the convoy. As Mark Strahl explained on Twitter (now X): 'She gave $50 to the convoy when it was 100% legal. She hasn't participated in any other way. Her bank account has now been frozen. This is who Justin Trudeau is actually targeting with his Emergencies Act orders.'[4]

By Wednesday, 15 February, the various protests and bridge blockings elsewhere had been cleared and the only protest remaining was in Ottawa.

On Friday, 17 February, police began a three-day operation to clear out protesters still occupying the city. Hundreds of 'mostly peaceful' police in riot gear, armed with stun grenades, pepper spray and big sticks, and supported by mounted police, attacked protest camps in the city centre and forced demonstrators to disperse. In one incident, mounted police rode their horses directly into a crowd of non-violent protesters and knocked over an elderly lady with a walker, who was then trampled underfoot. The horse was unharmed, tweeted Ottawa police.[5]

On Saturday at 4:58pm, Benjamin Dichter, one of the protest leaders, took to Twitter to urge protesters to leave: 'One of #freedomconvoycanada drivers had his truck windows smashed by Ottawa Police, guns drawn & dragged out of his vehicle by force. It's time to leave. @OttawaPolice please allow the remaining trucks to leave in #Peace.'[6] By Sunday protesters and their vehicles had been cleared and police set up concrete barriers and high metal fences to prevent them returning.

[4] See https://twitter.com/markstrahl/status/1495472037438967808. Accessed 2 February 2026.
[5] See https://x.com/OttawaPolice/status/1494847518844276741. Accessed 4 February 2026.
[6] See https://twitter.com/BJdichter/status/1494717870407888896. Accessed 4 February 2026.

During the operation, police had arrested 191 people, of whom 103 were charged, and over 70 vehicles had been towed away (Barrett, 2022). Protesters were not to be let off the hook, however. As the Ottawa Chief of Police Steve Bell stated on 20 February, the police were still going to go after them: 'If you were involved in this protest we will actively look to identify you and follow up with financial sanctions and criminal charges, absolutely' (quoted in Nightingale, 2022).

On 23 February, Trudeau then announced that the use of emergency powers was to be revoked on the grounds that the emergency was over. 'Today's announcement is proof that the prime minister was wrong when he invoked the Emergencies Act', said Conservative interim leader Candice Bergen.[7] 'Nothing has changed between Monday [20 February, when the Commons approved the emergency powers bill] and today [23 February] other than a flood of concerns from Canadian citizens, bad press, and international ridicule' (quoted in Boisvert, 2022).

The violent aggression of the government response and the unnecessary invocation of emergency powers to deal with a peaceful protect sent shock waves around the world and did immense damage to Canada's reputation. To illustrate, during a visit to the European Parliament a month later, Trudeau was positively excoriated by two MEPs. Croatian MEP Mislav Kolakušić said Canada has gone from being a symbol of the modern world to a 'symbol of civil rights violation' under Trudeau's 'quasi-liberal boot'. He went on: 'We watched how you trample women with horses, how you block bank accounts of single parents so they can't even pay their children's education and medicine, that they can't pay utilities, mortgages for their homes. … for many citizens of the world, [this] is a dictatorship of the worst kind.' German MEP Christine Anderson then said: 'A prime minister who openly admires the Chinese basic dictatorship, who tramples on fundamental rights by persecuting and criminalizing his own citizens as terrorists just because they dared to stand up to his perverted concept of democracy should not be allowed to speak in this house at all.' Trudeau was a 'disgrace for any democracy … Please spare us your presence' (Interim Staff, 2022).

Dichter, who had all his bank accounts and credit cards frozen, spoke of the experience feeling like 'being banished from the [medieval] village [and] left to die.'[8] His experience shows that governments do not need

[7] This claim was later confirmed by a Federal Court in January 2024 (Nardi, 2024).

[8] See https://twitter.com/jordanbpeterson/status/1495091321261989889?s=21. Accessed 4 February 2026.

CBDCs to give people the digital ostracism treatment, but have the means to do that already. David Sacks (2022) pointed out that Trudeau had created a new caste of economic untouchables, people 'whom no one will dare to transaction with or help' because those who do so would be financially deplatformed themselves. 'It's a Western version of China's social credit system that does not altogether prohibit political dissent but makes it so costly that it becomes impractical to the ordinary citizen.'

The Canadian government's overreach spelt doom for the Canadian CBDC, however, because it destroyed much of the public trust that a CBDC might otherwise have enjoyed. A November 2024 Bank of Canada study found that 'a significant number' of Canadians 'reject' digital currency, but, as it patronisingly put it, for some 'mindset fragments, their lack of interest in a hypothetical digital Canadian dollar was heavily influenced by perceptions of government overreach' (see Murdoch, 2024). But those 'mindset fragments' were enough to kill off the digital Loonie and well done, I say! It was clear, even to the Bank of Canada, that the public did not want it, and plans for the launch of a Canadian CBDC were shelved.

### 11.4.2 Vaccine Hesitancy in Pakistan

In Pakistan widespread vaccine hesitancy had led to very low rates of vaccine take-up among the population by June 2021.[9] Authorities responded with campaigns to force vaccination. In the Punjab, they sought to enforce vaccination by switching off SIM cards in the mobile phones of people who were not fully vaccinated. Punjab Health Minister Dr Yasmin Rashid stated

> We are doing all we can to *compel* people to get vaccinated ... The government cannot allow individuals, who do not want to get vaccinated, to risk lives of those who are already vaccinated. (Khan, 2021, my italics)

One critic, however, pointed out that this measure would be counterproductive:

> In many rural areas where phones are critical to transfer money, take micro-credit, etc., and where vaccines are not readily available, this approach is not likely to work. In fact, it will create further problems. There are not enough vaccines at this point either. (Usman, 2021)

[9] For more on this case, see Durden (2021c), Shah and Gillani (2021), ur-Rehman (2021) and Usman (2021).

Said another:

> This is a regressive step as it affects the right to freedom of speech of citizens. What is required is to raise awareness about vaccinations, and not coercion. During the pandemic, mobile phones are important for people to connect with others and to receive information. (Mashkoor, 2021)

The province of Sindh proposed similar measures. The Sindhi information minister, Syed Nasir Hussain Shah, simply stated that a decision not to get a shot is '*unacceptable*' (ur-Rehman, 2021, my italics).

Other measures to compel vaccination that were proposed included withholding the salaries of government employees who were not vaccinated, banning the unvaccinated from restaurants, malls and parks, subjecting them to travel restrictions and excluding them from public services such as collecting pension benefits, obtaining driving licences, registering property purchases or obtaining firearms licences.

### 11.4.3 Chinese Bank Depositors

Everyday life in China over the Covid crisis hinged on the approval of health code applications on mobile phones that were central to China's anti-Covid measures.[10] If a mobile phone gave a red result, then the individual concerned was suspected to have Covid or at least to have tested positive for it over the last fortnight, was immediately barred from access to all public places and amenities, and was required to quarantine themselves at home or in an official facility.

However, it was not long before some officials were using these tests as a tool of social control. In June 2022, officials in Zhengzhou, the capital of Henan Province, altered the codes of over a thousand people to red to prevent them from protesting against the potential loss of their savings in four local banks that had shut their doors.

Earlier that year, on 18 April, the four banks had frozen their deposits and told customers that they were upgrading internal systems. They then stopped communicating. The amounts at risk were estimated to be over $6 billion, according to one report, and a million people were said to be affected. Those affected were unable to access their savings, pay workers' wages, buy supplies or pay for regular medical care.

[10] This story is covered, e.g., in Dong (2022), Li (2022), Tham (2022) and Wong and *BBC Chinese* (2022).

There were protests outside the banks' branches, and some depositors travelled to the banks' headquarters, where there was a large violent confrontation with police on 23 May, when the police shut it down. Another protest was planned for 12 June and depositors from across the country went to Zhengzhou to take part. However, as they approached the city their health codes turned red, which meant that they could no longer move around. City officials had tampered with the software. 'The red code was definitely used to limit us depositors', one complained. 'It was a complete absurdity' (Dong, 2022).

One article reports of a depositor from nearby Hebei Province, who drove to Zhengzhou on 12 June. He ended up stranded on a highway when his health code turned red. He was required to return home – police threatened to send him to a quarantine centre if he refused. But he could not return home either: he was not allowed to take a break or use the toilets at a service station while driving back, and he was then blocked trying to exit the highway. I hope he made it home.

Another depositor was quoted as saying: 'I can't do anything. I can't go anywhere. You're treated as though you're a criminal. It infringes on my human rights' (Tham, 2022).

Reports of depositors' experiences went viral on Weibo and provoked a public outcry. The news fuelled concerns that Covid-19 curbs were being used by the CCP to strengthen social controls. 'It's so scary', one user wrote. 'If the health code is abused – it could be putting legal handcuffs on us. Everyone will become a prisoner from now on and could be stopped anywhere, anytime.'

## 11.5 DEBANKING

Debanking is the removal of banking services from clients who had hitherto enjoyed them, typically carried out with little notice and no explanation being given to the people affected. Debanking came to prominence in the UK as a public issue in June 2023, when the British politician Nigel Farage revealed that his account with the private bank Coutts was to be closed. Coutts claimed that his account was closed for standard commercial reasons, but it later came out that Farage's account was closed in part because Coutts felt that his beliefs and values did not align with theirs. Internal memos described him as 'at best seen as xenophobic and pandering to racists' and a 'disingenuous grifter' (*Sky News*, 2023), and bragged about how their bank had 'single-handedly driven [Mr Farage] out of the country' (Rayner, 2024). The CEOs of Coutts and NatWest, which owns Coutts, were forced to resign in the ensuing scandal. The Farage affair was seen by many as an example of cancel culture whereby unpopular views – or more to point, views that were unpopular among the elite – were punished.

It subsequently turned out that many others had been debanked too. A 2023 study by the UK's Financial Conduct Authority found that in 2021/22, UK banks had closed 343,000 accounts, up from 45,000 in 2017 when the latest UK money laundering regime was implemented (Brignall, 2023). In about half of those cases, the reason given was that the bank could not satisfy itself to the required standard that the customer was not involved in money laundering or other financial crimes. More precisely, certain kinds of customers present a relatively high prima facie risk of being involved in money laundering, but the cost of discovering whether they were really involved in criminal activity was not worth investigating, so the banks close their accounts even though they know that most of these people are innocent of wrongdoing. The banks' response appears to have been commercially rational given that the fines for being deemed non-compliant could be in the billions, that responsible staff could face serious personal penalties and that complying with AML regulations already costs UK banks £34 billion a year – which is twice the total spent on policing all other crimes put together (Whyte, 2024, p. 6).[11] The same report also claimed not to have found a single case where a person was debanked for their political views, but this finding is hard to take seriously given that there are numerous reports of, for example, individual Christians and Christian organisations being debanked because their bankers did not approve of their views regarding the promotion of homosexuality: think of 'Pride' here (see Simpson, 2023). To quote former Icelandic PM David Gunnlaugsson:

> All too often, the results of these kinds of regulations only become apparent when it's too late. I can't tell you the amount of times I've heard parliamentarians complaining about how rules they once backed have caused their parents, children, aunts and uncles great difficulty with their banks due to them now being considered to be Politically Exposed Persons (PEPs). Recently, when a young woman working for my party gave birth, she received a letter from her bank two days later, informing her that her daughter is now a politically exposed person. (Gunnlaugsson, 2023)

[11] Given the figures Whyte cites, the implication is that the UK government apparently regards it to be better that 169 innocent people be punished than that one guilty one go free.

Debanking is also an issue in the United States, where prominent people who have been debanked include Donald Trump, his wife Melania and their son Barron. However, the Trump family are far from alone in having been debanked. To quote Justin Haskins, the Director at the Heartland Institute, 'There is a mountain of evidence that shows many of America's largest and most powerful banks are discriminating against customers because of their ideological, social, cultural, religious, or political views' (quoted in Stockland, 2023).

The sources of the debanking problem in the United States are to be found in the erosion of the right to financial privacy that we discussed in the previous chapter, whereby financial institutions were deputised into becoming law officers required to surveil their clients and were forbidden to inform clients of the reports the banks were submitting about them to authorities. This regulatory system then created the incentives to carry out shallow prima facie 'risk assessments' and to debank customers if in any serious doubt on the grounds that it is better to be safe than sorry. It also left politically exposed people at the mercy of bankers who assumed the right to punish them for views they disliked.

The question is then what to do about it. Preventing banks from debanking is hardly a solution, because banks surely have a right to choose who to do business with, and preventing banks from ending a relationship with a customer would also discourage them opening new accounts. Another possibility would be to give victims of debanking the right to a notice period (e.g., sixty days) and the right to demand an explanation. Such a reform might help debanking victims, but further increases the costs to banks, which must then be passed on to someone else. A much better solution to the problem is to reform the AML regulatory structure that creates incentives to debank in the first place. A step in the right direction would be for Congress to repeal the confidentiality requirements that prevent financial institutions from telling customers why their accounts were closed. However, a better approach would be to target the main source of the problem: misguided laws and regulations that allow the government to pressure these businesses in the first place and, ideally, this regulation would be scrapped entirely.

## 11.6 GOVERNMENTS COULD TRACK, BLOCK OR RATION SPECIFIC PURCHASES

These cases illustrate the extent of governments' existing powers – whether legal or otherwise – and the extent to which governments across the world are willing to go in their efforts to suppress perceived opposition to their policies. During these experiences, they *already had powerful means* to suppress dissent. In Canada they had the means to block people's bank accounts, in Pakistan they could block people's SIM cards to pressure them to get vaccinated, and in China they could abuse people's health code tests to keep bank depositors at home. In truth, governments have been oppressing those they see as their opponents for centuries: in Russia, from before Fyodor Dostoyevsky to Alex Navalny, and modern critics such as Carlos Chamorro in Nicaragua, Jimmy Lai in Hong Kong, and of course Julian Assange and Ed Snowden have all received or would have received similar treatment.

But though governments and central banks already have the means to identify an individual user, currently existing payments systems imply that governments and central banks still cannot track what people spend their money on or block specific types of purchase before they are made.

Yet one could envisage future changes that *would* give governments the means to start tracking and blocking purchases which are not approved by the governing elite.[12] A glimpse of these possibilities comes from a 2024 California bill that requires that digital payment providers introduce a new four-digit code in digital payment systems that identifies the retail outlet as a gun shop (see Adams, 2024, or Moeller, 2024). The law makes purchases made at a certain type of retail outlet – in this case a shop that sells guns and ammo – trackable and, in principle, preventable at the point of sale. Thus, the authorities could presume that guns and/or ammo are being bought when that payment code is used, and track or prevent the transaction.

Such a check would be applied whatever the digital payments medium offered by the prospective buyer. This check might be some social credit check, but could also take the form of an old-fashioned National Instant Criminal Background Check System (NICS) against a police record base as is currently required by law in the US. This check is to establish that the would-be purchaser does not have a criminal record or is not otherwise ineligible to make the purchase.

Similar eligibility checks could be applied to would-be payments offered in cash. Alternatively, cash payments for such goods could be banned.

[12] I take as read that the central bank would share the information it collects with the national tax authority and that this information would be used to invent new means to oppress taxpayers further.

One could then imagine such a system being expanded to do the same for other retail outlets that are deemed to sell 'unapproved' products. For a UK example, consider the Tobacco and Vapes Bill passed by the UK House of Commons on 26 March 2025.[13] This Bill proposed to ban tobacco products to people born after 1 January 2009. Everyone born before that date would be free to continue to purchase them, but everyone born after that date would be banned from doing so, forever. The products it applies to include tobacco, cigarettes, cigars and even shisha. In this case, there would be no need for a social credit or police record check: a would-be purchaser could simply be required to furnish proof of age.

In cases where a CBDC is offered as a means of payment, there would be no need for any separate eligibility checks. Whatever the goods to be purchased – guns, tobacco or whatever – the CBDC system would automatically check the eligibility of the would-be purchaser to make the desired purchase, and would approve or reject the transaction accordingly. If the proposed purchase is tobacco, CBDCs would offer a more efficient (and less avoidable) way to implement an anti-smoking policy. CBDCs could also be used not only to control whether a sale should take place, but also how much is permitted to be sold, that is, to enforce government rationing.

To give one more example, one can already obtain a credit card that only allows you to spend if you have a low enough carbon footprint. To quote Aaron Day:

> The Doconomy Mastercard, a co-branded card with the United Nations, takes programmability a step further by tying financial transactions to carbon emissions. The card uses algorithms to track the carbon footprint of every purchase, and if a user's carbon spending exceeds a certain limit, the card can be declined or even shut off. This social engineering is achieved through a complex system that assigns a carbon score to each merchant and transaction, considering factors such as the type of goods or services being purchased, the location, and the mode of transportation used. The algorithm then calculates the user's total carbon footprint and compares it to a predetermined limit, which can be adjusted based on the user's individual carbon budget. If the limit is exceeded, the card can be restricted or shut off, limiting the user's access to their money. (Day, 2024)

Personally, the only reason I can think of to use one of these would be to signal one's carbon consciousness when the time comes to pay the bill, but to each their own.

[13] For more on this Bill, see, e.g., Ibrahim (2024). The Bill failed to be enacted after the recent UK General Election was called, but it is expected that the new Labour government will introduce a similar bill.

Once the principle of central bank or government control over purchases is conceded, one could imagine a similar approach being applied to other commodities too. One could easily imagine, for instance, a similar approach being used to apply limits to petrol consumption based on a new petrol consumption payment code. Or one could imagine sugar consumption being controlled using a sugar payment code. Or one could imagine the dreary prospect of a 'sin list' of proscribed or discouraged commodities that presumably would grow year by year. It could apply to guns or tobacco in the first instance, but would gradually be expanded to cover booze, gambling, porn, escort services and whatever else some busybody in authority takes a dislike to, in addition to petrol and sugar. The implementation might involve the use of a 'sin code' that identifies the transaction as a 'sin' activity. The conditions to permit such 'sins' could then be tightened up gradually over time until 'sin' is proscribed altogether and sinning becomes a fond memory. We would then live in a joyless world reminiscent of Mencken's description of Puritanism, the haunting fear that someone, somewhere might be doing something that makes them happy, and that could not possibly be allowed.

Similar methods might be used for more blatant political agendas of social control rather than merely to satisfy the latest sumptuary fad. One can imagine the results:

> BEEP! You have exceeded your Non-Essential Worker Fuel Allowance. Transaction Terminated. Thank you for your cooperation with our Carbon Zero Policy.
>
> BEEP! Payment declined. Your card has been flagged for misgendering a member of staff. Please wait for a Correctional Officer who will assess your need for Re-education.

And such like. These were actual comments posted on Dominic Frisby's song, 'Programmable Money'. Here are some of the lyrics:

> We'll monitor every purchase you make,
> Every transaction or decision you take.
> If you're not doing wrong, what is there to hide?
> How you spend money is for us to decide.
>
> We'll take your dough if we think it's owed.
> No matter if you do not think it's so.
> Taxes and fines fares fees of all kinds.
> All embedded in the lines of code.
>
> Hail Big Brother!
> We will implant you with a microchip,

AI and other forms of censorship.
We will decide what is good for you.
Total control there's nothing you can do.[14]

The decision to block or limit purchases could be based on a social credit system whose scores would reflect the agendas of the governing elite. Those agendas might be based on their views about gender, ethnicity, climate, health or religious issues. Those who promote these agendas might see themselves as redressing gender inequities (e.g., 'we are fighting the patriarchy'), promoting a race agenda (e.g., 'we are promoting "anti-racism"'), saving the environment ('there is a climate emergency on, don't you know?'), stopping us harming ourselves ('we are doing this for your own good') or promoting one religion over another ('we are doing this to save your souls'). Whoever controls the agenda could then seek to remodel society in their own image and use their control over the social credit and payments systems to compel everyone else to fall into line with their own preferred vision of an Ideal Society. Or else.

As Frisby remarks in one of his blog postings

> CBDCs allow for almost unimaginable interference in our lives, intrusions on our privacy and liberty, never mind meddling in the economy. Chinese social credit scores would be just the start of it.
>
> When you combine the instincts of, say, the current Labour administration to intervene, together with its incompetence, the ramifications are truly horrifying. (Frisby, 2024)

Let's say 'No' to all that stuff, thank you.

## 11.7 WEAPONISED CBDCS

Governments have been weaponising payments systems against opponents and critics or anyone else they disfavoured since forever. Moreover, even pre-CBDC approaches – such as blocking access to bank accounts or misusing Covid controls – can be highly effective, even to the point of ostracising those individuals by throwing them out of the monetary economy into the wilderness, where they could be left to die like outcasts from a medieval village.

[14] Do check it out: www.youtube.com/watch?v=W1i728D7V_U. Lyrics are at www.paroles-musique.com/eng/Dominic-Frisby-Programmable-Money-lyrics,p9509275. Accessed 23 January 2026.

FIGURE 11.1 A panopticon

The arrival of CBDCs enables this weaponisation to go to an altogether higher level.

The point to appreciate here is that a CBDC has the power to oversee all payments made within the system, that is, a CBDC has the powers of a panopticon, as shown in Figure 11.1. Jeremy Bentham's panopticon prison system enables a single guard to see everything that prisoners do without necessarily being seen himself. In the nineteenth century a number of prisons around the world were modelled on it. The panopticon was said to be a device of such monstrous efficiency that it left no room for basic humanity.

A CBDC not only enables the issuer to see all the payments made in the CBDC system, but it also enables the issuer to block any payments it wishes, so it can also control the payments made within it.

The central bank initially introduces a CBDC in an innocuous manner and gives the population time to get used to it ('See, it's quite harmless!'). Once the CBDC has settled in, the central bank quietly begins to weaponise it by giving it ever more monopoly privileges, leading eventually to the point that the central bank might require that all payments be made in the CBDC. Think of a frog slowly being boiled alive: at no particular point does the frog realise what is happening to it, but it is eventually boiled all the same. By the end of the process, people would then have no choice but to use a CBDC if they wished to spend at all, and the central bank would end up with absolute power over whether requests to spend are approved or not.[15]

Thus, the key to weaponising a CBDC is not the mere introduction of the CBDC itself. The introduction of a CBDC per se does little damage if the public are free to use alternatives. Instead, the real damage from a CBDC arises when the CBDC comes with regulations that restrict the public from using those alternatives. The more oppressive those regulations are, the more damage the CBDC can do.

It would seem to me to be foolish for governments to open such control opportunities to their central banks. If governments do not wish central banks to abuse CBDCs in such ways then they should make it impossible for their central banks to acquire such powers in the first place and the only way to do that is to prohibit CBDCs entirely. And if governments *do* wish central banks to acquire such powers, then I would challenge them to openly say so to give the hoi polloi the opportunity to get their pitchforks sharpened.

[15] Once a central bank can force the public to hold its CBDC, it no longer needs to offer competitive rates on it and can then charge customers high rates to hold it. The possibility is thus opened for CBDCs to earn a positive seigniorage that would otherwise have been impossible.

# 12

# A Reform Agenda for an Efficient Payments System

Main Points

I propose a radical reform agenda consisting of four key principles:

First, a gold standard in financial privacy should be re-established so that the financial system can operate efficiently free from the burden of AML/KYC regulations.

Second, central banks should be prohibited from issuing any kind of CBDC.

Third, the central bank should be required to establish a competitive legal framework for the issuance of payments media, which would require the central bank to establish a *level playing field* between alternative payments media.

Fourth, the central bank should not issue any payments media and instead leave the issue of currency entirely to the private sector.

## 12.1 BETTER TO BE LAST IN THE CBDC RACE

'In the CBDC race, it's better to be last', J. P. Koning recently wrote.

> That's because there is no first-mover advantage to issuing a central bank digital currency. With many products, being the first out the door is important to achieving brand dominance. But central bank digital currency is characterized by last-mover advantage, not first-mover advantage. Best to sit back and learn from the less-patient central banks as they struggle with their new digital projects. ... By going last, the Federal Reserve has the benefit of the most information. ...
>
> But at all costs, avoid being the first.

> The problem with a game in which no one wants to go first is the game never gets going. If CBDC is ever going to happen, it needs some reckless first movers. (Koning, 2020a)

Since most central banks are actively considering entering this game, the best way to ensure a good outcome is to pass legislation to prohibit central banks from engaging in any CBDC activity *at all.*

In truth, the CBDC 'race' analogy is just an analogy, and not an especially good one. The only thing that matters in this game is to get the domestic regulatory structure right.

I would suggest the following agenda to govern how payments media should be regulated in a market economy.

## 12.2 RESTORE A GOLD STANDARD IN FINANCIAL PRIVACY

First, as a preliminary, a gold standard in financial privacy should be re-established to allow the financial system to operate efficiently without the burden of AML/KYC regulations, which as we saw in Chapter 10 are highly inefficient and almost completely ineffective. For the US (and there would be similar reforms in other countries), the 1970 Bank Secrecy Act and its derivative legislation should be abolished with a revised Right to Financial Privacy Act to restore financial privacy to at least 1960s standards, but with added safeguards to restrain government attempts to violate financial privacy again. The Financial Crimes Enforcement Network (FinCEN) and the whole apparatus of AML/KYC etc. regulation should then be torn down. Law enforcement would then be forced to entirely rethink how they tackle criminal money transfers.

## 12.3 PROHIBIT RETAIL CBDCS

Next, central banks should be prohibited from issuing any retail CBDCs. To quote a tweet from Libertarian Party former Congressman Justin Amash, 'When government can simply flip a switch to block all your transactions, it controls your entire life.'[1]

In the US, a number of recent bills to prohibit CBDCs have been proposed in Congress. One such is the CBDC Anti-Surveillance State Bill proposed by Representative Tom Emmer (R-MN) on 21 February 2023. This measure proposed 'To amend the Federal Reserve Act to prohibit the

[1] See https://x.com/justinamash/status/1592919434112700416. Accessed 25 January 2026.

Federal Reserve banks from offering certain products or services to an individual, to prohibit the use of central bank digital currency for monetary policy, and for other purposes.'[2] He explained further on his official blog site:

> Unlike decentralized cryptocurrencies, like Bitcoin, a CBDC is a digital form of sovereign currency that is designed and issued by a government and transacts on a digital ledger that is controlled by that government. . . . a CBDC is government-controlled programmable money that, if not designed to emulate cash, could give the federal government the ability to surveil Americans' transactions and choke out politically unpopular activity.
>
> Specifically, the CBDC Anti-Surveillance State Act prohibits the Federal Reserve from issuing a CBDC directly to individuals, ensuring the Fed cannot mobilize itself into a retail bank able to collect personal financial data on Americans. It prohibits the Fed from indirectly issuing a CBDC to individuals through an intermediary, preventing the Fed from launching a retail CBDC through our two-tier financial system. Finally, it prohibits the Fed from using any CBDC to implement monetary policy, ensuring the Federal Reserve cannot use a CBDC as a tool to control the American economy. The legislation protects innovation and any future development of digital cash.(Emmer, 2023)

The Bill was passed as the CBDC Anti-Surveillance State Act on 23 May 2024 (see Centers, 2024). The key elements were to define a CBDC for the purposes of the Act and then state clearly that the Fed is forbidden to use CBDCs in any way. For these purposes, a CBDC might be defined as a retail digital currency issued directly by a central bank, treasury or other monetary authority to individual persons or firms or issued indirectly to them through any intermediary.

Comparable legislation for other countries could be along similar lines.

However, within the US, states can also play a useful role in opposing CBDCs. In 2023, Indiana and then Florida passed measures to exclude CBDCs from the definition of money under the Uniform Commercial Code in their states, and similar measures were passed in South Dakota, Tennessee and Utah the next year (for more information, see, e.g., Cortez, 2024, Maharrey, 2024 and Anthony, 2024d). In 2024, Indiana also passed a bill prohibiting it from accepting payments in CBDCs and from participating in CBDC programs. There is debate over how easy it would be for the federal government to override these measures by invoking the federal supremacy clause (Clause 6, Article 2 of the US Constitution), but

[2] H.R. 6415, www.congress.gov/117/bills/hr6415/BILLS-117hr6415ih.pdf. Accessed 25 January 2026.

there is little doubt that these measures pose further obstacles against the introduction of a nationwide CBDC.

In January 2024, US presidential candidate Donald Trump condemned CBDCs as 'very dangerous' and vowed to block them if he became President. A year later, in January 2025, he followed through on this promise and banned CBDCs in the United States.

## 12.4 ESTABLISH A COMPETITIVE LEGAL FRAMEWORK FOR THE ISSUANCE OF PAYMENTS MEDIA

The next issue is to establish a suitable legal framework for the issuance of currency. I would suggest that this legal framework be based on the foundational principle of creating a level playing field between all competing currencies and means of payment. Such a framework should be competitive, open to new entrants and, as far as possible, neutral in its impact on competing providers, whether they be providers of deposits, cash, digital dollars, cryptos, stablecoins, synthetic CBDCs, or gold or silver currency, in whichever allocations the market will bear. Within this monetary universe, people would be free to use whichever monetary instruments they wish depending on their preferences for features such as anonymity, cost, convenience and so forth, but there would be no place for CBDCs.

I am glad to see that the Fed accepts the principle of a level playing field so I do not have to argue the point. As former Fed Vice Chair Lael Brainard stressed in a speech to Congress, recent 'events underscore the need for clear regulatory guardrails to provide consumer and investor protection, protect financial stability, and *ensure a level playing field for competition and innovation across the financial system*' (Brainard, 2022, my italics).

Let us accept Ms Brainard's comments at their face value and see how this idea could be implemented across different digital currencies and gold and silver payments media.

### 12.4.1 Regulating Stablecoins, Synthetic CBDCs and Narrow Money

In a recent article, Norbert Michel and Jennifer Schulp (2021) offer a simple and reasonable proposal for regulating stablecoins (and by implication, synthetic CBDCs and narrow money schemes too). This proposal is a set of straightforward rules to prevent fraud and promote transparency. They observe that the biggest risk for most stablecoin holders is whether the issuing entity has the reserves it claims to have. A lack of transparency about the reserves that are used to stabilise the coin's value prevents a holder from evaluating the issuer's claims about the financial safety of the stablecoin and leaves holders exposed to possible fraudulent misconduct. They suggest a regulatory definition of a stablecoin as a 'limited purpose investment company' that 'engages in the business of issuing digital tokens, with a value anchored, pegged, or otherwise tied to the price of national currencies, such as the United States dollar'. They then propose that this entity be subject to a boilerplate set of reserve requirements and the mandatory disclosure of relevant information about its reserve holdings. These regulations could be applied to any stablecoins or synthetic CBDCs, including any offered by the big fintech firms, including, for example, any future version of Libra/Diem.

Michel and Schulp also suggest that the regulator should be the Securities and Exchange Commission (SEC) or perhaps the Commodities Futures Trading Commission (CFTC). This suggestion is much better than having the Fed as the regulatory, because it avoids the Fed's conflict of interest issues which arise when the Fed regulates a payments system that competes against it, and we already noted in Chapter 4 the problems that have arisen already with the Fed regulating narrow money.

### 12.4.2 Regulating Other Cryptocurrencies

Then there is the difficult issue of how or if to regulate other cryptocurrencies. I would suggest that such cryptos be left unregulated: the only obligation of the state towards cryptos should be to allow courts to enforce crypto contracts. A reason for making this suggestion is that cryptos can be *extremely useful* to people trapped under dysfunctional or repressive regimes. People who might live in Cuba, Iran, Lebanon or Venezuela, say, are at the mercy of the financial repression imposed by their governments; being able to move their money around in the form of Bitcoin or alt currencies then gives them some relief from this financial repression. There is no good reason to interfere with cryptos performing this vitally important function.

### 12.4.3 Regulating Gold and Silver Currency

The comparatively recent experiences of e-gold[3] and the Liberty Dollar[4] illustrate that private sector gold and silver currencies can be successfully issued in both physical and digital form:

[3] For more details see Dowd (2014, pp. 27–37).

[4] More details in Dowd (2014, pp. 28–38).

e-gold was founded in 1996 by Doug Jackson, an oncologist with a passion for Austrian economics. Envisaged as a private international gold currency, e-gold was registered in Nevis in the Caribbean and was legally a payment system rather than a money transmitter. By 2005, it was second only to PayPal in online payments, by which point it had 1.2 million accounts and payments that year reached $1.5 billion. Dr. Jackson worked closely with law enforcement in tracking down criminals until the U.S. Secret Service for reasons best known only to themselves raided the company in December 2005 and arrested him. They subsequently persuaded him to accept a plea to a felony conviction. e-gold was a major commercial success and shutting it down was a massive own goal for law enforcement. (Dowd, 2014)

The Liberty Dollar was founded by Bernard von Nothaus in 1998 to provide a private voluntary barter currency as an alternative to the US dollar. It existed in specie, paper and digital form and rose to become the second most popular currency in the United States after the US dollar. From 1998 to 2007 it issued up to perhaps $85 million in Liberty Dollars and had 250,000 customers. The government initially turned a blind eye to it until the US Mint declared in 2006 that the use of the Liberty Dollar for currency purposes was a federal crime. Von Nothaus was subsequently convicted of crimes including counterfeit despite having never attempted to counterfeit the US dollar. In the aftermath of the verdict, the US District Attorney concerned made a series of claims so absurd that they have become legendary. These include the memorable 'Attempts to undermine the legitimate currency of this country are simply a unique form of domestic terrorism.'[5] Given Mr von Nothaus's commitment to non-violence and the Fed's own inflation record, this claim must rank as one of the dumbest statements by a prosecutor in the history of American jurisprudence. 'This is the United States government', he told the *New York Times*. 'It has nuclear weapons, and it's worried about some ex-surfer guy making his own money? Give me a break' (Feuer, 2012).

Private currency issuers can be regulated under the same legal framework that would regulate stablecoins, synthetic CBDCs/narrow money schemes or any other private currency schemes.

In the centuries before digital currencies, private coinage was sometimes permitted and, when it was, had a good historical track record.[6] However, in the US, there needs to be legislative changes if physical

[5] See FBI archives, https://tinyurl.com/mr2jzwcu. Accessed 4 February 2026.

[6] See, e.g., Brough (1898) or Selgin's 2011 case study of the private mints in Birmingham in the late eighteenth and early nineteenth centuries.

versions of such currencies are to be permitted again. To quote Nick Anthony:

> Mending the law should begin with 18 U.S.C. Section 485. Currently, the law prohibits coins that have a 'resemblance or similitude' to U.S. coins, but it fails to define the necessary resemblance a coin must have to be considered an unlawful counterfeit of an existing U.S. coin. To clarify the law, Congress should add that a coin must possess some combination of official phrases (i.e., United States of America, Liberty, In God We Trust, and E Pluribus Unum) and imagery. Congress would need to amend 18 U.S.C. Sections 487–491 to accommodate this change, but it would only be a matter of updating the language for consistency.
>
> Congress should also amend 18 U.S.C. Section 486, in which the law specifically forbids not just counterfeit coins, but also coins of original design. This change could be as simple as striking 'or of original design' from the record. (Anthony, 2022b, p. 4)

In the US there is also a strong constitutional case for gold and silver to be restored their original legal tender status.[7]

## 12.5 A CENTRAL BANK SHOULD NOT BE A PLAYER IN THE PAYMENTS MARKET

The final principle is that the central bank should not be a player in the payments market at all because it would then be conflicted between its interest in promoting its own payment systems against competitors and its broader duty to act as an impartial referee or regulator of the payments system as a whole. These two roles of player and referee conflict and *at a fundamental and damaging level.* If you disagree, then imagine how that would work out in competitive sports. It would not matter how badly you played, all that would matter is that you have the referee on your side. The Fed's status as a competitor *and* a regulator means that it is able to write the rules, play the game and act as the referee. Moreover, the Fed does not even need to worry about earning a profit, because it has many opportunities to hide its costs and cross-subsidise its activities in ways that are almost impossible for an outsider to detect.

George Selgin elaborated on these problems in his 2019 testimony to Congress:

[7] 'No State shall … make any Thing but gold and silver Coin a Tender in Payment of Debts …' (United States Constitution, Article 1, Section 10, Clause 1). Legal tender means that the instrument can be used to pay taxes or fines to the government.

> As a rule, competition is an effective – if not the most effective – means for encouraging providers of services to price those services equitably, to produce them efficiently, and to improve their quality over time. However, these outcomes depend on the presence of a level playing field on which all providers compete – that is, they depend on the various providers having roughly equal legal privileges and obligations. In the absence of a level playing field, the presence of multiple providers alone does not guarantee good outcomes. Instead, special care must be taken to guard against bad ones.
>
> The Federal Reserve banks enjoy many legal advantages over private suppliers of payment services. They command a monopoly of bank reserves that serve as means of final payment; they are empowered to regulate commercial banks and some other private-sector payment service providers; and they are exempt from antitrust laws. Finally, although the 1980 Monetary Control Act requires that the Fed charge prices for its services that recover those services' capital and operating expenses, it only needs to do so over a 'long run' of unspecified length, and then only according to accounting methods of its own choosing that are not subject to external review. . . .
>
> These and other Fed privileges mean that, when it enters into direct competition with private-sector payment service providers, it does so on a playing field that it can easily slant in its favor. (Selgin, 2019)

A poignant example of the Fed being conflicted arises with suggestions that the Fed should regulate stablecoins. However, the Fed is the wrong regulator for stablecoins.

As Schulp and Solowey (2024) observe:

> As an alternative payment service, stablecoins compete with the Fed's own payment infrastructure, including FedNow, the central bank's instant payment service. The Fed's consideration of a central bank digital currency would leave it further conflicted when regulating privately issued stablecoins, as those two digital representations of the dollar can be seen as substitutes. Any government body, the Fed included, would struggle to objectively analyze private payment innovations that compete with its own services. Giving the Fed the authority to regulate stablecoins unfairly stacks the deck against payment alternatives. Simply put, the fox shouldn't be allowed to guard the henhouse.

In this context, we should also keep in mind the Fed's opposition to narrow money, a position that makes no rational sense until we realise that the Fed is merely putting its own narrow self-interest above the broader interests of achieving a level playing field.

Unfortunately, asking governments and central banks to provide a level playing field is to ask them to go against their own institutional self-interest and reverse their usual historical practice, which is to suppress competition against their own products. We have seen this pattern of behaviour again and again in the historical record on money and banking. For long periods of time the private minting of coins was often suppressed, then when banknotes appeared, competition in the issue of banknotes was sooner or later suppressed as well. Both the freedom to mint coins and the freedom to issue banknotes are still suppressed or at least heavily curtailed in many countries around the world. The pattern now repeats itself with cryptocurrencies and CBDCs. For example, Ecuador launched its CBDC and banned cryptos in 2015, China launched its CBDC pilot in December 2019 and banned cryptos almost two years later, India announced its CBDC pilot in February 2022 and had banned cryptos the year before, and Nigeria launched its CBDC scheme in October 2021 and banned banks from being involved with crypto exchanges two months later. These examples suggest that some of the same countries that are launching or intending to launch CBDCs are also seeking to suppress cryptos. Banning cryptos may not be inherent to the core design of a CBDC, but the repeated combination of promoting CBDCs while suppressing cryptos strongly suggests that CBDCs are part of a broader agenda – governments' *perennial agenda* – to protect or enhance the state's monopoly privileges over the control of money and never mind the resulting deterioration in the quality of the product for the people who use it.

Remember that it is not the mere issue of a CBDC as such that should concern us: when considering the dangers of CBDCs what we should fear most is a system of controls against the use of alternative media of payments, for therein lies their power.

The historical experience of free banking and private minting suggests that the best monetary systems are private ones. If they want the best money attainable, monetary authorities should resist the temptation to promote their own interests. Simply put, the historical record suggests that good money and monetary monopoly do not coexist. Therefore we need to be clear which we prefer.

# Bibliography

Adamoleikun, R. (2023) "Nigeria's Cash Crisis Driving Digital Transactions to All-Time High". *Premium Times* (15 April).

Adams, J. (2021) "The Potential Orwellian Horror of Central Bank Digital Currencies". LewRockwell.com (13 July).

Adams, J. (2024) "Will California's Gun Laws Place a Target on Card Networks?" *American Banker* (February 12).

Adrian, T. (2019) "Stablecoins, Central Bank Digital Currencies, and Cross-Border Payments: A New Look at the International Monetary System". Remarks at the IMF-Swiss National Bank Conference, Zurich (14 May).

Adrian, T., and T. Mancini-Griffoli (2019) "The Rise of Digital Money". *IMF FINTECH NOTES 19/01* (July).

Advani, R. (2024) "Stablecoins: Apac's Regulatory Edge in Shaping the Future of Digital Finance". The Edge Singapore (13 Dec).

Almeida, D. (2024) "Pix foi o meio de pagamento mais popular do Brasil em 2023". *Agência Brasil* (12 March).

American Bankers Association (2021) "ABA Statement for the Record" before the Subcommittee on Economic Policy of the Committee on Banking, Housing, and Urban Affairs, for the hearing, "Building a Stronger Financial System: Opportunities of a Central Bank Digital Currency" (9 June).

Andersson, F. N. G., and L. Jonung (2020) "Don't Do It Again! The Swedish Experience with Negative Central Bank Interest Rates in 2015–2019". *VoxEU* (8 May).

Andolfatto D. (2015) "Fedcoin: On the Desirability of a Government Cryptocurrency". *MacroMania* (3 February).

Andolfatto, D. (2021) "Assessing the Impact of Central Bank Digital Currency on Private Banks". *The Economic Journal*, 131 (February): 525–540. (a)

Andolfatto, D. (2021) "Some Thoughts on Central Bank Digital Currency". *Cato Journal*, 41(2) (Spring/Summer): 343–351. (b)

Andolfatto, D. (2021) "Does Canada Need a Central Bank Digital Currency?" *Finances of the Nation* (30 September). (c)

Andolfatto, D. (2021) "On the Necessity and Desirability of a CBDC". *MacroMania* (30 November). (d)

Andolfatto, D. (2021) "On the Necessity and Desirability of a Central Bank Digital Currency". In D. Niepelt (ed.), *Central Bank Digital Currency: Considerations, Projects, Outlook*. London: Centre for Economic Policy Research, pp. 127–134. (e)

Anglin, H. (2022) "In Our Cashless Society, We Need to Take Digital Jail Seriously". *The Hub* (22 February).

Anonymous (2022) "The Crash at DCash – the Significance of Resilience in the Caribbean". *Vixio* (14 February).

Anonymous (2024) "A Look Forward: Digital Payments in Southeast Asia". *Qashier* (22 January).

Anonymous IT Reporter (2023) "Who's Afraid of CBDCs?" *The Daily Sceptic* (23 August).

Anthony, N. (2022) "Reporting FinCEN's Suspicious Activity". *Cato at Liberty* (13 April). (a)

Anthony, N. (2022) "Congress Should Welcome Cryptocurrency Competition". Cato Briefing Paper No. 138 (2 May). (b)

Anthony, N. (2022) "Stablecoin Issuers Should Not Have to Compete with the Federal Government". *PolicyCommons* (8 July). (c)

Anthony, N. (2023) "The Right to Financial Privacy Crafting a Better Framework for Financial Privacy in the Digital Age". Policy Analysis no. 945, Cato Institute, Washington, D.C. (2 May). (a)

Anthony, N. (2023) "Why Is the Fed Keeping Banker's Hours?" *Cato at Liberty* (10 April). (b)

Anthony, N. (2023) "Whose Liability Is It Anyway?" *Cato at Liberty* (7 August). (c)

Anthony, N. (2024) "'Privacy-Minded' CBDCs Are a Wolf in Sheep's Clothing". *CoinTelegraph* (24 June). (a)

Anthony, N. (2024) Bahamians Didn't Want CBDC – So Now They Are Being Forced to Use Them". *CoinTelegraph* (11 July). (b)

Anthony, N. (2024) "Thailand Uses Digital Wallet for 10,000 Baht Handout". *Cato at Liberty*. (August 30). (c)

Anthony, N. (2024) "State-Based Approaches to Countering Central Bank Digital Currency". *Cato Institute Testimony* (1 October). (d)

Anthony, N. (2024) *Digital Currency or Digital Control? Decoding CBDC and the Future of Money*. Washington, DC: Cato Institute. (e)

Antoine, T. N. J. (2021) "The ECCB's Digital Currency (DCash) Is a Critical Step in the Buildout of a Digital Economy in the ECCU". *ECCB Blog*.

Arauz, A., R. Garratt and D. F. Ramos (2021) "Dinero Electrónico: The Rise and Fall of Ecuador's Central Bank Digital Currency". *Latin American Journal of Central Banking*, 2(2): 100030.

Areddy, J. T. (2021) "China Creates Its Own Digital Currency, a First for a Major Economy". *Wall Street Journal* (5 April).

Arnold, M. (2021) "Digital Euro Will Protect Consumer Privacy, ECB Executive Pledges". *Financial Times* (20 June).

Attlee, D. (2024) "Robert F. Kennedy Jr Pledges to End U.S. Efforts to Move Toward CBDC". *CoinTelegraph* (29 January).

Auer, R., H. Banka, N. Y. Boakye-Adjei, A. Faragallan, J. Frost, H. Natarajan and J. Prenio (2022) "FSI Insights on Policy Implementation No 41: Central Bank Digital Currencies: A New Tool in the Financial Inclusion Toolkit?" Bank for International Settlements and World Bank (April).

Baer, G. (2021) "Central Bank Digital Currencies: Costs, Benefits and Major Implications for the U.S. Economic System". Bank Policy Institute Staff Working Paper (7 April).

Baer, G., and B. Nelson (2021) "A Costly Misunderstanding about CBDC". Bank Policy Institute (17 December).

Baer, G., and P. Paridon (2022) "The Waning Case for a Dollar CBDC". Bank Policy Institute (18 February).

Bakx, K., and M. Read (2024) "Bank of Canada Shelves Idea for Digital Loonie". *CBC News* (18 September).

Banco Central Do Brazil (2024) "Pix Is Now the Most Widely Used Payment Method in Brazil", www.bcb.gov.br/en/pressdetail/2588/nota. Accessed 3 February 2026.

Banco de la República Colombia (2024) "Relevance and Risks of Issuing a Central Bank Digital Currency in Colombia". Report (15 July).

Banescu, S., B. Borodach and A. Lannquist (2021) "4 Key Cybersecurity Threats to New Central Bank Digital Currencies". weforum.org, Topic: "Financial and Monetary Systems" (20 November).

Bank of Canada (2024) "Digital Canadian Dollar". Bank of Canada web archive, www.bankofcanada.ca/digitaldollar/. Accessed 3 February 2026.

Bank of England (2015) "One Bank Research Agenda" (February). https://tinyurl.com/yrjubrn6. Accessed 3 February 2026.

Bank of England (2020) "Central Bank Digital Currency: Opportunities, Challenges and Design". Discussion Paper (March). (a)

Bank of England (2021) "New Forms of Digital Money". Discussion Paper (7 June).

Bank of England and HM Treasury (2023) "The Digital Pound: A New Form of Money for Households and Businesses". Consultation Paper (February).

Bank of England and HM Treasury (2024) "Bank of England and HM Treasury Respond to Digital Pound Consultation". News Release (25 January).

Bank Policy Institute (2018) *Getting to Effectiveness – Report of U.S. Financial Institution Resources Devoted to BSA/AML & Sanctions Compliance* (29 October). Washington, D.C.: Bank Policy Institute.

Barrdear, J., and M. Kumhof (2016) "The Macroeconomics of Central Bank Issued Digital Currencies". Bank of England Staff Working Paper No. 605 (July).

Barrett, E. (2022) "Pepper Spray, Tow Trucks, and Bitcoin Seizures: How Canada Finally Ended the Weeks-Long Freedom Convoy Protests in Ottawa". *Fortune* (21 February).

*BBC News* (2020) "Thousands of Mobiles and Laptops Lost by UK Government in a Year" (20 February).

Benes, J., and M. Kumhof (2012) "The Chicago Plan Revisited" (1 August). IMF Working Papers 2012(202). Washington, D.C.: International Monetary Fund.

Bextc, K. (2022) "FINTRAC Says Convoy Posed No Violent Threat, Accounts Still Frozen". *The Counter Signal* (28 February).

Bhandhakavi, S. (2024) "134 Countries Now Exploring CBDCs, Atlantic Council Study Finds". *TechMonitor* (17 September).

Bindseil, U. (2019) "Controlling CBDC through Tiered Remuneration". SUERF Policy Note No. 95.

Bindseil, U. (2022) "The Case for and against CBDC – Five Years Later". Mimeo (19 February).

BIS (2020) "Central Bank Digital Currencies: Foundational Principles and Core Features: Report Number 1 in a Series of Collaborations from a Group of Central Banks" (9 October). Joint report by the Bank of Canada, European Central Bank, Bank of Japan, Sveriges Riksbank, Swiss National Bank, Bank of England, Board of Governors of the Federal Reserve and Bank for International Settlements, www.bis.org/publ/othp33.htm. Accessed 3 February 2026.

BIS (2021) "Central Bank Digital Currencies: Financial Stability Implications" (September), Joint report by the Bank of Canada, European Central Bank, Bank of Japan, Sveriges Riksbank, Swiss National Bank, Bank of England, Board of Governors of the Federal Reserve and Bank for International Settlements, www.bis.org/publ/othp42_fin_stab.pdf. Accessed 3 February 2026.

Black, D. B. (2022) "DCash Shows Why Fedcoin Could Be a Disaster". *Forbes* (28 February).

Blackstone, B. (2019) "Negative Rates, Designed as a Short-Term Jolt, Have Become an Addiction". *Wall Street Journal* (20 May).

Bloomberg (2023) "Chaotic Cash Shortage at ATMs Force Nigerians to Wait Hours for $43". *Bloomberg* (4 February).

Board of Governors of the Federal Reserve System (2019) "Regulation D: Reserve Requirements of Depository Institutions, 12 CFR Part 204". *Federal Register*, 84(48) (12 March).

Board of Governors of the Federal Reserve System (2022) "Money and Payments: The U.S. Dollar in the Age of Digital Transformation". Washington, D.C.: Board of Governors of the Federal Reserve System (January).

Boisvert, N. (2022) "Trudeau Ends Use of Emergencies Act, Says 'Situation Is No Longer an Emergency'". *CBC News* (23 February).

Bordo, M. D., and A. T. Levin (2019) "Improving the Monetary Regime: The Case for U.S. Digital Cash". *Cato Journal*, 39(2) (Spring/Summer): 383–405.

Bossone, B., and A. Faragallah (2022) "Expiring Money (Part One)". *World Bank Blogs* (2 November). (a)

Bossone, B., and A. Faragallah (2022) "Expiring Money (Part Two)". *World Bank Blogs* (7 November). (b)

Bovard, J. (2024) "One Hundred Years of IRS Political Targeting". *The Libertarian Institute* blog (15 April).

BPI Staff (2020) "Bank On and CRA: A Powerful Yet Simple Change That Can Increase Financial Inclusion" (16 March). Washington, D.C.: Bank Policy Institute.

Brainard, L. (2022) "Digital Assets and the Future of Finance: Examining the Benefits and Risks of a U.S. Central Bank Digital Currency". Speech before the House Committee on Financial Services (26 May).

Brancaccio, D., A. Schroeder and R. Conlon (2022) "The Argument against the Fed Creating a Central Bank Digital Currency". *Marketplace Morning Report* (2 June).
Brignall, M. (2023) "UK Banks Are Closing More Than 1,000 Accounts Every Day". *The Guardian* (30 July).
Broadbent, B. (2016) "Central Banks and Digital Currencies". Speech to the London School of Economics (2 March).
Brough, W. (1898) *Open Mints and Free Banking*. New York: Putnam.
Brown, S. (2019) "Brown Statement on Payment Providers Declining to Join Facebook's Libra Association". Minority Press Releases (11 October).
Brunnermeier, M. K., and D. Niepelt (2019) "On the Equivalence of Private and Public Money". *Journal of Monetary Economics*, 106: 27–41.
Bull, G., W. Cook, M. Kerse and S. Staschen (2021) "Is Financial Inclusion a Reason to Push Central Bank Digital Currencies?" CGAP blog (13 May).
Burton, D. R., and N. J. Michel (2016) "Financial Privacy in a Free Society". Backgrounder No. 3157 (23 September), Heritage Foundation.
Callahan, S. (2023) "Why a CBDC Will NOT Promote Financial Inclusion". *Swan Private Insight*, Issue 20 (14 February).
*CanadianLibertarian* (2022) "Trudeau Calls Unvaccinated Canadians Extremists, Misogynists, and Racists" (7 January).
Capurro, M. E. (2024) "Brazil's Wildly Popular Instant-Payment System Is Going Global". *Bloomberg* (24 February).
Carstens, A. (2019) "The Future of Money and Payments". Whitaker Lecture, Central Bank of Ireland, Dublin (22 March).
Carstens, A. (2020) Speech to IMF seminar event "Cross-Border Payments – a Vision for the Future" (19 October).
Carstens, A. (2021) "BIS's Carstens: Digital Currencies and the Future of the Monetary System". *The Asian Banker* (28 January).
Casey, D. (2022) "Doug Casey on the WEF's Plan for Mankind and What Comes Next". *ZeroHedge* (10 November).
Cecchetti, S., and K. Schoenholtz (2017) "Banking the Unbanked: The Indian Revolution", www.moneyandbanking.com (6 November).
Cecchetti, S., and K. Schoenholtz (2021) "Central Bank Digital Currency: Battle for the Soul of the Financial System". *VoxEU* (8 July).
Cecchetti, S., and K. Schoenholtz (2022) "Let Crypto Burn". *Financial Times* (17 November).
Centers, J. (2024) "Republicans Fight Back against Central Bank Digital Currencies". *Blaze Media* (25 May).
Central Commission for Discipline Inspection and the National Supervisory Commission (2024) "Yao Qian, Former Director of the Science and Technology Supervision Department of the China Securities Regulatory Commission, Was Expelled from the Party and Removed from Office for Using Virtual Currency to Trade Power for Money" (11 November).
Chan, S. P. (2023) "Sunak's Britcoin Ambitions Hit by Huge Public Backlash". *Daily Telegraph* (3 July).
Chaum, D. (1983) "Blind Signatures for Untraceable Payments". In D. Chaum, R. L. Rivest and A. T. Sherman (eds), *Advances in Cryptology*. Boston, MA: Springer, pp. 199–203.

Cheng, J. (2020) "China Rolls Out Pilot Test of Digital Currency". *Wall Street Journal* (20 April).

Chiu, J., M. Davoodalhosseini, J. Jiang and Y. Zhu (2020) "Bank Marketing Power and Central Bank Digital Currency: Theory and Quantitative Assessment". Bank of Canada Staff Working Paper (2010–20).

Choi, J. (2023) "Digital Yuan Transactions Growing Rapidly, PBOC Says". *CoinTelegraph* (25 July).

Chorzempa, M. (2021) "Promise and Peril of Digital Money in China". *Cato Journal*, 41(2): 295–306.

Cochrane, J. (2019) "Fed Nixes Narrow Banks Redux". *The Grumpy Economist* (30 May).

Cœuré, B. (2021) "Central Bank Digital Currency: The Future Starts Today". Speech to the Eurofi Financial Forum, Ljubljana (10 September).

Cœuré, B., and J. Loh (2018) "Central Bank Digital Currencies". Committee on Payments and Market Infrastructures, Bank for International Settlements (March).

Coghlan, J. (2022) "Former Chinese Central Banker Says Digital Yuan 'Usage Has Been Low'". *CoinTelegraph* (30 December).

*CoinTelegraph* (2022) "The Caribbean Is Pioneering CBDCs with Mixed Results Amid Banking Difficulties" (29 September).

Corbishley, N. (2022) "Unbeknown to Most, a Financial Revolution Is Coming That Threatens to Change Everything (and Not for the Better)". *Naked Capitalism* (25 March).

Corbishley, N. (2023) "Nigerian Central Bank's 'Drive to Entrench' a 'Cashless Economy' Is Creating a World of Pain for Nigerian Citizens". *Naked Capitalism* (21 February). (a)

Corbishley, N. (2023) "The Central Bank of Nigeria Just Paused Its Demonetisation Program after Visiting Untold Damage on Nigeria's Economy". *Naked Capitalism* (17 March). (b)

Cortez, J. P. (2024) "Nebraska Ends Income Taxes on Gold and Silver, Declares CBDCs Are Not Lawful Money". *Power & Market*, Mises Institute (8 May).

Crapo, M. (2020) "Crapo Statement at Digital Currency Hearing". Majority Press Releases (30 June).

Crawley, J. (2024) "China's Digital Yuan Isn't Taking Off Despite State Employee Salary Trial: Report". *CoinDesk* (13 May).

Croce, B. (2021) "Idea of Central Bank Digital Currency Gains Traction among More Countries". *Pensions and Investments* Special Report (19 April).

Cunliffe, J. (2023) "The Digital Pound". Speech at UK Finance (7 February).

Dai, W. (1995) "Law vs Technology". Cypherpunks Mailing List (10 February), https://cypherpunks.venona.com/date/1995/02/msg00508.html. Accessed 25 January 2026.

Danezis, G., and S. Meiklejohn (2016) "Centrally Banked Cryptocurrencies". http://dx.doi.org/10.14722/ndss.2016.23187.

Daniel, E. (2020) "Cambodia's Serey Clarifies: 'Bakong Is Not [Central Bank] Digital Currency". Radio Finance, https://tinyurl.com/45vfmzce. Accessed 25 January 2026.

Das, K. N., and J. Spicer (2016) "How the New York Fed Fumbled over the Bangladesh Bank Cyber-Heist". *Reuters* (21 July).

Davis, I. (2023) "Central Bank Digital Currency Is the Endgame – Part 1". *Iain Davis Substack* (2 March).

Day, A. (2024) "Fifty Shades of Central Bank Tyranny". Brownstone Institute (30 August).

De Bode, I., M. Higginson and M. Niederkorn (2021) "CBDC and Stablecoins: Early Coexistence on an Uncertain Road". McKinsey & Company (11 October).

de los Rios, A., and Y. Zhu (2020) "CBDCs and Monetary Sovereignty". *Staff Analytical Note 2020–5* (February), Bank of Canada.

Dietz, C. (2022) "eNaira Paves the Way to Cashless Economy in Nigeria – CBN's Emefiele". *African Business* (30 October).

Dong, J. (2022) "A Chinese City May Have Used a Covid App to Block Protesters, Prompting an Outcry". *New York Times* (16 June).

Dowd, K. (2014) *New Private Monies A Bit-Part Player?* London: Institute of Economic Affairs.

Dowd, K. (2023, ed.) *The Experience of Free Banking*, second edition. London: Institute of Economic Affairs.

Dowd, K., and M. Hutchinson (2010) *Alchemists of Loss: How Modern Finance and Government Intervention Crashed the Financial System*. New York: Wiley.

Durden, T. (2017) "Bundesbank's Weidmann: Digital Currencies Will Make the Next Crisis Worse". *ZeroHedge* (14 July).

Durden, T. (2019) "12 Reasons Why Negative Rates Will Devastate the World". *ZeroHedge* (17 August).

Durden, T. (2021) "China's Digital Yuan Comes with an Expiration Date". *ZeroHedge* (12 April). (a)

Durden, T. (2021) "'I'm Not at All Excited': China's Digital Yuan Is Turning into a Giant Flop". *ZeroHedge* (12 May). (b)

Durden, T. (2021) "No Vax, No Phone – Pakistan Province Blocks Sim Cards of the Unvaccinated". *ZeroHedge* (12 June). (c)

Durden, T. (2022) "Ontario Government Employee Fired over $100 Contribution to Freedom Convoy". *ZeroHedge* (19 February).

Durden, T. (2023) "FinTech CEOs Expose How Feds Colluded in 'Debanking' Schemes after Andreessen 'Opened the Floodgates' on Rogan". *ZeroHedge* (30 November).

Durden, T. (2024) "Trump Vows to "Never Allow" a Central Bank Digital Currency". *ZeroHedge* (18 January).

Earle, P. C. (2021) "Make No Mistake: Programmable Digital Currencies Are Weaponizable Money". *The Daily Economy*, American Institute for Economic Affairs (24 April).

ECCB (2022) "Region-Wide Service Interruption of DCash Platform" (14 January).

ECCB (2023) "East Caribbean Central Bank Annual Report, 2022–2023".

Editorial Board (2020) "China Is Exporting Its Digital Authoritarianism". *Washington Post* (5 August).

Editorial Board (2022) "Justin Trudeau's Liberal Tyranny". *Wall Street Journal* (22 February).

Ekins, E., and J. Gygi (2023) "Poll: Only 16% of Americans Would Support the Government Issuing a Central Bank Digital Currency". Cato Institute *Survey Report* (31 May).

Elder, B. (2024) "Even Central Bankers Are Losing Faith in CBDCs". *Financial Times* (26 November).

Eleanya, F. (2022) "eNaira Fails to Entice Merchants, Banks". *Businessday* (31 May).

Ellwood, J. (2021) "Archbishop Vigano, a Beacon of Light". *The Conservative Woman* (24 October).

Ely, J. E. (2007) *The Guardian of Every Other Right: A Constitutional History of Property Rights*, third edition. New York: Oxford University Press.

Emmer, T. (2023) "Emmer Reintroduces CBDC Anti-surveillance State Act", emmer.house.gov. Accessed 4 February 2026.

Falodun, H. (2023) "As Its Central Bank Limits Cash and Pushes a CBDC, Nigeria Needs Bitcoin". *Bitcoin Magazine* (11 February).

Fanti, G., J. Lipsky and O. Moehr (2022) "Central Bankers' New Cybersecurity Challenges". *Finance & Development*, IMF (September): 30–32.

Federal Deposit Insurance Corporation (2020) *How America Banks: Household Use of Banking and Financial Services*. Washington, D.C.: FDIC.

Federal Deposit Insurance Corporation (2021) *2021 FDIC National Survey of Unbanked and Underbanked Households – Executive Summary*. Washington, D.C.: FDIC.

Federal Reserve System (2019) "Advanced Notice of Future Rulemaking" (March). Washington, D.C.: Federal Reserve System.

Feuer, A. (2012) "'Liberty Dollar' Creator Awaits His Fate Behind Bars". *New York Times* (24 October).

Financial Conduct Authority (2024) "Financial Services and Electronic Money – the FCA's Role under the Payment Services Regulations 2017 and Electronic Money Regulations 2011" (November). London: Financial Conduct Authority.

Fingerhut, H., L. Packard and J. Wright (2022) "Central Bank Digital Currencies Increase Financial Inclusion" (10 March). Tony Blair Institute for Global Change.

Fischer, M. S. (2021) "The 10 Most-Fined Financial Services Firms". *ALM ThinkAdvisor Newsletter* (9 March).

Fisher, I. (1933) "The Debt-Deflation Theory of Great Depressions". *Econometrica*, 1(3): 337–357.

*Forkcast.news* (2023) "ECB's Lagarde Gets Pranked, Reveals Digital Euro Will Have 'Limited' Control". *Yahoo Finance* (7 April).

Frisby, D. (2022) "Paypal, Bitcoin, and the Weaponisation of Money". Moneyweek.com (22 September).

Frisby, D. (2024) "The Orwellian Horror of Central Bank Digital Currencies – and Why It Won't Happen". *The Flying Frisby* (8 December).

Frontini, P. (2024) "Brazil's PID to Reach 40% of Online Payment Market by 2026, Ebanx Study Finds". *Reuters* (25 January).

Garcia, J. (2019) "Keep Big Tech Out of Finance Act". H.R. 4813, United States Bill (13 November).

Gerard, D. (2020) "Avant Card – a Central Bank Digital Currency from 1990s Finland". *Attack of the 50 Foot Blockchain* (25 January). (a)
Gerard, D. (2020) "Sistema de Dinero Electrónico (2014–2018) – Ecuador's Sort-of-CBDC". *Attack of the 50 Foot Blockchain* (8 September). (b)
Gerard, D. (2020) "Book Except: Libra Shrugged – How Facebook Tried to Take Over the Money". *Revenge of the 50 Foot Blockchain* (10 November). (c)
Gerard, D. (2022) "News: World Wildlife NFT, Diem Sale Details, ECCB DCash Offline". *Attack of the 50 Foot Blockchain* (7 February). (a)
Gerard, D. (2022) "Regulatory Clarity: Doomed US Crypto Bills, Nigeria's CBDC Lacks Repeat Users, Central Banks Don't Like Crypto Either". *Attack of the 50 Foot Blockchain* (27 August). (b)
Gesell, S. (1891) *Die Reformation des Münzwesens als Brücke zum sozialen Staat*. Self-published, Buenos Aires.
Giambruno, N. (2022) "Another CBDC Flop . . . Here's What Really Comes Next (and It's Not What the Elite Hoped For". *ZeroHedge* (2 November).
Gladstein, A. (2021) "Financial Freedom and Privacy in the Post-Cash World". *Cato Journal*, 41(2): 271–293.
Global Coin Research (2018) "What Would a Successful Stablecoin Look Like? A China Perspective on Tether and Stablecoins". *Medium* (17 October).
Goodhart, C. (1988) *The Evolution of Central Banks*. Cambridge, MA: MIT Press.
Gorton, G., and D. J. Mullineaux (1987) "The Joint Production of Confidence: Endogenous Regulation and Nineteenth Century Commercial-Bank Clearinghouses". *Journal of Money, Credit and Banking*, 19: 457–468.
Government of Canada (no date) Emergency Measures Regulations (SOR/2022-21). Justice Laws Website, www.laws-lois.justice.gc.ca/eng/regulations/SOR-2022-21/index.html. Accessed 25 January 2026.
Grym, A. (2020) "Lessons Learned from the World's First CBDC". *Bank of Finland Economics Review*, No. 8/2020. Helsinki: Bank of Finland.
Guida, V. (2017) "Justice Department to End Obama-Era 'Operation Choke Point'". *Politico* (17 August).
Gunnlaugsson, D. (2023) "We Need to Take Back Control from the Banks". *Spiked* (10 August).
Haldane, A. G. (2015) "How Low Can You Go?" Speech at Portadown Chamber of Commerce (18 September).
Hall, I. (2022) "Bahamas Central Bank Shares CBDC Lessons from Sand Dollar's First Two Years". *Global Government Fintech* (9 November).
Hanke, S. H., Z. Ma and R. Cheng (2022) "On the Quantity Theory of Money: Some Monetary Facts". *Studies in Applied Economics No. 224* (December), Johns Hopkins University Institute for Applied Economics, Global Heath, and the Study of Enterprise.
Hartnell, N. (2023) "'Barely Scratching Surface' on Sand Dollar's Adoption". *The Tribune* (6 April).
Heeb, G. (2022) "A Digital Dollar for the Unbanked? Banks, Consumers See Pitfalls". *Bloomberg Law* (22 June).
Himes, J. (2022) "Winning the Future of Money: A Proposal for a U.S. Central Bank Digital Currency". White Paper (22 June).

Hoffman, S., J. Garnaut, K. Izenman, M. Johnson, A. Pascoe, F. Ryan and E. Thomas (2020) "The Flipside of China's Central Bank Digital Currency". Australia Strategic Policy Institute International Cyberpolicy Center Policy Brief Report No. 40/2020.

House of Lords Economic Affairs Committee (2022) "Central Bank Digital Currencies: A Solution in Search of a Problem?" HL Paper 131 Published by the Authority of the House of Lords (13 January).

Hughes, E. (1993) *A Cypherpunk's Manifesto* (9 March), https://nakamotoinstitute.org/cypherpunk-manifesto/. Accessed 25 January 2026.

Hustle Escape (no date) "CBDCs: A Monetary Highway to Hell". Hustle Escape (12 September).

Hutchinson, M. (2012) "Sado-Economics". *The Bear's Lair* (24 December).

Hutchinson, M. (2013) "Banking Secrecy Is a Key Civil Liberty". *The Bear's Lair* (29 April).

Hutchinson, M. (2022) "The Anti-industrial Complex". In M. Walsh (ed.), *Against the Great Reset: Eighteen Theses Contra the New World Order*. New York: Bombardier, distributed by Simon & Schuster, pp. 289–310.

Hyman, V. (2023) "Your Guide to Understanding CBDCs". *Perspectives*, Mastercard Newsroom (1 August).

Ibrahim, R. (2024) "The Tory Tobacco Bill Is All Smoke and Mirrors". *CapX* (16 April).

Idris, A. (2021) "Africa's First e-Currency Is Off to a Shaky Start". *Rest of World* (19 November).

Interim Staff (2022) "European Parliamentarians Condemn Trudeau". *The Interim* (20 May).

Jackson, D. (2018) "Debunking Blockchain". Global Standard Mimeo.

Jackson, D. (2019) "CBDCs Are a Terrible Idea". Global Standard Extended Abstract (9 May).

Jackson, D. (2020) "'Global Stablecoin' Challenges: Response to FSB Consultation Document". Global Standard Mimeo (7 December).

*Jamaica Observer* (2022) "JAM-DEX ... Finally" (26 July).

Jaremski, M., S. Fleitus and S. P. Schuster (2020) "The US Postal Savings System and the Collapse of Building and Loan Associations during the Great Depression". Utah State University Center for Growth and Opportunity Working Paper (30 April).

Jeftovic, M. E. (2023) "Freedom Convoy's B. J. Dichter: We Live in a Belief-Based Society". *Bombthrower* (4 May).

Jones, H., and D. Milliken (2021) "'Britcoin' Not Bitcoin? UK Considers New Digital Currency". *Reuters* (19 April).

Jonung, L. (2023) "Free Banking in Sweden". In K. Dowd (ed.), *The Experience of Free Banking*, second edition. London: Institute of Economic Affairs, pp. 285–313.

Jossey, P. H. (2022) "Central Bank Digital Currencies Threaten Financial Stability and Financial Privacy". *Competitive Enterprise Institute Issue Analysis 2022 Number 1* (February).

Kaaru, S. (2024) "Jamaica's Largest Bank Casts Doubt on CBDC". *CoinGeek* (23 August).

Kantchev, G., C. Whittall and M. Inada (2016) "Are Negative Rates Backfiring? Here's Some Early Evidence". *Wall Street Journal* (8 August).

Kempe, F. (2021) "Why the US Can't Afford to Fall Behind in the Global Digital Currency Race". *Inflection Points*, Atlantic Council (28 February).

Khan, R. (2021) "Punjab to Block SIM Cards of Unvaccinated". *The Express Tribune* (11 June).

Kiff, J., J. Alwazir, S. Davidovic, A. Farias, A. Khan, T. Khiaonarong, M. Malaika, H. Monroe, N. Sugimoto, H. Tourpe and P. Zhou (2020) "A Survey of Research on Retail Central Bank Currency" (26 June). IMF Working Papers 2020(104). Washington, D.C.: International Monetary Fund.

Killian, A. (2020) "A Deep Dive into Bitcoin Scalability" (3 January). crypto.com.

Klein, A., and G. Selgin (2020) "We Shouldn't Have to Wait for FedNow to Have Faster Payments". *American Banker* (28 February).

Knightly, K. (2021) "Programmable Digital Currency: The Next Stage of the New Normal?" *Off-Guardian* (1 October).

Knightly, K. (2022) "Ukraine Crisis Accelerating Rise of Central Bank Digital Currencies". *Off-Guardian* (19 March).

Kobie, N. (2019) "The Complicated Truth about China's Social Credit System". *Wired* (6 July).

Koning, J. P. (2013) "Why the Fed Is More Likely to Adopt Bitcoin Technology Than Kill It Off". *Moneyness Blog* (14 April).

Koning, J. P. (2014) "FedCoin". *Moneyness Blog* (19 October).

Koning, J. P. (2018) "Anonymous Digital Cash". *The Daily Economy*, American Institute for Economic Affairs (24 February). (a)

Koning, J. P. (2018) "Money Is Privacy". *The Daily Economy*, American Institute for Economic Affairs (4 September). (b)

Koning, J. P. (2018) "Swedish Betrayal". *Moneyness Blog* (27 December). (c)

Koning, J. P. (2019) "The Fed Wants to Close the Window on Narrow Banks". *AIER Blog* (28 May). (a)

Koning, J. P. (2019) "Who Should Provide Central Bank Digital Currency?" *AIER Blog* (1 September). (b)

Koning, J. P. (2020) "In the CBDC Race, It's Better to Be Last". *CoinDesk* (2 November). (a)

Koning, J. P. (2020) "Programmable Money Isn't New, We've Had It for Ages". *Moneyness Blog* (19 November). (b)

Koning, J. P. (2021) "To CBDC or Not to CBDC?" *AIER Blog* (5 July).

Koning, J. P. (2022) X post (8:18 pm, 4 April), https://x.com/jp_koning/status/1511060784889143298. Accessed 3 February 2026.

Kumar, A. (2022) "A Report Card on China's Central Bank Digital Currency: The e-CNY". *GeoEconomics Center* (1 March).

Kumhof, M., M. Pinchetti, P. Rungcharoenkitkul and A. Sokol "CBDC Policies in Open Economies". BIS Working Papers No 1086 (April).

Lagarde, C. (2018) "Winds of Change: The Case for New Digital Currency". Speech to Singapore Fintech Festival (14 November).

Lannquist, A., and B. Tan (2023) "Central Bank Digital Currency's Role in Promoting Financial Inclusion". IMF Fintech Note 2023/011. Washington, D.C.: International Monetary Fund.

*Ledger Insights* (2022) "Report: Only 80 Merchants Signed Up for Nigerian CBDC" (31 May).

*Ledger Insights* (2024) "Fed's Powell Says Don't Worry about CBDC. It's Not Happening Any Time Soon" (8 March).

Lee, A. (2021) "What Is Programmable Currency?" *FEDS Notes* (23 June).

Lee, I. (2021) "Bank of England Official Says Britcoin CBDC Launch Is 'Probable'". *Business Insider* (14 May).

Leopold, J., A. Cormier, J. Templon, T. Warren, J. Singer-Vine, S. Pham, R. Holmes, A. Ghorayshi, M. Sallah, T. Kozyreva and E. Loop (2020) "The FINCEN Files – Thousands of Secret Suspicious Activity Reports Offer a Never-before-Seen Picture of Corruption and Complicity – and How the Government Lets It Flourish". *BuzzFeedNews* (20 September).

Levi, M., and P. Reuter (2006) "Money Laundering". In M. Tony (ed.), *Crime and Justice: A Review of Research*, Vol. 34. Chicago: University of Chicago Press, pp. 289–375.

LexisNexis Risk Solutions (2022) *True Cost of Financial Crime Compliance Study United States and Canada Edition* (September).

Li, D. (2022) "Chinese City Uses COVID-19 App to Prevent Bank Protesters from Gathering, Depositors Say". *The Epoch Times* (16 June).

Lian, K. W. (2024) "Here Comes the Wave of Insurance Claims for the CrowdStrike Outage". *Business Insider* (22 July).

Libra Association Members (2019) "An Introduction to Libra". Libra Association (18 June).

Lindrea, B. (2023) "China's Digital Yuan Nears $250B Transaction Volume – China Bank Governor". *CoinTelegraph* (20 July).

Lloyd, M. (2023) *Central Bank Digital Currencies: The Future of Money*. Newcastle upon Tyne: Agenda Publishing.

Lowe, P. (2021) "Payments: The Future?" Speech given to the Australian Payments Network (9 December).

Ludwin, A. (2016) "Keynote Address". 16th Annual International Conference on Policy Challenges for the Financial Sector, co-hosted by the FRB, IMF, WBG, 1–3 June, Washington, D.C.

Luther, W. J. (2022) "The CBDC Tradeoff". American Institute for Economic Research blog (9 October).

Luther, W. J. (2024) "CBDCs Undermine Financial Privacy". *The Daily Economy*, American Institute for Economic Research (3 October).

Lyddon, B. (2023) "Why the Bank of England Is Beyond Control". Global Britain.

Lyons, N. S. (2023) "Just Say No to CBDCs". *The Upheaval* (10 March).

Macleod, A. (2015) "From ZIRP to NIRP". *GoldMoney* (24 September).

Maharrey, M. (2024) "Several States Take Steps to Block a Central Bank Digital Currency". *ZeroHedge* (21 May).

Marr, B. (2017) "A Short History of Bitcoin and Crypto Currency Everyone Should Read". *Forbes* (6 December).

Mashkoor, L. (2021) "Punjab Province in Pakistan to Block SIM Cards and Salaries of Unvaccinated People". *The National* (11 June).

Matthieu, E. (2024) "Mobile Money Accounts Are Surging Globally, Especially in Africa and Asia". *Daily Data Insights* (4 June).

McAndrews, J. (2017) "The Case for Cash". ADBI Working Paper No. 679. Tokyo: Asian Development Bank.

McCloskey, D. N., and A. Mingardi (2020) *The Myth of the Entrepreneurial State*. Great Barrington, MA: American Institute for Economic Research/Adam Smith Institute.

McGrogan, D. (2023) "On the Right to Property, Central Bank Digital Currencies, and Excellent Tyranny". *Uncibal blog* (18 January).

McGrogan, D. (2024) "Not Everything Is Bad, But Everything Is Dangerous". *Uncibal blog* (18 January). (a)

McGrogan, D. (2024) "A 'National Conversation about the Future of Money'". *Uncibal blog* (13 February). (b)

McGrogan, D. (2024) "Baby It's Cold Outside (the Central Bank's Core Ledger)". *Uncibal blog* (26 April). (c)

Meiklejohn, S., M. Pomarole, G. Jordan, K. Levchenko, D. McCoy, G. M. Voelker and S. Savage (2013) "A Fistful of Bitcoins: Characterizing Payments among Men with No Names". Proceedings of the Internet Measurement Conference, ACM. *Communications of the ACM* 59(4).

Michel, N. (2022) "The U.S. Should Disavow CBDCs and Set the Standard for Protecting Financial Privacy". *Forbes* (2 March). (a)

Michel, N. (2022) "Central Bank Digital Currencies Are about Control – They Should be Stopped". *Forbes* (22 April). (b)

Michel, N. (2023) "Not Just Another Form of Money". *Forbes* (6 March). (a)

Michel, N. (2023) "Central Bank Digital Currencies, under Any Name, Threaten Privacy and Freedom". *Forbes* (2 May). (b)

Michel, N. (2023) "Cato Survey Shows Few Americans Support Central Bank Digital Currencies". *Forbes* (31 May). (c)

Michel, N. J., and J. Schulp (2021) "A Simple Proposal for Regulating Stablecoins". Cato Briefing Paper No. 128 (5 November).

Milne, A. (2024) "The Digital Pound: A Plan Designed to Fail". Working paper, Loughborough University Business School (14 April).

Milne, R., and M. Arnold (2020) "Why Sweden Ditched Its Negative Rate Experiment". *Financial Times* (20 February).

Moeller, K. (2024) "California Guns Shops to Require Separate Merchant Codes to Track Suspicious Purchases". *CBS News* (12 February).

Molyneux, P., A. Reghezza and R. Xie (2019) "Bank Margins and Profits in a World of Negative Rates". *Journal of Banking and Finance*, 107: 1–11.

Molyneux, P., A. Reghezza, J. Thornton and R. Xie (2020) "Did Negative Interest Rates Improve Bank Lending?" *Journal of Financial Services Research*, 57: 51–68.

Monnet, E., A. Riva and S. Ungaro (2021) "Bank Runs and Central Bank Digital Currencies". *VoxEU* (1 May).

Moran, A. (2023) "CBDCs with Expiration Dates, Restrictions Could Target Social Policies, Economist Tells WEF". *ZeroHedge* (1 July).

Motamedi, S. (2014) "Will Bitcoins Ever Become Money? A Path to Decentralized Central Banking". Tannu Tuva Initiative (21 July).

Mullin, J. (2022) "Fed Eyes Central Bank Digital Currency". *Econ Focus* (Second Quarter), Federal Reserve: 10–13.

Munshi, N. (2021) "Nigerians Cautious over Africa's First Digital Currency". *Financial Times* (7 November).

Murdoch, A. (2024) "Bank of Canada Admits 'Significant' Number of Citizens Would Resist Digital Dollar". *InfoWars* (1 November).

Murphy, H., and K. Stacey (2022) "Facebook Libra: The Inside Story of How the Company's Cryptocurrency Dream Died". *FT Magazine*(10 March)

Mutton, T. (2021) "Central Bank Digital Currency: An Update on the Bank's Work". Speech at FS Tech: The Future of Fin Tech Conference (17 June).

Nakamoto, S. (2008) "Bitcoin: A Peer-to-Peer Electronic Cash System" (21 August), https://ssrn.com/abstract=3440802. Accessed 28 January 2026.

Nardi, C. (2024) "Court Rules Liberals' Use of Emergencies Law Was Unjustified, Unreasonable". *National Post* (23 January).

National Bank of Cambodia (2024) "Annual Report 2023 and Target for 2024" (May 10).

Naughtie, A. (2022) "Trudeau Accuses Canada Truckers of 'Hate, Abuse and Racism' as He Tests Positive for Covid after Evacuation". *Independent* (31 January).

New, F. (2023) "BPUK Response – the Digital Pound: A New Form of Money for Households and Businesses?" *Bitcoin Policy UK* (31 May).

Niepelt, D. (2021) "'Reserves for All': Political Rather than Macroeconomic Risks". In D. Niepelt (ed.), *Central Bank Digital Currency: Considerations, Project, Outlook*. London: Centre for Economic Policy Research, pp. 39–44.

Nigeria Inter-Bank Settlement Systems (2022) "E-Payment Transactions in Nigeria Hit N38.9 Trillion in November 2022". Nairametrics.com (9 December).

Nightingale, H. (2022) "WATCH: New Ottawa Police Chief Says Freedom Protesters Will Be Punished Financially and Criminally". *PM* (20 February).

Nivtric (2018) "The Miracle of Wörgl". *The Plan for the Future* (19 June).

Nwite, S. (2023) "Nigeria's Electronic Payment Transactions Volume Was N135trn in Q1, 2023". *Tekedia* (18 April).

O'Connell, O. (2022) "'It Has to Stop': Trudeau Demands End to Trucker Protest Saying 'People Waving Swastikas' Don't Represent Canada". *Independent* (8 February).

Oliver, E. W., and L. Svalgaard (2005) "The 1859 Solar-Terrestrial Disturbance and the Current Limits on Extreme Space Weather Activity". *Solar Physics*, 224 (1–2): 407–422.

Orcutt, M. (2023) "What's Next for China's Digital Currency?" *MIT Technology Review* (3 August).

Osae-Brown, A., M. Fatunde and R. Olurounbi (2022) "Digital-Currency Plan Falters as Nigerians Defiant on Crypto". *Bloomberg* (25 October).

O'Sullivan, A. (2020) "China Is Rolling Out a Government Digital Currency. We Shouldn't Try to Copy Them". *Reason* (28 April).

Pandey, G. (2024) "Why India's Latest Sun Mission Finding Is Crucial for the World". *BBC News* (27 November).

Paravacini, G. (2018) "Europe Is Losing the Fight against Dirty Money". *Politico* (2 April).

Partz, H. (2022) "Some Central Banks Have Dropped Out of the Digital Currency Race". *CoinTelegraph* (9 November).
Patel, B. (2020) "Cambodia Edges Towards Digital Payments". OMFIF.org (22 June).
People's Bank of China (2021) "Progress of Research & Development of E-CNY in China". Report: Working Group on E-CNY Research and Development of the People's Bank of China.
Pol, R. F. (2020) "Anti-money Laundering: The World's Least Effective Policy Experiment? Together, We Can Fix It". *Policy Design and Practice*, 3(1): 73–94, DOI: 10.1080/25741292.2020.1725366.
Pooler, M. (2023) "Brazil Counts Success with Pix Payments Tool". *Financial Times* (18 September).
Prasad, E. (2021) "The Case for Central Bank Digital Currencies". *Cato Journal*, 41(2) (Spring/Summer): 251–258. (a)
Prasad, E. (2021) *The Future of Money: How the Digital Revolution Is Transforming Currencies and Finance*. Cambridge, MA: The Belknap Press of Harvard University. (b)
Prasad, E. (2024) "Thailand May Tell Us a Great Deal about the Future of Money". *Financial Times* (6 August). (b)
Quarles, R. K. (2021) "Parachute Pants and Central Bank Money". Speech to the 113th Annual Utah Bankers Association Convention, Sun Valley, Idaho (28 June).
Qureshi, H. (2019) "The Cypherpunks". *Nakamoto* (29 December).
*Rate Captain* (2023) "Naira Scarcity: N20TrN Lost to Reduction in Economic Activities, Says CPPE" (14 March).
Rayner, G. (2024) "NatWest Staff 'Gloated That They Had Driven Nigel Farage Out of the Country'". *Daily Telegraph* (23 October).
Ree, J. (2023) "Nigeria's eNaira, One Year After" (16 May). IMF Working Papers 2023(104). Washington, D.C.: International Monetary Fund.
Reserve Bank of Australia and Government of Australia (2024) "Central Bank Digital Currencies and the Future of Money in Australia". Report (September).
*Reuters* (2016) "Federal Reserve Was Hacked More Than 50 Times in the Past Five Years". *The Guardian* (1 June).
*Reuters* (2021) "Fed's Powell 'Legitimately Undecided' on Central Bank Digital Currency" (15 July).
*Reuters* (2022) "In a Rare Move, Trudeau Uses Measures to Cut Off the Protesters' Funding". *Global Times* (15 February). (a)
*Reuters* (2022) "Fed's Brainard Sees Case for U.S. Central Bank Digital Currency" (18 February). (b)
Richards, J. (2022) "Biden's Most Enduring Legacy". *ZeroHedge* (1 September).
Riksbank (2017) "The Riksbank's e-krona Project – Report 1". Sveriges Riksbank (November).
Riksbank (2018) "The Riksbank's e-krona Project – Report 2". Sveriges Riksbank (October).
Rogoff, K. (2016) *The Curse of Cash*. Princeton, NJ: Princeton University Press.
Rosalsky, G. (2019) "The 'Strange, Unduly Neglected Prophet'". *NPR Planet Money* (27 August).

Ross, M. (2024) "Sweden Has Stopped Using Cash – and Fraudsters Are Having a Field Day". *The Daily Telegraph* (11 July).

Roubini, N. (2018) "Why Central Bank Digital Currencies Will Destroy Cryptocurrencies". *Project Syndicate* (19 November).

Roubini, N. (2019) "Nouriel Roubini on Fintech Revolution". YouTube (uploaded 1 February), www.youtube.com/watch?v=97keNLmxPoc. Accessed 3 February 2026.

Sacks, D. (2022) "David Sacks: Trudeau Creates a Caste of Economic Untouchables in Canada". *National Post* (22 February).

Sams, R. (2015) "Which Fedcoin?" cryptonomics.org (5 February).

Sandbu, M. (2019) "How Facebook's Libra Fuelled Push for Central Bank Digital Currencies". *Financial Times* (23 September).

Sandor, K. (2023) "Ron DeSantis Promises to Ban CBDCs if Elected President". *CoinDesk* (17 July).

Saphir, A. (2021) "Fed's Brainard: Can't Wrap Head around Not Having U.S. Central Bank Digital Currency". *Reuters* (31 July).

Sarkar, A. (2024) "India Preparing for a CBDC-Driven Economy – Central Bank Governor". *CoinTelegraph* (11 December).

Scherer, S., D. Ljunggren and N. Saminather (2022) "Canada's Trudeau Invokes Emergency Powers in Bid to End Protests". *Reuters* (15 February).

Schneier, B. (2006) "The Eternal Value of Privacy". *Schneier on Security* (18 May).

Schoenholtz, K., and S. Cecchetti (2018) "Banking the Masses: 2018 Edition". *VoxEU* (26 June).

Schrodt, P. (2016) "Edward Snowden Just Made an Impassioned Argument for Why Privacy Is the Most Important Right". *Business Insider* (15 September).

Schulp, J., and J. Solowey (2024) "The Fed Is the Wrong Regulator for Stablecoins". *CoinDesk* (23 October).

Selgin, G. (2011) *Good Money: Birmingham Button Makers, the Royal Mint, and the Beginnings of Modern Coinage, 1775–1821*. Ann Arbor: University of Michigan Press.

Selgin, G. (2019) "Facilitating Faster Payments in the U.S." *Testimony*, Cato Institute (25 September).

Selgin, G. (2021) "Central Bank Digital Currency as a Potential Source of Financial Stability". *Cato Journal*, 41 (Spring/Summer): 333–341. (a)

Selgin, G. (2021) "In Defense of Bank Deposits: An Open Letter to Professor Omarova". *Alt-M* (13 October). (b)

Selgin, G. (2021) "George Selgin on Bitcoin and the Future of CBDCs". *Macro Musings Podcast*, Mercatus Center (25 October). (c)

Shah, S., and W. Gillani (2021) "In Pakistan, Saying 'No' to Covid-19 Vaccine Carries Consequences". *Wall Street Journal* (22 June).

Shen, T., and T. Zuo (2023) "China's Digital Yuan Needs WeChat, Alipay to Boost Adoption, Experts Say". *Forkast* (16 January).

Shoniwa, R. (2023) "The Bank of England's CBDC 'Consultation' and How to Respond, Part 1". *TCW Defending Freedom* (29 May).

Shurk, J. B. (2023) "The World Economic Forum's 'AI Enslavement' Is Coming for You!" Gatestone Institute (1 March).

Simpson, P. (2023) "Woke Bankers Are the 21st Century Pharisees". *TCW Defending Freedom* (30 July).

Skingsley, C. (2016) "Should the Riksbank Issue e-krona?" Speech to FinTech Stockholm (16 November).

Sky News (2023) "Key Points from Coutts' Dossier on Nigel Farage". *Explainer* (28 July).

Srivastava, V. (2023) "The Curious Case of the Missing CBDC Users". GT School of Public Policy Internet Governance Project (30 January).

Steward, R. (2022) "Nigerian Governor Announces Second Phase of CBDC Project". *Central Banking* (24 August).

Stockland, K. (2023) "Banks Take the Lead in Establishing Personal Social Credit System, Critics Charge". *ZeroHedge* (1 August).

Stoller, M. (2019) "How Monopolies Broke the Federal Reserve". *BIG* (13 August).

Subramanya, R. (2022) "The TRUTH about the Freedom Convoy: RUPA SUBRAMANYA Spoke to Close to 100 Protesters. She Didn't Find a Single Insurrectionist, White Supremacist, Racist or Misogynist. She Did Find a Diverse Group of Decent People, Who've Had Enough". *Mail Online* (10 February).

Sutton, S. (2022) "Banks, Crypto Lobby Clash with Lawmakers over Fed Digital Dollar". *Politico* (22 August).

Tham, E. (2022) "China Bank Protest Stopped by Health Codes Turning Red, Protesters Say". *Reuters* (16 June).

Thomas, K. (2022) "Legault Expresses Concern over Use of Emergencies Act in Quebec". *Montreal Gazette* (14 February).

Todd, S. (2015) "The Case for a Government-Backed Cryptocurrency". *American Banker* (29 March).

TT/*The Local* (2023) "Swedish Inquiry Calls for State-Run Digital ID and Low-Risk Bank Accounts". *The Local* (31 March).

Tumilty, R., and C. Nardi (2023) "Trudeau Expresses Regret for Denouncing Freedom Convoy as 'Fringe Minority'". *National Post* (17 February).

Turley, J. (2022) "Turley: Canada Extends Trudeau's Emergency Powers ... after the Protest Has Ended". *ZeroHedge* (22 February).

Turton, J. (2022) "House of Lords Report: Digital Pound Could Lead to Run on Banks". *Professional Adviser* (13 January).

Ujah, E. (2022) "e-Naira Transactions Hit N4bn – Emefiele". *Vanguard* (19 August).

Usman, M. (2021) "Millions of Pakistanis Threatened with Cell Phone Cut-Off if They Don't Get a COVID Vaccine". *CBS News* (24 June).

ur-Rehman, Z. (2021) "Unvaccinated in Pakistan? You Might Lose Your Cellphone License". *New York Times* (15 June).

Viganò, C. M. (2021) "Archbishop Issues New Emergency Message Warning People of the Great Reset". *InfoWars* (21 December).

Vollgeld Initiative (2018) "A Respectable Result for the Sovereign Money Initiative (Vollgeld-Initiative)". Press Release (10 June), Wettingen, Switzerland.

Walker, C. W. (2022) "How Is the 'World's Most Advanced Central Bank Digital Currency' Progressing?" London School of Economics blog (22 November).

Wallace, T. (2021) "Bank of England Tells Ministers to Intervene on Digital Currency 'Programming'". *Daily Telegraph* (21 June).

Waller, C. J. (2016) "Negative Interest Rates: A Tax in Sheep's Clothing". *On the Economy*, Federal Reserve Bank of St. Louis (2 May).

Waller, C. J. (2021) "Central Bank Digital Currency: A Solution in Search of a Problem?" Speech at the American Enterprise Institute, Washington, D.C. (5 August).

Warmbrodt, Z. (2019) "Fear of Facebook Spurs Momentum for Fed to Build Its Own Digital Currency". *POLITICO* (15 October).

Watson, P. (2023) "'Rich Dad, Poor Dad' Author Warns "Dystopian" CBDCs Will Allow Governments to Track All Purchases". *ZeroHedge* (28 April).

White, L. H. (2014) "What You Should Know about Free Banking History". *Cato at Liberty* (28 April).

White, L. H. (2018) "The World's First Central Bank Electronic Money Has Come – and Gone: Ecuador, 2014–2018". *Alt-M* (2 April). (a)

White, L. H. (2018) "Central Bank Digital Currency Threatens Financial Privacy and Economic Growth". *Cato at Liberty* (4 December). (b)

White, L. H. (2019) "Efficient 'Central Bank Digital Currency' Is a Fantasy". *Alt-M* (11 February). (a)

White, L. H. (2019) "Libra's Unresolved Puzzles". *Alt-M* (2 July). (b)

White, L. H. (2021) "Should the State or the Market Provide Digital Currency?" *Cato Journal*, 41(2) (Spring/Summer): 237–249. (a)

White, L. H. (2021) "Should We Fear Stablecoins? *Alt-M* (24 June). (b)

White, L. H. (2024) "Should the Sstate or the Market Provide Digital Payment Media?" IIMR Webinar (5 March).

The White House (2025) "Strengthening American Leadership in Digital Financial Technology" Executive Order (23 January), https://tinyurl.com/2r79f4yu. Accessed 4 February 2026.

Whyte, J. (2024) "Debanked: The Economic and Social Consequences of Anti-money Laundering Regulation". IEA Discussion Paper No. 125 (May).

Wong, T. and *BBC Chinese* (2022) "Henan: China Covid App Restricts Residents after Banking Protests". *BBC News* (14 June).

Young, P. (2023) "A Britcoin Digital Currency Is an Accident Waiting to Happen". *CapX* (6 April).

Zuluaga, D. (2021) "Which Type of Digital Currency for Financial Inclusion?" *Cato Journal*, 41: 413–421.

Zywicki, T. J., G. A. Manne and J. Morris (2014) "Price Controls on Payment Card Interchange Fees: The U.S. Experience". George Mason University Law and Economics Research Paper Series 14–18.

# Index

For EU product safety concerns, contact us at Calle de José Abascal, 56–1°,
28003 Madrid, Spain or eugpsr@cambridge.org.

www.ingramcontent.com/pod-product-compliance
Ingram Content Group UK Ltd.
Pitfield, Milton Keynes, MK11 3LW, UK
UKHW040719180726
473384UK00009B/283

* 9 7 8 1 0 0 9 7 5 8 4 6 8 *